WHITENESS

INTERRUPTED

MARCUS BELL

WHITENESS

INTERRUPTED

White Teachers and Racial Identity in
Predominantly Black Schools

DUKE UNIVERSITY PRESS   *Durham and London*   2021

Designed by Courtney Leigh Richardson
Typeset in Minion Pro and Trade Gothic by Copperline Book Services

Library of Congress Cataloging-in-Publication Data
Names: Bell, Marcus, [date] author.
Title: Whiteness interrupted : white teachers and racial identity
in predominantly Black schools / Marcus Bell.
Description: Durham : Duke University Press, 2021. | Includes
bibliographical references and index.
Identifiers: LCCN 2021005979 (print)
LCCN 2021005980 (ebook)
ISBN 9781478013709 (hardcover)
ISBN 9781478014638 (paperback)
ISBN 9781478021933 (ebook)
Subjects: LCSH: Teachers, White—United States—Attitudes. | Whites—
Race identity—United States. | Teaching—Social aspects—United States. |
Education, Urban—United States. | Racism in education—United States. |
African Americans—Crimes against—Public opinion. | Racism—
United States—Public opinion. | United States—Race relations.
Classification: LCC LB1775.2 .B43 2021 (print) |
LCC LB1775.2 (ebook) | DDC 370.890973—dc23
LC record available at https://lccn.loc.gov/2021005979
LC ebook record available at https://lccn.loc.gov/2021005980

Cover and title page art: Marker lines. Courtesy Ron Dale/Shutterstock.

CONTENTS

Preface and Acknowledgments   vii

Introduction: Whiteness in America   1

1. White Racelessness   17
2. The Color Line and the Classroom   38
3. Becoming White Teachers   63
4. The White Race Card   85
5. Colorblind   117

Conclusion: White Identity Politics
and the Coming Crisis of Place   153

Appendix: Methodology and Research Design   166

Notes   179
Bibliography   219
Index   241

PREFACE AND ACKNOWLEDGMENTS

Perhaps it is easy for those who have never felt the stinging darts of
segregation to say, "wait." But when you have seen vicious mobs lynch your
mothers and fathers at will and drown your sisters and brothers at whim;
when you have seen hate-filled policemen curse, kick, and kill your black
brothers and sisters . . . when you are forever a degenerating sense of
"nobodiness"—then you will understand why we find it difficult to wait.
—MARTIN LUTHER KING JR., "Letter from a Birmingham Jail"

White ignorance is the axis around which white Americans construct
our political identity. . . . The white eye is socialized to see lynchings
and racialized torture as entertainment worthy of picnics and
postcard reproductions.—ALISON BAILEY, *Strategic Ignorance*

I can't breathe.
—GEORGE FLOYD JR.

Everything felt different. From all outward appearances, something about
the country had changed. While any commitment to greater racial justice in
America requires measured optimism, the spring and early summer of 2020
offered the most visible opportunity for change in modern American history.
Looking back, was it a moment of fundamental change, or was it a temporary fad that soon faded from memory? Was it a moment of honesty, cour-
age, and moral clarity, or was it an opening for career opportunism, media
grandstanding, and hashtag activism? Was the year 2020, a year full of pain,

suffering, and rage, the moment when America—despite what it meant for individual Americans—acknowledged and confronted institutional racism on a national scale, or was it destined to become a political football, yet another weapon in our never-ending culture war? Though time has dampened the optimism shared by many in the spring of last year, it remains unquestionably true that in real time, the march toward racial equality, literally and symbolically, felt real.

On May 25, 2020, George Perry Floyd Jr. was killed by police officers in Minneapolis, Minnesota. He was forty-six years old. Accused of passing a counterfeit twenty-dollar bill, Floyd was confronted by several police officers, arrested, and physically restrained. One of the officers, Derek Chauvin, who is white, was filmed kneeling on the back of Floyd's neck. Several other officers were also present. Two of them helped Chauvin restrain Floyd, while another stood around nonchalantly, appearing to be unbothered by Floyd or the numerous bystanders pleading on his behalf. On the video, Floyd can be heard begging for his life, calling for his late mother, and, through fear and clear physical distress, forcing out the words, "I can't breathe."[1] After six minutes, Floyd, handcuffed and lying face down in the street, went motionless. After nine minutes and twenty-nine seconds, he was dead.

Eric Garner, Tamir Rice, Walter Scott, John Crawford, Freddy Gray, Mike Brown, LaQuan McDonald, Philando Castile, Stephon Clark, Botham Jean, Breonna Taylor, and now George Floyd, together constitute but a fraction of the African American men, women, and children who have been killed by police officers in recent years.[2] Now a common occurrence, extrajudicial killings of African Americans are the most extreme example of a criminal justice system that, from drugs to death row, disproportionately—and negatively—affects black communities all across the United States. Each death, controversial in its own way, engendered a public backlash: those of Brown and Gray caused weeks of sometimes violent protests in Ferguson, Missouri, and Baltimore, Maryland, respectively. Though not the only death to be captured on film, Floyd's murder, virtually overnight, set off a wave of protests unlike anything we have seen since the assassination of Martin Luther King Jr. over fifty years ago.[3]

In the immediate aftermath of Floyd's murder, hundreds of thousands of Americans marched in protest.[4] From big cities to small cities, suburbs to farm towns, protestors took to the streets in all fifty states, the District of Columbia, and multiple countries abroad.[5] Public support for Black Lives Matter increased significantly among white Americans, and police practices, from choke holds to no-knock warrants, came under increased scrutiny.[6]

Politicians from both major parties participated in protests, and the parties themselves each initiated police reform packages in Congress.[7] Corporations ranging from Microsoft to Ben and Jerry's released statements condemning racism and white supremacy, and professional sports leagues, including the NBA and the NFL, initiated difficult conversations about police brutality and America's ugly history of antiblack racism.[8] Celebrities and professional athletes used their considerable influence to call attention to racial inequality and white privilege, and many of them pledged millions of dollars in donations to black communities and black businesses.[9] Books about antiracism soared to the top of the *New York Times* Best Sellers list. Netflix and Amazon Prime offered free programming centered around African American history.[10] NASCAR banned Confederate flags from all of its events, and the Pentagon proposed renaming any military base named after a Confederate general.[11] Also, multiple memorial services to George Floyd were carried live on local news, cable news, and social media networks.[12] Having taken place in the span of three weeks, these and a host of other responses combined to make the spring of 2020 feel, in a word, different.

A BOOK ABOUT WHITENESS

Why start here? Why start a book about whiteness with the murder of George Floyd and the ensuing aftermath? Why start a book about white teachers in urban education with yet another deadly example of the criminalization of blackness? Finally, why start a book about white racial identity with a discussion of black pain, black suffering, and national resistance? After all, this is not a book about African Americans or social movement activism. This is not a book about criminal justice or mass incarceration, and this is not a book about policing. So, once more, why start here? The answer is simple. What made the spring of last year seem so remarkable, what made it simultaneously a reason for hope and a cause for concern, what made it so difficult to understand or envision what it meant for the future, was not marches or protests, not rioting or looting, not social media posts by celebrities or outspoken professional athletes. What made that particular moment seem different was white America.

Though by no means universal, the response of white Americans to the murder of George Floyd, at the time, seemed nothing short of astonishing. Old and young, suburban and urban, rich, poor, and everything in between, they joined African Americans and other people of color on the front lines, standing up for racial equality and against police brutality. To be clear, going all the way back to the movement to abolish slavery, some white Americans have been willing to fight, kill, and die in the battle against white supremacy. Comparatively, however, in very few moments in American history has white public opinion—and white public action—shifted so far and so fast in the direction of *greater* racial equality. Given that policing was at the center of the George Floyd tragedy, and given the traditional standing that police officers hold within the broader white community, it was all the more surprising that the budding movement to rethink and reform policing, at least initially, garnered so much white support.

With the luxury of time, I can now state that our national moment of hope and optimism for a more just, racially egalitarian society was just that: a moment. Over the course of the summer and then into the fall and winter of 2020, the unity displayed earlier in the year dissipated, rendering the possibility of meaningful and lasting change all but moot. Yes, the marches were real. The protests were widespread, they were genuinely multiracial, and, in real time, they were meaningful. What they were not, however, was lasting. They were not without resistance, they were not without violence, and, like so many other aspects of our society, they were not immune to broader social and political forces. Contextualized by a deadly pandemic and a contentious presidential election, over time, the multiracial marches waned and public support for Black Lives Matter declined. By the time a record number of Americans headed to the voting booth to cast their ballot in the 2020 presidential election, peaceful protests against police brutality were deliberately— and often inaccurately—associated with rioting, looting, and the contemporaneous rise in violence in many American cities. Tellingly, the biggest decline in support for Black Lives Matter and the broader movement for racial justice was among white Americans.[13]

So what should we make of all this? How should we process it? Beyond the spring of 2020, and as I detail in this book, America has been through a decade of racial progress *and* racial tumult. We have seen the election and reelection of an African American president, as well as the election and defeat of a man who, for years, led a racist conspiracy that questioned his citizenship. We have seen a renewed call for racial reparations. We have seen a rise in racially motivated hate crimes. We have seen political polarization dovetail with racial polarization. And we have also seen the reemergence and rebranding of white nationalism. Perhaps most salient, or at least most germane to this book, is that the past ten years have offered multiple concrete examples of a darkening country. That is, contextualizing everything—the good, the bad, and the deadly—are rapid cultural and demographic changes that are now being felt by much of white America.

In this book I tell a story. I tell a story about the malleability of racial identity, as well as the durability of racial ideology. I also tell a story about local environments and the importance of racialized space. Boiled down to its essence, stripped of all academic jargon, I tell a story about a group of white teachers who work in schools where the majority of students are black. These teachers, most of whom are from middle-class and affluent backgrounds, spend their days in spaces that are racially and economically segregated and around people who, demographically, look nothing like them. Their training, including college courses on whiteness and white privilege, student teaching in inner-city schools, and professional development seminars focused on diversity and cultural sensitivity, did not fully prepare them for life in an environment where race and racial identity could not be escaped. While experience within these spaces did show the possibility of satiation, at no time could white teachers become complacent, as race—particularly the racial disparity between teachers and students—*always* had to be navigated.

This book would not have been possible without teachers. Contacted by a stranger asking to talk with them about whiteness, they opened up and shared their lives with me in illuminating ways. Our interviews—humorous, emotional, gut-wrenching, and heart-warming—both intrigued and challenged me, and they form the basis for a much-needed course correction in the study of white racial identity. While I do not know what you think of me or how you will react to this book, I am grateful to each and every one of you. I thank you for your dedication to your profession and your commitment to your students. Teaching in doubly segregated, inner-city schools can be a difficult and thankless job, so please know that I appreciate and respect all of the hard work you put in as educators and as professionals. Again, thank you for making this project possible.

I would also like to thank a number of people who supported me throughout the entirety of this process. To Lisa LaMontagne, Tristan Teater, Amy Lutz, Arthur Paris, Barbara Applebaum, Mario Rios Perez, Prema Kurien, and Marjorie DeVault, thank you for your guidance, your support, and your patience as this project went from idea to study to actual book. White racial awareness and white racial identity are not easy topics to study, and through it all—the frustration, the confusion, and long nights of writing—you made finishing this project possible by providing a welcoming and understanding support system. Also, to my daughters, Maliah Pearl and Viola Rose, thank you for lighting up my life. The two of you are my world, and I am lucky to call myself your father. I only hope to make you proud. Finally, I would like to thank the numerous scholars of racial identity and racial inequality who came before me. Without your tireless scholarship, my own simply would not be possible. From methods to theory, from reflexivity to ethics, I put my all into this book; it is my sincere hope that it makes a substantive contribution to our national conversation on race.

INTRODUCTION: WHITENESS IN AMERICA

Whiteness, as a set of cultural practices, is visible most clearly to those
it definitively excludes and those to whom it does violence. Those who are
securely housed within its borders usually do not examine it.
—RUTH FRANKENBERG, *White Women, Race Matters*

One of the privileges of whiteness is to be able to remain invisible,
unnamed. As in a child's "peek-a-boo" game, as white people we are able
to cover *our* eyes to consciousness of "race."
—KARYN D. McKINNEY, *Being White*

The study of white racial identity in the United States can greatly
benefit from moving away from simply naming whiteness as an overlooked,
privileged identity.—MONICA McDERMOTT AND FRANK SAMSON,
White Racial and Ethnic Identity

MARCH 2011

"You're so lucky you're not white." Mrs. Wilkes, then a twenty-nine-year-old
English teacher and colleague of mine at Capitol Heights Public School, an-
grily walked into my classroom during our lunch break.[1] She was visibly upset and on the verge of tears. At the time, Mrs. Wilkes and I were two of the

few Capitol Heights staff members under the age of thirty, so in some ways we felt drawn to each other through the shared experience of being of the same generation. On this day, she was upset because she had just come from a meeting with the mother of one of her students, the actual student, and the school principal. According to Mrs. Wilkes, she was made to sit through twenty-five minutes of being told how racist she was and how she didn't like black people; how due to, at best, a racial disconnect, and at worst, racial prejudice, she mistreated the student in question and unfairly stigmatized him because of his race. As a proud liberal who had purposely chosen to teach in an urban, predominantly black school, Mrs. Wilkes—who is white—was hurt that anyone would accuse her of being a racist, and as a teacher, she was outraged by the suggestion that her pedagogical practices were discriminatory against students of color. After insisting that she was raised not to see color, Mrs. Wilkes surprised me when she looked me straight in the eyes and flatly said, "I'm telling you, Mr. Bell, you're so lucky you're not white."

These words, hanging in the air like a thick fog, left me dumbfounded. "Lucky," then and now, is not the first word that comes to mind when I think about life as a black man in America. For my entire life, I have recognized my race. As far back as childhood, I knew that I was black and I knew that it meant something. Although I could not always say what that something was, I did know that being black was relevant in some way and that it was both meaningful and consequential. Perhaps it was the fact that for most of my life, the neighborhoods I lived in and the schools I attended were overwhelmingly black. Perhaps it was the fact that employees, white and black alike, would follow me around grocery stores, apparently waiting for me to shoplift or otherwise do something illegal. Perhaps it was the fact that when I was growing up, black people told me that I "talked like a white boy," and as I got older, white people told me I was "articulate for a black guy." Or perhaps it was the explicit racialized warnings about police officers and other authority figures— commonly referred to as "the talk"—that I regularly received from my parents throughout my teenage years. Any one of a thousand people or a thousand experiences may have helped to shape my racial identity, and at no point during this process of racial socialization did I think of myself as lucky.

Although I was initially confused and taken aback, very quickly my confusion turned into curiosity. I asked Mrs. Wilkes to elaborate, and she did so by telling me that she and many of the other white teachers in the school felt that they were often mistreated and disrespected by the predominantly black student body, by black parents or guardians, and at times even by black members of the faculty and staff. What's more, according to Mrs. Wilkes, the reason for this mistreatment and disrespect had nothing to do with them as individual teachers, but everything to do with the fact that they were white. That is, for many white teachers Capitol Heights was more than just a school with a predominantly poor, predominantly black student body; it also served as a physical space where being white was a disadvantage, a space where whiteness itself was unnecessarily and unfairly stigmatized.

Conversely, according to Mrs. Wilkes, within this same space, being black was an advantage, one she regarded as a relevant factor in the overwhelmingly positive relationship I had with black students and their families. While she, a white teacher, experienced racial discrimination at Capitol Heights, I, a black teacher, enjoyed racial privilege. In her mind, simply not being white provided me with a leg up in building meaningful relationships with black students, parents, and primary caregivers. To be clear, Mrs. Wilkes was *not* making general claims about racial advantage and disadvantage in the American stratification system; rather, she was specifically referencing the local environment of Capitol Heights. Somewhat skeptical, I asked Mrs. Wilkes, who was now sitting across from my desk with her head down, if she sincerely believed that she was a victim of racial discrimination or that her job as an educator would be easier if she were black. After a brief pause, she snapped her head up and pointedly replied, "In this school, absolutely."

As a white teacher at Capitol Heights, an urban school with a predominantly black student body, Mrs. Wilkes did not see whiteness as the raceless norm; instead she thought of it as a stigma, the mark of the racial other. Her status as a racial minority was constantly on her mind: being white became a social reality that she could not escape. According to Mrs. Wilkes, her students saw her as white, her students' families saw her as white, and even many of her nonwhite coworkers saw her as white, all leading to a surprising and somewhat disturbing development; she started to see herself as white. Over time, through this more local form of socialization, Mrs. Wilkes came to adopt a specific and *situated* racial identity.[2] She found herself trying to make sense of a new and, at times, emotionally challenging racial classification system. She struggled with it individually; she openly discussed it with other white teachers; and eventually she came into my classroom and voiced her concern about antiwhite discrimination. For her, our school represented a space where whiteness was neither a meaningless demographic marker nor an invisible or privileged identity. Instead, for Mrs. Wilkes, as well as other white teachers at Capitol Heights, whiteness was interrupted.

What does it mean to be white? How do white Americans see (or not see) themselves racially, and how do they make sense of an interpersonal, institutional, and seemingly entrenched racial stratification system? These are empirical questions that legal scholars, historians, sociologists, and other social scientists have spent decades trying to answer.[3] Among the numerous findings put forth, scholars have shown that whiteness is largely constructed as the raceless norm, that whiteness is a form of structural privilege, and that whiteness emanates from a particular standpoint, "a place from which white people look at ourselves, at others, and at society."[4] Scholars have also shown that today white racial identity is socially constructed from a pantheon of European ethnic identities and that whiteness—akin to private property—has been granted the legal right to exclude.[5] American institutions, from education to criminal justice, from the labor market to the law, privilege and protect whiteness, and American culture, from discourse to ideology, and from styles of dress to standards of beauty, reflects and reifies the preferences of white people.[6]

Although insightful and highly influential to the overall study of race in America, the literature on whiteness and white racial identity suffers from several limitations.[7] First, even across different disciplines, theoretical models, and research methodologies, few empirical studies focus on the racial dimensions and racializing effects of physical space. Far too often, race scholars speak of racial categories and racial experiences in broad, spatially generalized terms. For example, one of the most robust and consistent findings— white racial invisibility[8]—presupposes a static, unchanging racial environment. To the extent that variation in racialized experience is examined at all, it is typically examined along other prominent demographic classifications, such as class, gender, and, increasingly, age, ability, and sexual orientation.[9] In this sense, within the existing literature, racialized experience may vary by class, gender, sexual orientation, and so on, but it is assumed to be lived within a static, racially monolithic physical space.

In addition to overlooking the importance of physical space, scholars have largely failed to systematically examine the awareness and experiential nature of white racial identity *after* it has been made visibly meaningful to actual white people. Put differently, what happens to white racial identity once the veneer of normalcy is stripped away and its racialized dimensions are laid bare? How do white people in America respond to being seen, being addressed, and, from their perspective, being treated as white? Though adept at detailing the way white Americans conceptualize white racial identity generally, scholars have been far less successful in examining how white Americans conceptualize white racial identity locally.[10] Given the inherent heterogeneity within any racial group, it seems theoretically flawed and empirically limiting to assume that spatial variation has no meaningful bearing on how white people experience, understand, and make sense of their own lives in racial terms. Even with the rise of critical whiteness studies, relatively little is known about the localized experiential dynamics of white racialization.[11]

In this book I seek to address these and other limitations by explicitly making physical space the center of my analysis. Moving beyond the general question *What does it mean to be white?*, I ask more specifically, *What does it mean to be white in nonwhite racialized spaces?* I use in-depth interviews to study the daily experiences and discursive practices of white teachers who currently work in urban, predominantly black schools. Focusing on the "localness of race," I empirically examine a subset of white Americans who have experienced, and continue to experience, what Charles Gallagher terms a *momentary minority status.*[12] As white teachers who often found themselves surrounded by nonwhite students, my interview respondents were able to speak comprehensively, if clumsily, to the significance of physical space and localized racial identities.

Over the course of nineteen months, I interviewed thirty-two white teachers from the Brick City School District, a poor, inner-city, racially segregated district in Upstate New York. Identified and recruited through a combination of purposeful and snowball sampling, all teachers came from schools with predominantly black student populations. Although preceded by detailed email and telephone conversations, the face-to-face interviews afforded me the opportunity to examine white racial identity and the effects of socialization on a deeper and more intimate level. In the interviews I asked teachers about their racial identities in a general or more abstract sense, as well as how they experienced white racial identity within predominantly black schools. We talked about their childhoods, their decisions to become educators, their teacher preparatory programs, and the multitude of paths that led them to urban, racially segregated schools. More than anything else, though, we talked about race: the race of the teachers, the race of the students, and, indeed, the race of the schools themselves. After just a handful of interviews, it was clear that the complexities of white identity construction required considerably more empirical and theoretical scrutiny. I attempt to offer such scrutiny in the pages and chapters to come.

In 2014, for the first time in American history, the majority of public school students were nonwhite.[13] Although non-Hispanic whites still constituted the single largest bloc of public school students, collectively, the percentage of nonwhite students surpassed that of white students. As a whole, slightly more than 50 percent of all public school students are now students of color.[14] This new majority-minority status of public school students is not congruent with the racial (and gender) homogeneity of public school teachers. While a slight majority of all public school students are nonwhite, over 80 percent of all public school teachers are white.[15] In fact, in twenty-four states, the percentage of white public school teachers exceeds 90 percent; in fourteen of those states, it surpasses 95 percent.[16] As we move further into the twenty-first century, neither the trend of an increasingly nonwhite student body nor that of a predominantly white teaching staff shows any signs of slowing down, let alone reversing.[17]

In tandem with the rapid resegregation of public schools, the racial disparity between teachers and students has led to a number of schools in which the teaching staff is predominantly white, while the student body is predominantly nonwhite.[18] The demographic gap between teachers and students in many public schools all but ensures that a number of white teachers will spend a significant amount of time in nonwhite racialized spaces. While scholars have consistently shown that such racial disparities can often lead to negative outcomes for students of color, comparatively little is known about how this pattern affects white racial identity.[19] Of particular concern in this book is how white teachers negotiate and navigate race and racial identity within physical spaces that are themselves demographically and discursively racialized. One such space is the Brick City School District (BCSD), the site of this study.

The Brick City School District is a severely impoverished, underperforming, and hypersegregated school, primarily serving students of color. To be more precise, the BCSD has a student body that is over 70 percent nonwhite; 53 percent of its students identify as African American. Also, the pattern of housing segregation in Upstate New York has resulted in a number of BCSD schools becoming predominantly black, predominantly Hispanic, or predominantly white. For example, there are several BCSD schools in which African Americans compose more than 90 percent of the student population. At other schools in the district too, the student bodies are more than 60, 70, and 80 percent African American. While predominantly black student bodies are quite common, there are exactly zero BCSD schools where the majority of the faculty and staff are nonwhite. It is from these schools, schools with an African American student population of 60 percent or greater, that *all* of my interview respondents were selected.

In their respective schools, as well as their individual classrooms, the teachers I interviewed consistently found themselves interacting with people who did not talk, act, or look like them. On almost a daily basis, they were confronted with the reality of race, and unlike in their lives outside work—which took place in overwhelmingly white spaces—they were not afforded the luxury, or privilege, to pretend otherwise. Whether addressing behavioral misconduct, calling parents at home, or even planning a lesson, white Brick City teachers came to see race as an explicit and inevitable feature of their professional lives. Within Brick City schools, there was no ambiguity or vacillation, no disinclination or pretense; black students, as well as their parents and primary caregivers, named whiteness directly, leaving white teachers with little ideological space to obfuscate what quickly became a social fact;[20] white racial identity was salient, it was substantive, and it was also scary.

As white teachers immersed within an explicitly racialized environment, the women and men I spoke to were forced to grapple with their own racial identity in real and meaningful ways.[21] For most of them, this was the first time in their lives that they had had to take their own racial identity seriously, as their daily interactions within Brick City schools made it impossible for them to construct it as raceless or simply "normal." Teachers who thought of themselves as both believers and practitioners of colorblindness became enveloped by race, and over time being white took on a more prominent meaning. Similar to Mrs. Wilkes, who began this chapter, white teachers found their occupational status as racial minorities to be highly significant, and it altered, at least temporarily, the way they experienced and made sense of white racial identity. As the following pages will show, this new form of racial socialization, engendered in part by a heightened sense of white racial awareness and a weakened sense of white racial autonomy, is connected to, and has important lessons for, race throughout the broader United States.

THE INTERVIEWS: MEETING FACE TO FACE

I completed all of my interviews during a nineteen-month period from October 2014 to May 2016. While conducting fieldwork, I met with teachers in a variety of locations, including coffee shops, cafés, public libraries, school classrooms, their homes, and, on one occasion, a public park. Interviews ranged from ninety minutes to over two hours. Even though I had spoken to each teacher on the phone before meeting them face to face, the interviews themselves had a surreal quality to them. In a way, despite having recruited these teachers specifically because of their race and occupation, I was often surprised by the overwhelming whiteness of teachers in public education.[22] It is one thing to read about the demographic gap between white teachers and nonwhite students,[23] but it is something else entirely to give it a name, a face, and a voice. Thus, interviewing white teachers about their various constructions of white racial identity, at least initially, proved to be a bit of a culture shock for me and, on several occasions, for the teachers as well.

My first interview was with Leah Thompson, thirty-three, a middle school art teacher of nine years. Leah, a single mom, has worked at two different schools throughout her career, both of which had majority-black student populations. Leah invited me to her home on a weekday evening after she had put her son to bed. As I prepared for the interview, I could see that Leah appeared to be nervous. I double-checked to see whether she wanted to go through with the interview, and she reassured me that not only did she want to go through with it but she was also "kind of excited" to speak with me. When I remarked about her apparent nervousness, she explained that she was more excited than nervous and that she had been looking forward to the interview for quite some time. As I turned on my recorder and began to ask my first question, Leah blurted out, unsolicited, "Please don't make me sound racist."

With these words—"Please don't make me sound racist"—Leah voiced a concern that would cast a shadow over the entire data collection process. As ensuing chapters will show, with great specificity, teacher after teacher expressed thoughts and feelings about black students and black families that can be considered, at best, racially insensitive, and at worst, blatantly racist. A common concern that spanned multiple interviews was the idea that, as white teachers speaking openly about black students, their words would not only be seen as racist but could also be used against them and could endanger their careers. This feeling on the part of multiple teachers caused me to begin each of my interviews, whether solicited or not, with an emphasis on confidentiality. I started every interview with an intentional effort to reassure interviewees that nothing they said could be traced back to them. Thus, despite a great deal of initial concern on the part of my research participants, I was ultimately successful in gaining their trust and conducting meaningful and thematically rich interviews.[24]

For the most part, the tenor and tone of my interviews followed a familiar pattern. First, teachers would express an excited trepidation about speaking openly about race, urban education, and white racial identity. Next, I would reassure them that the interview was 100 percent confidential and that nothing they said could be traced back to them. Then, slowly but surely, their comfort levels with me and the subject material would grow, causing them to open up about their experiences in the BCSD. Finally, the words, stories, and experiences would come in bunches, providing me with an in-depth and intimate portrait of how they socially construct whiteness in nonwhite racialized spaces. Not only did teachers go into detail about a whole range of experiences, but they also, with the help of me probing, expressed and examined their interpretations of those experiences. As these teachers spoke, I listened carefully and paid close attention to their words. I made note of their facial expressions, discursive patterns, and general body language, and I followed each interview with a detailed summary memo. In the end, this process led to the collection of rich, sophisticated, and illuminating interview data.

WHITENESS, WHITE PEOPLE, AND RACIALIZED SPACE: A BRIEF NOTE ON TERMINOLOGY

Throughout this book, I refer to "whiteness" and "white people" on a regular basis, therefore it is necessary to flesh out how they are conceptualized within this study. While the terms "white people" and "whiteness" are inextricably linked, I do not think of them as interchangeable.[25] At their most basic levels, one term refers to individuals, while the other refers to a system. Those individuals who fall under the racial classification of white are, in the eyes of most, deemed white people. This, in itself, is significant, because for most of American history—including today—being racially designated as white was, and is, admission into the dominant racial group. To be racially classified as white is to be a member of the racial majority, which in turn imbues one with a set of racial privileges, including the privilege of just being "normal."[26]

On the other hand, whiteness is a system, one built on the historical foundation of white racial domination and maintained through institutional racism and a racialized social system.[27] Systems are bigger, more expansive, and in many ways more consequential than individual people. For example, while individual white people can be racially prejudiced and even act in racially discriminatory ways, whiteness, as a system, "*is racial domination normalized.*"[28] That is, within a white-identified and white supremacist society, the systematic domination of people of color seems normal, as opposed to being the result of unequal power relations.[29] As a result, institutional efforts to promote racial equality, such as affirmative action, are widely considered to be overt examples of reverse discrimination, ostensibly because they violate the ideological norms of colorblindness and meritocracy.[30]

Also, as a system, whiteness represents more than a collection of white citizens. Looking at the historical arc of race and racial identity in the United States, whiteness has been the archetype of what it means to be American.[31] Many social and political battles have been fought to protect whiteness from outside incursions, and, like private property, whiteness has been granted the legal authority to exclude.[32] Numerous immigrant groups, including those who are racially classified as white today, had to effectively work toward whiteness, enduring vitriol and discrimination from the dominant group along the way.[33] With this in mind, whiteness should not and, indeed, *cannot* be conceptualized in the same way as blackness, brownness, and so on. As the normative system of racial classification, whiteness represents the default American and it is deeply invested in the maintenance and reproduction of racial inequality.[34]

Finally, racialized space also needs to be deconstructed. Even though all space is racialized space, the very term "racialized space" can unwittingly reinforce whiteness as the raceless norm. If space is only racialized once it becomes occupied by people of color, then, by definition, whiteness, white people, and white space are not racialized. In order to avoid the reification of white racelessness, in this book I use the term "nonwhite racialized spaces" when describing Brick City schools and the neighborhoods that house them. Nonwhite racialized spaces are physical and social environments where white racial consciousness cannot be escaped. Within these spaces, whiteness is denormalized, or interrupted, by the cultural practices and people within them, and even by the physical spaces themselves. Whereas segregated white neighborhoods and schools are indeed racialized spaces, they are often interpreted by white people as simply neighborhoods and schools, respectively. Within nonwhite racialized spaces, however, white visibility and white racial awareness are heightened by the physical dimensions, racial demographics, cultural mores, and interactional practices *of those* particular spaces. Although there is often a distinction between the way Americans construct white versus nonwhite racialized space, it is important to me that I do not reinforce the process of white normalization.

Before I outline the plan for the book, I think it is important for me to be clear about what I did, *and did not*, write. I did not write a book about education. While sites of great importance, schools, *as schools*, are not the primary focus of this study. To the extent that schools are my focal point, it is due to their historical construction—and contemporary existence—as race-making spaces, including in the minds of white teachers.[35] Furthermore, I did not write a book about education policy. Institutionalized disinvestment in public schools, the decimation of teacher protections, high-stakes testing, the proliferation of charter schools, and other features of neoliberal education policy—though instrumental to the very existence of the BCSD—do not receive extensive attention in this book.[36] Finally, this is not a book about inequality. A lot has been and will be written about education as a site of racial and economic inequality, and a lot has been and will be written about the impact that inequality has on student outcomes.[37] Topics such as the achievement gap, inequitable funding and access to technology, racialized tracking, and the school-to-prison pipeline, to name but a few, have been, and will remain, of great interest to educational scholars.[38] Again, though, despite their importance to education specifically, and to the country as a whole, these and other examples of inequality *are not* the primary focus of this study.

This book is about identity. More specifically, this book is about white racial identity.[39] My primary objective in writing this book is to demonstrate, empirically, that white racial identity is constructed, and often reconstructed, based on localized interactions.[40] This book is also about socialization. Socialization, not biology, is what leads so many white Americans to construct raceless identities for themselves,[41] and as I will cover in great detail, local resocialization processes have the power to interrupt this normative construction. This book is about physical space. Space does not exist in a vacuum, and it is not immune to the social, political, and discursive processes of racialization.[42] The same controlling images that have constructed African American women as "mammies" or "jezebels," and African American men as "thugs" or "gang members," have also constructed "urban schools" as "black schools."[43] One of my chief objectives in this book, then, is to examine the racial construction of space and the impact this process has on white racial identity. Finally, this book is about ideology. How does local space, and the resocialization it engenders, affect the racial ideologies of colorblindness and postracialism, both of which are normative in much of white America?[44]

That is, does a heightened racial awareness reinforce or challenge white racial ideology?[45] These are the questions I attempt to answer in writing this book.

Chapter 1, "White Racelessness," begins where a great deal of the research literature ends, with a discussion about, and analysis of, the so-called invisibility of whiteness and normalness of white racial identity. After briefly reviewing the literature on white racelessness, I show how, consistent with this literature, white teachers constructed whiteness as the invisible, raceless norm. As long as my questions were framed in an abstract fashion—"What does it mean to be white?"—teachers, with few exceptions, struggled to discuss or describe white racial identity in a meaningful way. The data presented in this chapter lend empirical support for the long-held belief that, owing to their social positioning, many white Americans do not see themselves as racial beings or see their lives in racialized terms. Two thematic concepts, rhetorical incoherence and white deflection, are introduced and discussed at length.

Chapter 2, "The Color Line and the Classroom," highlights the concept of racialized space, as well as the interactive processes that help to engender racial identities among white Brick City Teachers. Focusing on historical, political, and legal changes, I detail the racialization of urban schools in the public imagination. I also show how Brick City teachers, without exception, *all* conceptualized their schools as black schools. Due to a variety of factors, namely the physical nature of the school, the predominantly black student body, and the presence and consistency of explicit racialized discourse, white teachers distinctly thought of their respective workplaces as racialized spaces. Compounding this process was the culture that purportedly engulfed Brick City schools. From styles of dress and modes of talk to so-called pathological or oppositional behavior, *black culture*—as represented by black students and black families—all but cemented the racialization of these particular spaces.

Chapter 3, "Becoming White Teachers," explores how white teachers are locally socialized regarding race, whiteness, and white racial identity. More specifically, I detail how nonwhite racialized space interrupts the normality of whiteness. Contrary to whiteness as an invisible identity, this chapter shows how, within certain local environments, white teachers are resocialized to constantly see and think about what it means to be white. For these teachers, their sense of whiteness as the raceless norm was eroded by the explicitly racialized dimensions of Brick City schools. From their position as the numerical, social, and cultural minority, white teachers in the BCSD saw themselves not as the raceless norm but as the racial other. Such a process is incongruous with their past life experiences, as well as their current realities outside of work.

Chapter 4, "The White Race Card," examines the specific type of racial identity developed by white teachers in predominantly black schools, namely their construction of whiteness as the marked and maligned racial other. This chapter uses interview data to show how the racial dimensions of Brick City schools caused white teachers to develop a heightened sense of racial victimization. Within these schools, not only did whiteness become visible; it also became a liability. To varying degrees, the teachers I interviewed expressed a spatially situated racial identity, one fueled by what they considered antiwhite prejudice and reverse discrimination. From getting called a racist for punishing students to being distrusted and mistreated by black parents who "just can't stand white people," teacher after teacher constructed whiteness in the BCSD as a disadvantage. In this chapter I also discuss the spatial construction of "black privilege."

In chapter 5, "Colorblind," I compare the racial discourse of white teachers when talking about race and racism in general with how they describe their personal experiences within predominantly black schools. In the former, with little exception, white teachers professed a strict belief in colorblindness. As long as they were speaking in broad or general terms, nearly every teacher in this study downplayed the significance of racial inequality in the contemporary United States. In the latter, again, with little exception, these same teachers were highly cognizant of race, as it was pronounced throughout their descriptions and depictions of being the racialized other within Brick City schools. In a stark departure from their general belief in colorblindness and postracialism, when referencing their schools, white teachers were not only color-conscious but also went into detail about the realness and relevance of racial discrimination. When I pointed this out to them, the juxtaposition led to a discursive negotiation in which white teachers tried to rationalize and make sense of their spatially contingent, ideological contradictions.

Finally, in the conclusion, "White Identity Politics and the Coming Crisis of Place," I end the book with a discussion that goes beyond the Brick City School District. Specifically, I discuss what this study suggests about race, white racial identity, and race relations throughout society as a whole. To do so, I situate my findings within the larger context of a rapidly changing—and rapidly darkening—United States. Following the trajectory of public schools, America is moving closer to becoming a majority-minority country. Experientially, this will lead to fewer and fewer predominantly white spaces, with still fewer exclusively white spaces. What this means for white racial identity remains to be seen, but there are several indications that such demographic shifts, along with the economic and cultural changes that are perceived to accompany them, have ignited a white backlash, one that includes the rise of white nationalism and the election of Donald Trump as the forty-fifth president of the United States. Limitations and suggestions for future research are also discussed.

THINKING DEEPER: RESEARCH AND REFLEXIVITY

Whiteness interrupted is a process, one that challenges assumptions about white socialization and disrupts the development of normative white racial identities. As this book demonstrates, the institutional, ideological, and interactive processes that cast doubt on white racialization can be ruptured, leaving whiteness exposed and causing individual white people to experience life as racial actors. What's more, whiteness interrupted is ongoing; it does not result from solitary encounters. Although they recalled individual experiences that could be dramatic, for most teachers it was the iterative nature of it all that, over time, shattered the illusion of white invisibility. Finally, whiteness interrupted is spatial. It stems from localized dimensions of space, not simplistic generalities or essentialist notions of distinct racial categories. In order to better understand this process, I had to first step outside myself, challenging my own constructions of whiteness and white racial identity.

It is not lost on me that, as an African American, my speaking empirically about the racial experiences of white Americans may come across as somewhat peculiar. Neither is it lost on me that, as a man, my speaking empirically about the lived experiences of women might come across as somewhat paternalistic. Finally, as a black man, it is not lost on me that there is a complex and, quite frankly, tortured history between African American men and white women in the United States.[46] No matter how conscientious and reflexive one claims to be, there is no surefire methodological way for researchers to completely shield their own experiences and perspectives from the study of race, class, gender, or any other form of identity.[47] For this study, all of my interview respondents were white, and the vast majority of them were women. I, an African American man, am neither. The racial and gender incongruity between myself and my interview respondents was more than noticeable to me, and on more than one occasion it was verbally recognized by the interviewees themselves. This, I believe, speaks to both the salience of racial identity and the necessity for self-reflection and reflexivity.[48]

When I was interviewing white teachers for this project, there were times when their words made me cringe. Permeated with racial stereotypes at best, and racial vitriol at worst, many of the statements made by these teachers were hostile to black people and what they perceived to be black culture. For some, this hostility seemed to bubble just beneath the surface of their words, while for others, the prefixes "This might sound bad, but . . ." or "I have nothing against black people, but . . ." served as ominous precursors to a litany of racially insensitive, or downright racist, commentaries about black students and black families. As someone who has experienced overt racial discrimination firsthand, on several occasions I found myself thinking, "This person should not be teaching black children." The separation of my personal thoughts and feelings from my role as a researcher, while not always easy, was something I focused on and took great pains to maintain. Still, even as I write these words, I cannot be sure that I was completely successful in this endeavor.

As my interviews proceeded, something unexpected happened. The complexities of race, racial identity, and racial discourse began to stand out in ways that were hard to make sense of, particularly given the antiblack sentiment that was expressed earlier in my respective interviews. Many of the teachers who made disparaging remarks about black students and black families would later speak of them with great fondness, empathy, and compassion. The same teachers who early in the interview made me cringe, later in the same interview made me smile with their genuine concern and encouraging remarks. Though not always in the same order, or in response to the same questions, racial stereotypes *and* racial compassion could be found in nearly every one of my interviews. In a very real sense, the teachers who participated in this study seemed conflicted, and at times even confused, about their own feelings toward and their relationships with the black students who were entrusted to their care. Still, in the end, they opened up to me, choosing to tell their stories and share their experiences in their own words.

In the following pages, many of the statements and opinions that you will read can, and likely will, come across as racist. Some cases will speak for themselves, as they undoubtedly reflect racist hostilities toward African Americans. In most cases, though, these seemingly racist statements reflect real people grappling with the day-to-day logistics of a difficult job, all while trying to make sense of a racial identity that is experientially unfamiliar to them. To put it differently, these words exemplify members of the dominant racial group desperately trying to restore and get back to what sociologist Margaret Hagerman refers to as "the existing racial order."[49] As with the meeting that caused Mrs. Wilkes to burst into my classroom back at Capitol Heights, white teachers were often forced to confront their racial identity as a defense against charges of racism. Lashing out was just one of the many defense mechanisms they used to shield themselves against racialized stress. This is not to make excuses for teachers who hold on to or express racial stereotypes, and it is certainly not meant to rationalize racism, but as you read this book, it is important to remember—just as I had to—that context matters. More specifically, racial context matters.

1. WHITE RACELESSNESS

Central to the meaning of whiteness is a broad, collective American silence. The denial of white as a racial identity, the denial that whiteness has a history, allows the quiet, the blankness, to stand as the norm.
—GRACE ELIZABETH HALE, *Making Whiteness*

For many white people, the idea that we have racial identities is difficult to come to terms with. We usually see ourselves as simply people. Whiteness, by virtue of its status as the dominant social position, is unmarked.
—CYNTHIA KAUFMAN, "A User's Guide to White Privilege"

The truth is that whiteness is not an illusion but a historically evolving identity-formation that is produced in diverse locations, while constantly undergoing reinterpretation and contestation.
—LINDA MARTIN ALCOFF, *The Future of Whiteness*

Silence. Amid the hustle and bustle of a crowded café, Paige Vincent, a middle school health teacher, sat across from me in complete silence. Up to that point, Mrs. Vincent had been extremely talkative. She told numerous, if not random, stories about teaching at Medgar Evers Middle School. In a somewhat disjointed, nonlinear fashion, Mrs. Vincent responded to my initial rapport-building questions with long responses that included personal and professional anecdotes, rants about student work ethic or the lack thereof, and, on numerous occasions, homages to those teachers who have inspired—and continue to inspire—her to become a better educator. Mrs. Vincent described herself as someone who "loved to talk," and during our interview, she did so with great passion and excitement. As we went back and forth about a number of topics, I eventually asked the question that would come to stump the majority of my interview respondents: *What does it mean to be white?* Almost immediately, Mrs. Vincent, who, again, was extremely talkative, stopped talking. For close to three minutes, we sat in silence. Finally Mrs. Vincent, in a more muted and far less enthusiastic tone, replied, "I don't know how to answer that question."

Mrs. Vincent was not alone in struggling to articulate what it means to be white. In nearly all of my interviews, teachers paused, stuttered, stumbled, and, similar to Mrs. Vincent, went silent when trying to talk about white racial identity. This was true of female teachers and male teachers, experienced teachers and new teachers, introverted teachers and extroverted teachers. Collectively, when it came to talking about their own racial identities, gender had no impact, age had no impact, and years of experience had no impact. Even for those teachers who were eager to share their thoughts about race more broadly, and African Americans in particular, the subject of whiteness had a muzzling effect, triggering a combination of silence and rhetorical incoherence. As a general concept, white Brick City teachers simply could not discuss white racial identity, at least not in a cogent or coherent manner.

In this chapter I briefly review the literature on the invisibility of whiteness, and I highlight the degree to which white teachers reinforced this literature. Interview data will show that, without specifically being situated, white racial identity remained elusive and was very difficult to see. As a general concept, being white held no specific meaning and served no significant purpose beyond demographic classification. According to my respondents, they were not white moms or white dads, white sons or white daughters, white brothers or white sisters, white husbands or white wives; they were "just people." For most of the teachers I interviewed, their personal sense of normality, or *white racelessness*, permeated their responses, and with regard to both content and form, they struggled to speak about themselves in racial terms. Substantively, white Brick City teachers could not articulate a meaningful racial identity, and structurally, they could hardly speak about it in complete and grammatically correct sentences, period. Also, teachers often deflected specific questions about white racial identity by propping up other, presumably more significant demographic identities, such as gender and, to a lesser degree, ethnicity. Thus, as I detail below, the concepts of *rhetorical incoherence* and *white deflection* remained constant across interviews, and together they demonstrate the degree to which white Brick City teachers endorse and exemplify white racelessness.

WHITENESS AS THE RACELESS NORM

Sociology has a long and distinguished history of applying the tools of social science to the study of race and ethnicity in America.[1] Although the American Sociological Society (now the American Sociological Association) was founded in 1905, in reality, people from numerous backgrounds have studied race and ethnicity going back to at least the eighteenth century.[2] Ever since the first Department of Sociology was formally founded in 1892, sociologists have employed a multitude of theoretical paradigms and research methodologies to study, analyze, and report on the realities of race and ethnicity in the United States. This has led to over a century of racial theorizing about the nature of races and the causes of racial inequality, including biological theories, cultural theories, and social structural theories.[3] Unfortunately, for the overwhelming majority of this history, race scholars have reflected the broader epistemology of ignorance, treating whiteness as invisible and focusing almost exclusively on the racial and ethnic other.[4]

Since its inception as an academic discipline, sociology has not only been complicit in the normalization of whiteness; it has been a willing and active participant.[5] In an effort to empirically analyze and better understand race and racial inequality, the discipline—from its scholarship to some of its most celebrated practitioners—trained its critical gaze on racial and ethnic minorities, and it shunned, if not excluded, sociologists of color.[6] This latter point is particularly unfortunate, because it was precisely these scholars who first took whiteness and white racial identity seriously.[7] Among others, Ida B. Wells was writing about the legal and cultural salience of white lynch mobs in the 1890s, W. E. B. Du Bois was interrogating the "souls of white folk" in the 1920s, and Joyce Ladner was calling for the "death of White Sociology" in the 1970s.[8] While sociology, as a discipline, may have treated the study of race as a nonwhite affair, these and other scholars of color have been interrogating and writing about whiteness and white people for well over a century.[9] Still, it wasn't until the late 1980s and early 1990s, when a number of white scholars took a sustained interest, that *whiteness studies* proliferated in the humanities and social sciences.

In 1993, the late Ruth Frankenberg wrote what was to become one of the foundational readings in the field of critical whiteness studies, *White Women, Race Matters: The Social Construction of Whiteness*. Frankenberg noted that "'whiteness' refers to a set of cultural practices that are usually unmarked and unnamed" and that "it is crucial to look at the 'racialness' of white experience."[10] According to Frankenberg, whiteness, as a racial category, had been given a free pass and needed to be subjected to far more theoretical and empirical scrutiny.[11] Similarly, according to sociologist Woody Doane, the historical "downplaying of 'whiteness'" has resulted in a "one-dimensional perspective on race relations, a sociology that by its neglect of the identity of the dominant white group has treated majority-minority relations as if were necessary to understand only one actor."[12] Beginning in the late 1980s and early 1990s, there has been a concerted effort among researchers to broaden their critical gaze and abandon the nearly unilateral focus on nonwhites.

For over thirty years, sociology and other disciplines have taken up the call to study the "racialness" of whiteness, effectively upending the study of racial inequality in the United States. The last three-plus decades have seen a proliferation of studies dedicated to the study of whiteness, both in America and abroad.[13] In addition to a bevy of scholarly books and peer-reviewed journal articles, novelists, clergyman, poets, and laypeople have also produced an impressive catalog on whiteness and white racial identity.[14] Although this shift has led to a number of empirical findings, few have been as pronounced, or as consistent, as the social construction of whiteness as the raceless norm. In his award-winning book *The Possessive Investment in Whiteness: How White People Profit from Identity Politics*, preeminent sociologist George Lipsitz succinctly summarizes this line of thinking when he writes, "As the unmarked category against which difference is constructed, whiteness never has to speak its name."[15]

Beyond Frankenberg, Doane, and Lipsitz, a multitude of studies have shown that, for many white people living in the United States, whereas nonwhiteness embodies a certain identity or way of being, whiteness, by comparison, is broadly conceptualized as regular or just normal.[16] According to a now copious literature, though white Americans are fully aware that they are in fact white, being white carries little weight as a meaningful racial identity.[17] To be clear, white racelessness is less about biology and more about socialization. As members of the racially dominant group, white people are often socialized to view whiteness as little more than a physical characteristic, a demographic trait devoid of any racially or culturally specific value.[18] That is, owing to social positioning, and despite their knowledge that they embody the demographic classification of white, a broad cross-section of white Americans do not view whiteness as an institutional or interpersonal organizing principle.[19]

RACELESS IDENTITIES

Consistent with much of the existing literature, white Brick City teachers repeatedly constructed whiteness as an invisible identity. When speaking in broad, abstract terms, they found it extremely difficult to articulate a coherent position on what it means to be white. In fact, whenever I asked them about white racial identity as a general concept, teachers almost immediately engaged in rhetorical incoherence. I define rhetorical incoherence as verbal gibberish. It is speaking in an unclear, distorted, and illogical manner. In almost every interview, I watched thoughtful and well-spoken teachers fall apart, discursively, as words became hard to find and sentences hard to form. To the limited extent that they made any sense at all, White Brick City teachers admitted that being white was something to which they had rarely, if ever, given serious thought.

Rhetorical incoherence was only one indicator of white racelessness; the other was white deflection. White deflection is the intentional use of other identity markers to deflect or distance oneself from questions about whiteness. While most teachers struggled to talk about white racial identity, they were able to speak fluidly and thoughtfully about their gender and ethnic identities. Many of my female respondents were acutely attuned to the historical and contemporary significance of gender as a system of male domination. During my time in the field, they offered a litany of stories that spoke powerfully to the reality of institutional patriarchy, and for the most part, they did so voluntarily. Relatedly, a smaller subset of teachers invoked ethnicity in responses to questions about racial identity, focusing especially on the ethnic-based discrimination endured by their parents and grandparents. Contextualized by rhetorical incoherence, white deflection was a common strategy employed by Brick City teachers, one that allowed them to avoid grappling with questions about white racial identity.

I Don't Know If I Ever Really Thought about It

Well, I think that, um, hmmm, I would say, that's a good question. I think that I, through my life experiences, I do realize that life might be laid out for me some. Uh, being a white woman, although I find, I do, uh, there are issues that, um, I don't know what I, I don't know. This is a tough question. I just want to, I want to make sure I, um, say what I want, um. Gosh, I don't know if I ever really thought about it. Wow, this is hard.

—ERICA MARTIN, 27

Whenever they spoke about race in general terms, white Brick City teachers consistently conceptualized whiteness as the raceless norm. Throughout my fieldwork, interview respondents routinely spoke in ways that reflected a white racial framing of society, one that reinforced themselves individually, and whiteness more broadly, as normal.[20] With few exceptions, the teachers I interviewed constructed whiteness as insignificant, as invisible, and as something that did not matter to them, or for them, in any real or meaningful way. For example, Allison Hall, a high school history teacher, described whiteness as something that held very little meaning to her. When asked to describe what it means to be white, Ms. Hall responded this way:

> MS. HALL: [*Laughs*] I don't know, I guess it doesn't, um, it hasn't really meant anything. I mean, what does it mean to have brown eyes or be left-handed, you know? It may help describe you, you know, but, um, physically, it doesn't tell you, um, anything about me, it doesn't mean anything. I don't think I really, or, you know [*pause*], I've never had to think about it, I guess. I never really thought of myself as white, I'm just me [*laughs*].

For Ms. Hall, the very question "What does it mean to be white?" immediately evoked laughter.[21] Her response was so instantaneous that it almost seemed instinctive, as if it was a visceral reaction to a question that had not occurred to her in her forty-plus years of life. Ms. Hall did not consider being white as anything more than a demographic marker, something as meaningless and insignificant as having brown eyes or being left-handed. In the abstract, whiteness held zero meaning for her as an organizing principle or an integral part of her personal identity. Yes, Ms. Hall self-identified as white, but it was a meaningless identification. She happened to be white just like she happened to have brown eyes. By openly proclaiming, "I'm just me," Ms. Hall made it clear that she did not see herself as someone whose personal identity was influenced or affected by racial group membership.

For most of her life, Ms. Hall—like the majority of my interview respondents—gave little thought to what it means to be white. Although she did better than most, it was difficult for her to articulate a cogent position on whiteness and white racial identity. As a whole, because it was something that they, by their own admission, rarely thought about, white Brick City teachers consistently became verbally incoherent when asked to talk about what it means to be white. The very question caused most of them to speak in disjointed and convoluted sentences, interspersed with long pauses and bouts of nervous laughter. Providing support for previous research, many of the teachers I interviewed found it extremely difficult to speak lucidly at all.[22] They stuttered and stumbled throughout their answers, and they repeatedly laughed—not in a mocking or condescending way, but more in a way that indicated discomfort and uncertainty, particularly as they openly struggled to come up with intelligible responses.

Hanna Walker, in her late fifties and enjoying her first year of retirement, struggled considerably when asked about white racial identity. Rhetorically, Mrs. Walker engaged in a combination of laughter, long pauses, and stuttering, while ultimately failing to articulate a clear position on what it means to be white. After several false starts and long pauses, Mrs. Walker eventually asked if we could return to this question later in the interview, while also intimating that she would remain preoccupied with coming up with a suitable answer.

BELL: In your own words, thoughts, feelings, could you please tell me what it means for you to be white?

MRS. WALKER: [*Long pause*] I don't know if I ever really thought about it [*laughs*]. Um [*long pause*], that's a tough question. Am I the only one that needs a little, um, a little time to think [*laughs*]? [*Long pause*] I don't know. Um, I never really thought about what it's like to be white because I've never been anything else. But I, um, I don't know. We'll have to come back to that one because you're going to make me be up half the night thinking about what it means to be white [*laughs*]. I don't know if I'm going to be able to stop thinking about it. That's an excellent question.

Mrs. Walker not only struggled to answer this question rhetorically but also began to squirm around in her seat, fidgeting and changing positions as she tried to come up with a response. Her combination of rhetorical and somatic uneasiness led me to double-check and make sure she was 100 percent comfortable with this line of questioning. I asked if she wanted to take a break or move on to a different topic, but Mrs. Walker assured me that she was perfectly fine and ready to continue. As she would later reveal, her seeming discomfort and uneasiness resulted not from my question about whiteness but from her inability to answer "such a simple question." We sat in silence for several minutes. I waited patiently while Mrs. Walker looked to the side and continued to ponder my question about her racial identity. Finally, shaking her head back and forth, she literally threw her hands in the air and said through laughter, "OK, I got nothing, I give up. Sorry."

Other teachers—though also displaying rhetorical incoherence—hinted at common sociological concepts such as white privilege and intersectionality, only to immediately minimize their significance, or subsequently attribute any advantages they possess to individual effort. Sophia Taylor, a middle school music teacher of eleven years, stumbled into an intersectional response after tacitly admitting to being privileged by whiteness. Seeking to clarify why she believed her life "might be easier," she shifted the focus from race to class, eventually introducing geography as a plausible explanation for the advantages she enjoyed growing up.

> BELL: In your own words, thoughts, feelings, could you please tell me what it means for you to be white?

> MRS. TAYLOR: Hmm, well, um, I guess growing up, um, hmm. I mean, just a, hmm. I've never really thought about that question. Um, I just, I guess in some ways, I've had, you know. Wow, I'm really struggling with this question. Well, let me back up. I think that being white, um, for me, um, maybe things are a little easier for me. I mean, I really can't say, but, you know, to be white, sometimes, I think sometimes we might have it easier. I mean, not all white people have it easier, my family has money, you know, so that definitely made things a little easier, plus it's not as bad as it used to be, but, uh, I, I don't know what I'm saying. I had it easier growing up, but I'm not sure that race or being white, um, maybe that wasn't really the reason. I mean we had other people, there was a black family on my block, you know. So, maybe it was the neighborhood. Oh my god, I must sound like a moron right now [laughs].

> BELL: Did you grow up in a diverse neighborhood?

MRS. TAYLOR: No, not really. I think that one black family was the only one in the neighborhood [*laughs*]. Um, but their kids had a pretty good life too, you know. They went to the same schools I did, they drove nice cars and wore name-brand clothes. Everything was easy for them just like it was for me, you know. That's why I brought them up.

Even though she did so in a somewhat clumsy manner, Mrs. Taylor put forth an intersectional explanation of advantage and disadvantage.[23] While her initial response hinted at white privilege—"maybe things are a little easier"— she used the presence of one black family in her affluent neighborhood to pivot to more of a class-based explanation of privilege. Curiously, though, Mrs. Taylor's long and convoluted answer was in direct response to a question about what it means to be white. That is, even though an intersectional approach to studying identity and inequality is warranted, Mrs. Taylor was not trying to be thorough or comprehensive in her response. She was not offering an analysis of compounding inequalities or the erasure of women of color; rather, she was attempting to find a nonracial explanation for why her life was "a little easier." Also of note, the structure of Mrs. Taylor's response was disjointed and extremely difficult to follow. She, like most of my other interviewees, became rhetorically incoherent when trying to explain white racial identity.

For white Brick City teachers, their display of white racelessness and rhetorical incoherence was no coincidence. As I mentioned previously, rather than some biodeterministic by-product of white skin, white racelessness typically results from a different and unique form of racial socialization. To be clear, by the term "racial socialization," I do not mean to imply that white children or those from any other race are mere passive recipients of adult messaging or existing ideology. As numerous scholars have argued convincingly, children are active participants in their own socialization.[24] They are not pieces of clay to be molded by the adults in their life; they think, they feel, they act and react. With this in mind, white kids are instrumental to the social construction of whiteness as the raceless norm.[25] For my interview respondents, this construction was so internalized that describing their own racial identities became a difficult, if not impossible, task. All told, the primary reason that white teachers struggled to recognize and talk about whiteness is that they were socialized not to. Cynthia Jarvis, a twenty-four-year-old health teacher, illustrates this process below.

MS. JARVIS: We barely talked about race in my house, and we certainly never talked about whiteness or being white or whatever. How would, um, what would that even sound like? How would that even come up? We didn't look at ourselves as white or anything like that, nobody cared, you know. We just saw people, race didn't matter.

BELL: Were there any black families or other people of color in your neighborhood?

MS. JARVIS: Um, no, not really. There was an immigrant family once, but they didn't stay for very long [*laughs*].

BELL: What about school? Were there many, or any, students of color that attended your school?

MS. JARVIS: [*Pause*] No, it was, um, I would say it was pretty normal.

BELL: Normal? Do you mean white?

MS. JARVIS: [*Laughs*] Yeah, there was no, um, my school was pretty white, yeah. That's what I mean. That, that, um, I don't mean that like we were racist or anything, it probably sounds bad, but we were just normal people. It's not like we said, "No blacks allowed" or anything like that, we just didn't, um, everybody was white. That probably sounds terrible [*laughs*].

BELL: When you say everybody, does that include your friends too?

MRS. JARVIS: Yeah. I didn't have any black friends [*laughs*]. How could I? There were no black people around. I mean, again, I don't want to make it seem like we did that on purpose or anything. We never said like, oh, "We don't want black girls hanging around us." We were just normal kids, we didn't care about race at all.

In this exchange, Ms. Jarvis indicated that her family, her friends, and her school—three primary agents of socialization—all participated in the normalization of whiteness and contributed to her development of an invisible racial identity. For most of her life, whiteness never came up. It did not come up in her home, it did not come up in her school, and it did not come up with her friends. Also revealing was that even though she lived in an all-white neighborhood, went to an all-white school, and had only white friends, Ms. Jarvis believed her childhood to be a raceless one, evidenced by her repeated use of the word "normal" when describing white spaces and white people. Thus, in large part due to the way she was socialized, Ms. Jarvis treated race as something that belonged only to nonwhites. Without the presence of African Americans or other people of color, race did not exist. Everything and everyone was just "normal."

Richard Marsh, fifty-four and a highly experienced urban school teacher, also demonstrated the centrality of socialization to the development of raceless identities. For him, the very idea of sustained and/or meaningful conversations about "being white" was so foreign that he found this line of questioning "ridiculous." When I asked him if he had, at any point in his childhood, discussed what it meant to be white, Mr. Marsh responded with incredulity and, unlike the majority of my other interview respondents, a bit of hostility.

BELL: Growing up, did you ever engage in any conversations about what it meant to be white?

MR. MARSH: Huh? I don't know if I understand, you're asking me if I ever talked about being white, like, as a kid?

BELL: Yes. Throughout your childhood, including adolescence, did anyone in your family or anyone that you were close to ever bring up the subject of whiteness with you? Or did you ever bring it up with them? Did you ever have any questions about your racial identity?

MR. MARSH: No. That's ridiculous.

BELL: Why do you say that?

MR. MARSH: Because it's a ridiculous question. Why would I ask anybody about being white? I know I'm white, I've always been white. But, um, I don't think, or, um, I don't see why that matters, or let me just say it never mattered to me.

BELL: Did it matter to anyone in your family?

MR. MARSH: Of course not. I don't know what you're implying here, but I honestly don't understand what you're trying to get at. I mean, I, look, I'm fifty-four years old. I was born in the sixties, you know. And, um, by the time I was, you know, old enough to know anything, the civil rights movement, all that was, um, I, it was done and over with. So, um, I think, as, I just think as a country, um, I think, we white people we're not the same as before, you know. We're in a much more tolerant, a much, much better place, you know. So we didn't need to talk about it. I think it would've been unnecessary to say the least.

In more ways than one, Mr. Marsh reinforced the importance of racial socialization, particularly white racial socialization in the post–civil rights era.[26] Initially taken aback, Mr. Marsh could not understand why I would ask a question about whiteness in reference to his childhood, even going as far as to call the question ridiculous. In addition to dismissing my question verbally, he also appeared to take issue with it physically, repeatedly frowning and rolling his eyes throughout the exchange. The actual substance of his response was also revealing. Mr. Marsh, like other white Brick City teachers, never talked about his own racial identity as a child. As he explained, given his birth cohort—and its temporal proximity to the civil rights movement—Mr. Marsh did not see the need for him or anyone in his family to broach the subject of being white. To do so not only was unnecessary but also would have reflected poorly on the racial attitudes of white people, possibly indicating that they harbored a pre–civil rights mindset. With this construction in mind, Mr. Marsh explicitly equated the recognition of race with racism, leading him to avoid the subject, both as a child and as an adult. Still, despite these noble intentions, Mr. Marsh was socialized to believe that racial identity *did not* belong to him, all but ensuring he would become a producer and practitioner of white racelessness.[27]

White racelessness and rhetorical incoherence were commonplace throughout my time in the field. In both content and form, the empirical claim that white Americans fail to see or recognize whiteness came to life as, across interviews, white Brick City teachers repeatedly described whiteness as normal or otherwise invisible. This pattern held true for the majority of respondents, even after I rephrased and varied how I framed the question. As long as I asked about white racial identity generally, it remained invisible and teachers found it difficult to discuss. When interview respondents did speak about meaningful identities, the identities in question had little to do with whiteness *as whiteness*. That is, white Brick City teachers discussed their gender and ethnic identities frequently, and they did so in a much more lucid and coherent manner. Thus, white deflection—the tendency to pivot to other, seemingly more meaningful identities in response to questions about being white—accompanied rhetorical incoherence throughout the interview process. Next I explore this concept in greater detail.

I Have Thought about Being a Woman. Like a Lot.

I really can't tell you. That's something I've never thought about, really. I don't think I know a single white person who could give you a clear answer to that question. It's funny, though, I have thought about being a woman. Like a lot. I always wonder how people see me. Do they see me as Melanie or do they see me as some random woman? That's something I've thought about pretty much my entire life.—MELANIE SCOTT, 49

Although white Brick City teachers struggled to discuss their racial identity, they spoke forcefully about other aspects of their lives and personal sense of self. Though not always in response to the same question, and certainly not to the same degree, gender and ethnicity were routinely cited in response to inquiries about whiteness. After struggling to make sense of white racial identity, teachers would shift the discussion to personal identities that were more visible to them. Given that the majority of my research participants were women, gender was by far the most frequent nonracial form of identity invoked by white Brick City teachers. Of all of my interviews with female participants, twenty-five in total, only five did not volunteer their thoughts about being a woman. Thus, for much of my fieldwork, gender was front and center, and although teachers also volunteered their thoughts about ethnicity, it was the historical and contemporary reality of sexism, misogyny, and patriarchy that was used most frequently to deflect questions about whiteness and white racial identity.

White deflection became apparent early on in the data collection process. Spanning from one of my first interviews to my last, white Brick City teachers deflected questions about white racial identity with detailed, and sometimes emotional, stories about gender and ethnicity. For example, Carrie Weaver, a middle school teacher, struggled when trying to talk about white racial identity but spoke clearly and openly about gender and how much it has impacted her life. When asked what it meant to be white, Mrs. Weaver immediately pivoted to gender, providing me with numerous thoughts and examples about what it means to be a woman.

MRS. WEAVER: Um, I don't know. I honestly never think, I don't really think of myself in terms of race, of being white, you know. I think of myself as more of a woman. Being a woman is something I think about all the time. Even as a teacher, you know, I'm expected, women are expected to be teachers, but if you look at who the principals and vice principals are, they're mostly men. I, um, I just don't see that as a coincidence.

BELL: Why do you think about gender and what that means to you, but not about race?

MRS. WEAVER: Um, hmmm [*pause*], I don't know, really. I just think of myself first and foremost as a woman. It's right there, you know. I think when people see me, they see a woman. When I look in the mirror, I see a woman. And as a woman, I'm certainly treated differently—I mean, not always, but there are times when I'm treated unfairly because I'm a woman. So it's definitely something I think about. Something I think about a lot. Being a woman is very important to me.

BELL: Do you consider being white as something that's very important to you?

MRS. WEAVER: Again, I just, I'm a woman. I don't really think of myself in terms of being white. I just never have [*laughs*]. I mean, I guess technically I'm a white woman, technically. But still, I think in reality, you know, at least for me, being a woman and dealing with all that being a woman entails, you know, being a working mom, um, is what I find to be most important.

Mrs. Weaver's response was emblematic of how gender was introduced into the interview process. Teachers, specifically female teachers, not only were keenly aware of gender as an identifying and institutional force but also stood ready to invoke it in direct response to my questions about white racial identity. In almost every instance where gendered experiences were volunteered, it followed a familiar pattern. After specific questions about white racial identity, teachers first would struggle to form and articulate a lucid answer. Then, very quickly, they would pivot to gender, an identity that they found more salient to their day-to-day experiences. Finally, after I would attempt to steer the conversation back to race, teachers would reiterate that they had not given much thought to what it means to be white but they had given considerable thought to what it means to be a woman.

Melanie Scott, a forty-nine-year-old high school science teacher, typified this process. A self-proclaimed "proud feminist bitch," Mrs. Scott—going all the way back to her time as a middle school student—offered a variety of personal stories about how gender has affected her life, both positively and negatively. Very attuned to various discriminatory processes, such as the gender pay gap and institutionalized rape culture, Mrs. Scott spoke of widespread and systematic patriarchy with incredible ease. Whenever I attempted to steer the conversation back to white racial identity, however, her rhetorical fluency and overall command of the facts diminished significantly.

MRS. SCOTT: Look, I'm a woman first, a woman second, and everything else third [*laughs*]. When it comes to being white or whatever, I, um, I just don't even think about it. It doesn't really mean anything. I guess, um, I think that, being a woman, it's, being white, I don't know about being white. But, I know I sound crazy, but stay with me. You want to talk about inequality, well, let me tell you about being a woman. As a man, I don't think you'll be able to understand this. I've been fighting against patriarchal bullshit since I was eleven years old, OK. I got sick of people telling me that my future consisted of finding a husband and having kids. So I spoke out. I spoke out. At home, at school, wherever. If I thought people were treating me differently because I was a woman, I would let them know about it. I was this way as a kid, I was this way in college, I was this way in my first marriage, I'm this way in my current marriage, and I'm still this way as a middle-aged adult. I've been a proud feminist bitch for a long time, and if people have a problem with it, that's on them, not me.

BELL: You say you're a woman first and a woman second, but do you think your experiences as a white woman are different from those of women of color?

MRS. SCOTT: I, hmm [*pause*]. That's an interesting question. I think as women, I mean, I think as a whole, women don't get a fair shake. We never really have. When I think about how hard it is as a teacher, you know, a so-called woman's job, I just get so upset because people have no idea how hard it is, you know. So, I don't know, I just think when people talk about things like racism or whatever, they should keep in mind that women are still women, and we're always fighting an uphill battle.

BELL: Just to be clear, in terms of lived experiences, do you feel like your experiences as a white woman are identical to those of women of color?

MRS. SCOTT: I honestly can't answer that question. I think, um, I have no reason to believe my experiences are dramatically different from say a black woman or an Asian woman. Maybe women from old money [*laughs*]. Even then, it's, um, I mean we're still women, right? At some point, it will catch up to you, no matter what race you are.

Mrs. Scott's experiences with institutional and interpersonal patriarchy, in part, have led to a heightened awareness of gender norms, gender politics, and gender discrimination. Although conceptually and empirically valid, Mrs. Scott's devotion to discussing gender and gender discrimination, particularly in response to my questions about whiteness, was a distancing strategy, one used by numerous teachers to compensate for their inability to talk about white racial identity.[28] Still, despite their attentiveness to the intricacies of gender, not one teacher who spoke openly—and accurately—about institutional patriarchy took racial variation among women into account. That is, intersectionality, or the "focus on *inclusion* of the experiences of multiply-marginalized persons and groups," was not something that white Brick City teachers took seriously, even as they spoke eloquently about the day-to-day reality of gender discrimination.[29]

Historically, the whitewashing of womanhood has been all too common, not just in terms of lived experiences but also in the areas of research and scholarship, popular culture, and social movement activism.[30] Beginning in the 1980s, a cadre of scholars, mostly women of color, introduced and developed the concept of intersectionality, providing a powerful analytical framework for the study of identity and inequality.[31] Among other things, these scholars pointed out that (1) women have been erased from social movements focused on race, (2) black women have been erased from social movements focused on gender, and (3) women of color were uniquely susceptible to symbolic, political, and physical forms of violence.[32] Debated and expanded over multiple decades, intersectionality has been applied in a multitude of ways, accounting for both interactional and institutional processes.[33] For the purposes of this study, I use intersectionality to highlight the socially constructed nature of race and gender, as well as the very real effects they have on lived experiences and life outcomes.

In their article "Practicing Intersectionality in Sociological Research: A Critical Analysis of Inclusions, Interactions, and Institutions in the Study of Inequalities," sociologists Hae Yeon Choo and Myra Marx Ferree offer a comprehensive review of the adaptations and applications of intersectionality.[34] They write, "Social constructionist understandings of intersectionality . . . highlight dynamic forces more than categories—racialization rather than races, economic exploitation rather than classes, gendering and gender experiences rather than gender—and recognize the distinctiveness of how power operates across particular institutional fields."[35] This formulation of intersectionality is instructive, specifically because it helps to explain why many of the women I interviewed could easily recognize their gender identities while remaining oblivious to their racial identities. As women living within a male-dominated society, lived experience across various institutional fields shaped their perception that they, *and not men*, were gendered. Conversely, as white women living within a white-dominated society, lived experience across those same institutional fields shaped their perception that nonwhites, *and not them*, were raced.[36] That is, prior to working in the Brick City School District, nowhere in their lives, personally or professionally, had they undergone the dynamic and experiential process of racialization.

Ethnicity, albeit to a significantly lesser extent, was also used to deflect inquiries into whiteness and white racial identity. Several teachers talked about their ethnic backgrounds, particularly as it pertained to their participation in cultural traditions and their fond memories of ethnic food. One teacher spoke affectionately about growing up celebrating "the feast of the seven fishes" at Christmas, while another jokingly admitted that she must "pretend to care about being Polish" to placate her "traditional mother." Still, while teachers offered their thoughts about, and experiences with, European ethnic culture, their most common invocation of white ethnicity came in the form of stories about the ethnic discrimination endured by their parents and grandparents. Of the teachers who deflected white racial identity with European ethnicity, no topic was discussed more than the ugly history of white-ethnic discrimination.[37] For example, Kate Meredith, a fifty-three-year-old English teacher, explained how her Irish background is a more salient identity marker than her "white skin" is.

MRS. MEREDITH: To be honest, I think of myself as more Irish than white, you know. I mean, um, I can't, off the top of my head, think of how being white has affected my life. At the end of the day, it's just white skin. I, um, I don't think it really means anything. But I'll tell you what, I'm Irish, you know. I'm sure you know the type of racism we faced when we first came here. I remember my grandfather telling me horrible stories, just godawful stories about what he and his wives went through. He was married three times [*laughs*]. But you get what I'm saying? I think that, you know, being Irish is more important than being white. At least it is for me.

Tellingly, during her description of white ethnic discrimination, Mrs. Meredith never once claimed that she had ever experienced it herself. Rather, in lieu of personal experiences with ethnic-based discrimination, she recounted the "godawful stories" told to her by her late grandfather. Still, despite her lack of firsthand experience with, or exposure to, anti-Irish discrimination, Mrs. Meredith equated the historical mistreatment of Irish immigrants to modern-day racism against people of color, ultimately using this equivalence as the basis for a heightened and more meaningful ethnic identity. Within the context of our interview, Mrs. Meredith used her ethnic identity, in part fueled by the very real, very ugly history of anti-Irish discrimination, to deflect my questions about whiteness and white racial identity. She was not the only teacher to do so.

Mrs. Vincent, a middle school health teacher from an Italian background, initially shut down when I asked her about white racial identity. She started and stopped several times, paused again, and eventually admitted that she did not know how to answer the question. After we moved further into the interview, Mrs. Vincent—*voluntarily*—came back to my question about whiteness. Cutting me off midquestion, she offered the following thoughts:

MRS. VINCENT: You know, I'm sorry, but I think I can maybe I can answer you better now, um, about being, what it means to be white.

BELL: OK. Sounds good.

MRS. VINCENT: The reason I think it was so hard is because I never really saw myself as white, you know. I don't mean it like that, of course I'm white, you know. But, um, what I mean is, like it never really meant anything.

BELL: Being white never meant anything?

MRS. VINCENT: Yeah, like I've always thought of myself as Italian, you know. I come from a big Italian family, and I've always been Italian first. That's how I've always saw myself, you know, a loudmouth Italian [*laughs*].

BELL: Did anyone in your family ever talk to you about being an Italian American?

MRS. VINCENT: Yeah, like all the time. Especially my grandmother. She was old school, you know, more traditional. And she overcame a lot to become a successful businesswoman. So, I just wanted to say, I know we were talking about something else, but if my poor, uneducated grandma, who was also a single mom, can overcome the racism of her day, I don't wanna hear excuses about racism today. I'm sorry, but we've all been through something.

BELL: That's OK, you're fine. I did want to touch on one thing, though.

MRS. VINCENT: Sure.

BELL: You said that you did talk about your Italian background while growing up. Does that include any conversations about whiteness? Did anyone ever talk to you specifically about what it means to be white?

MRS. VINCENT: Oh. No [*laughs*].

While initially struggling to articulate a coherent position on what it means to be white, Mrs. Vincent eventually found her footing and offered up her thoughts about her Italian identity. She readily admitted that, in no small part due to her ethnic socialization, she has long identified with her Italian background, even going so far as to describe herself as "Italian first." Whereas her family did not talk to her about what it meant to be white, they did talk to her about what it meant to be Italian, socializing her to embrace the latter and ignore the former. In a bit of a tangent, however, Mrs. Vincent veered off topic, conflating race and ethnicity and falling back on the neoliberal, meritocratic idea of rugged individualism. Based on her grandmother's success in overcoming ethnic discrimination, she chastised anyone who would complain about racial discrimination today. All told, within the span of this one exchange, Mrs. Vincent spoke to the importance of racial socialization, used her ethnic identity to deflect questions about her racial identity, and also engaged in what Charles Gallagher terms the *white ethnic card*, "selectively recalling ethnic family history" to equate the treatment and life experiences of European immigrants to those of racial minorities.[38]

In the cases of Mrs. Meredith, Mrs. Vincent, and several others, ethnic discrimination against European immigrants served as an important tool for white deflection. While it is certainly true that many European immigrants faced discrimination on arriving to the United States, over time these ethnic groups successfully assimilated into the dominant mainstream.[39] That is, as the 1800s faded into memory and we moved deeper into the twentieth century, Irish, Italian, Polish, Greek, and, to a lesser degree, Jewish identities all became intertwined and intimately associated with whiteness.[40] In fact, for many European immigrants, their passport to whiteness was stamped by embracing and outwardly participating in the dehumanization of racial minorities, particularly African Americans.[41] Thus, in falling back on the discrimination faced by their parents and grandparents, white Brick City teachers not only deflected questions about white racial identity but also obfuscated the role of antiblack racism in ethnic assimilation, reinforcing white racelessness and rationalizing systems of white domination in the process.

Although a form of discursive distancing, the term "white deflection" is in no way meant to dismiss the reality of sexism and patriarchy, nor is it meant to diminish the ugly history of ethnic discrimination suffered by Southern and Eastern European immigrants.[42] Furthermore, the concept is not intended to mock or make light of the importance that white teachers assign to their gender and/or ethnic identities. Specifically, in reference to gender, teachers spoke emotionally about the myriad ways that misogyny affected their lives, and they did so with a genuine concern about the existence of institutional patriarchy and the unique challenges they face as women. As a sociologist, as well as a male within a male-dominated society, it would be methodologically and ethically inappropriate for me to question women's experiences with sexism and gender discrimination.[43] Therefore, the concept of white deflection should not be taken as the minimization of gender and/ or ethnic identity, nor should it be interpreted as the infantilizing of gender and/or ethnic discrimination.

That being said, however, gender and ethnicity were consistently used as distancing strategies. Gender identity and examples of gender discrimination—and, to a lesser degree, ethnic identity and historical examples of ethnic discrimination—while genuine and important, were offered as a deflection, a shield against my questions about white racial identity. Even when I tried to steer the conversation back to race, teachers remained steadfast, delving deeper into the salience of gender and/or ethnicity. For example, with gender, despite knowing of, and sometimes speaking to, the experiential and epistemological dissonance that often accompanies privilege, many of the women who volunteered information about their gendered experiences remained blissfully unaware that they themselves displayed this very dissonance with matters of racial experience.[44] That is, while Mrs. Scott could accurately surmise that I, as a man, could never fully understand certain gendered realities, she could not bring herself to admit that she, as a white woman, could never fully understand certain racialized realities.[45] Even after I explicitly asked her about racial variation *among women*, Mrs. Scott continued to construct womanhood as a uniform experience, rendering women of color invisible and allowing her to deflect my questions about white racial identity.

CONCLUSION

As with a fish in water, total immersion within white racialized spaces can, and often does, normalize whiteness to the point of invisibility. This was clearly the case for the teachers who participated in this study. Owing to their unique form of racial socialization, white Brick City teachers acknowledged that open and candid conversations about being white were generally foreign to them. As products of white spaces and of the interactions within them, the teachers I interviewed had had little occasion to examine their lives as racial actors. The combination of growing up in predominantly or exclusively white neighborhoods, attending predominantly or exclusively white schools, and belonging to predominantly or exclusively white peer groups caused white Brick City teachers to construct whiteness as the raceless norm, leaving them devoid of meaningful racial identities. Thus, white racelessness, the theory that white Americans struggle to recognize whiteness and white racial identity, was heavily supported by the data presented in this chapter.

Taking the form of rhetorical incoherence and white deflection, white racelessness caused Brick City teachers to stutter and stammer their way through answers about white racial identity. Both concepts, together and in their own way, brought the research literature to life, giving concrete weight to theoretical claims about privilege and empirical claims about identity. With each "I don't know, I never thought about it," with every broken sentence or pivot to gender or ethnic identity, the concept of white invisibility leaped from the pages of sociological texts and landed in the form of a thinking, feeling Brick City teacher. Still, though illuminating, and in many ways confirmatory, representations of white racelessness did not hold. As I show in the chapters to come, within the physical space of predominantly black schools, whiteness, as an elusive identity and as the raceless norm, can be interrupted.

2. THE COLOR LINE AND THE CLASSROOM

The problem of the 20th century is the problem of the color-line.
—W. E. B. DU BOIS, *The Souls of Black Folk*

Education has been romanticized to the extent that, like religion,
it appears disconnected from the world of power, partisanship, and
the shaping of the social world.—WILLIAM H. WATKINS,
The White Architects of Black Education

The wider society is still replete with overwhelmingly white neighborhoods,
restaurants, schools, universities, workplaces, cosmopolitan spaces. . . . As
demographics change, public spaces are subject to change as well, impact-
ing not only how a space is occupied and by whom but also the way in
which it is perceived.—ELIJAH ANDERSON, "The White Space"

"Malcolm X. My kids love Malcolm X." Mrs. Martin, a veteran teacher of fifteen years, sat across from me in her own living room, explaining why her
school, as well as her individual classroom, was "decked out in blackface."
According to her, many of the students at Cass Tech High School were "really into civil rights," and as a result, the school principal had long since decided that civil rights imagery would be prominently featured throughout

the building. All teachers, regardless of their preferences or personal politics, were to contribute to the overall black cultural aesthetic of Cass Tech. While Mrs. Martin did see the utility in such a policy, it left her somewhat uncomfortable, specifically the numerous images of Malcolm X that were plastered throughout the school. As she stated during our interview, "Here you have a man who was unapologetically racist against whites, you know. He hated white people. Whatever good that folks see in Malcolm X, it's a known fact that he thought we were devils, and his picture is in the hall right outside my classroom." Although she would never venerate Malcolm X in her personal life, his picture, as well as those of other African American icons, lined the hallways and classroom walls of Cass Tech High School.

Throughout our interview, Mrs. Martin described the great lengths she went to in order to make her predominantly black student body feel welcome at Cass Tech. In her classroom alone, you can find numerous images of civil rights figures, as well as a small library filled with books about African American history and literature. Mrs. Martin wanted her students to feel comfortable, which in part meant that the "look and feel of the school" should reflect the types of students who attend the school. Therefore, even though she personally took issue with images of Malcolm X, she supported the idea of tailoring the school's overall aesthetic to the cultural preferences and historical iconography of its mostly black student body. Central to this logic was Mrs. Martin's personal construction of Cass Tech High as a black school. That is, Mrs. Martin, like each of my other interview respondents, viewed her school as an explicitly racialized space.[1]

In this chapter I highlight the degree to which white teachers distinctly identified Brick City schools as black schools. Interview data will show how a combination of factors, both institutional and interactional, led white teachers to conceptualize their respective schools as racialized spaces. Institutionally, their workplaces were located in, and physically surrounded by, racially segregated ghettos, and the schools themselves were aesthetically tailored to appeal to the broader black community. On a more intimate level, the sheer number of black students and black families, combined with speech patterns, modes of dress, and other indicators of what white teachers perceived to be "black culture," affected the day-to-day interactions within these physical spaces. Compounding matters further, student discourse about racism and racial inequality permeated the school environment, cementing the racialization of Brick City schools in the minds of white teachers.

I begin by reviewing the racialization of space. The physical structures and spatial surroundings that contextualize and, in many ways, shape our lives, are, just like people, subject to the forces of racialization.[2] Today states, neighborhoods, and schools, among other physical spaces, have taken on or have been assigned racial identities of their own.[3] Next I trace the racialization of urban schools, particularly in the political aftermath of the *Brown v. Board of Education* decision of 1954. Following the formal invalidation of state-mandated school segregation, a number of legal and social policies, individual choices, and the rise of neoliberalism all colluded to link urban centers to black and brown bodies.[4] Over time, the association of "the inner city" with blackness has become a social fact, as the two terms are now interchangeable in the national consciousness.[5] Finally, I present interview data. More specifically, I show how white Brick City teachers, without exception, conceptualized and characterized their schools as black schools, as explicitly racialized spaces.

THE RACIALIZATION OF SPACE

The importance of space in American society cannot be overstated.[6] Space, in the form of houses, neighborhoods, schools, parks, swimming pools, public transit, jails, movie theaters, cemeteries, and perhaps most (in)famously, water fountains, has been racialized for the greater part of American history.[7] Beyond racialization, space is also contested. Where one lives, where one works, what schools are available to one's children, indeed, where one is allowed to physically be, have all been, *and are*, sites of racialized conflict.[8] This is particularly true of white space, which, historically and today, is afforded protection from what are often perceived to be outside threats.[9] Informally, white space, in the form of the white neighborhood, the white school, and even the white body, is protected through physical and symbolic violence, and formally, white space is protected through the force and finality of law.[10] All told, the intersection of race and space has a long and fraught history, and numerous scholars have documented the resulting consequences of the racialization of space.

Sociologist George Lipsitz, in detailing the reciprocal history of race and space, writes, "Opportunities in this society are both racialized and spatialized." He continues, "The lived experience of race has a spatial dimension, and the lived experience of space has a racial dimension," and "the interconnections among race, place, and power in the United States have a long history."[11] In this sense, lived experience does not take place within a vacuum; it takes place within a physical space.[12] We live out our day-to-day lives not in some abstract, spaceless void, but in actual neighborhoods, actual schools, actual workplaces, actual hospitals, actual prisons, and actual homes. In this way, the forces of racialization that affect us as individuals and groups also come to affect the physical dimensions that shape our lives. As a result—and in a true personification of biography, society, and history—the very spaces that give context to our lives as people, over time, themselves become racialized.[13] Other sociologists too have offered a substantive analysis of race and space.

In his seminal article "The White Space," renowned urban ethnographer Elijah Anderson makes a distinction between various physical spaces that have been systematically racialized over the course of American history. On the one hand, black space, most powerfully symbolized by the *iconic ghetto*, is marked by extreme poverty, rampant drug use, and deadly violence and, according to Anderson, "appears to verge on self-destruction."[14] On the other hand, white space, while economically and politically diverse, is chiefly marked by the "overwhelming presence of white people" and the formal and informal "absence of black people."[15] In the broad spatial imagination, white and black spaces are diametrically opposed. While black spaces are commonly thought of as loud, dangerous, and unruly, white spaces are largely seen as quiet, peaceful, and orderly. In this regard, physical space can be symbolically linked to race in a manner that seems normal; or, as philosopher, Charles Mills, puts it, "The norming of space is partially done in terms the *racing* of space, the depiction of space as dominated by individuals (whether persons or subpersons) of a certain race."[16] The barrio for brown people and the ghetto for black people, for example, both attest to the racialized norming of space, as these terms, alone, often conjure specific and stereotypical racial imagery.[17]

Taking a macro view of the racialization of space, sociologists Matthew Desmond and Mustafa Emirbayer observe that "one of the most pernicious images of America is that the country is white."[18] That is, a broad swath of Americans view the country as a white country. This is true not only in an ideological or symbolic sense, but in a physical and numerical sense as well. The United States is, after all, a physical space, a populated land mass encompassed within socially constructed, geopolitical borders. As the single largest racial category, and as the group that wields a disproportionate amount of political influence and economic power, white people in America have come to represent the default American, the standard to which all other racial classifications are compared.[19] Thus, taken together, racial power, racial ideology, and racial demography have so thoroughly linked whiteness to the United States that, in the minds of many Americans, the former is now synonymous with the latter.[20] Such a connection has major implications for how we view and understand physical space.

If America is constructed as a white country, then the physical space that composes America is a white space. Any reference to the country, its history, its social norms, its cultural values, and so on is also (1) an implicit reference to the physical dimensions that make up the country, and (2), unless explicitly associated with people of color, an implicit reference to whiteness.[21] Given the racial and ethnic heterogeneity within the United States, however, as well as the historical legacy and contemporary reality of racial segregation, spatial racialization throughout the country is localized.[22] That is, while America as a whole may be constructed as a white space, there are a multitude of spatial localities that have and maintain different racial identities. Urban education, both as a social institution and a physical space, is one such locality. Next I examine the racialization of urban education.[23]

URBAN EDUCATION: THE MAKING OF A NONWHITE SPACE

Public schools in the United States cannot be separated from the white supremacist context in which they were born.[24] American schools were founded for the enrichment and enlightenment of white males and, as such, were originally conceived as white spaces.[25] From school teachers to school curricula, from school policy to actual schools, race was central to the founding of education, and just as was the case throughout the broader society, white people—or a subset of white people—were the primary beneficiaries.[26] As time moved on, the white supremacist roots of education led to over a century of political and legal battles that were fought to determine who should, and who should not, have access to schools, in terms of both education and the physical spaces themselves.[27] While progress has been slow and unsteady, the conflict has linked race and place to schooling in indelible and seemingly endemic ways.

Today public schools are increasingly being associated with students of color.[28] Although 2014 marked the first time in American history that nonwhite children composed the majority of public school students, the minoritization of urban education has been an ongoing process spanning the last half of the twentieth century.[29] Following the landmark *Brown v. Board of Education* decision of 1954, white people in the South began employing a series of tactics that were designed to reinforce the color line and protect racial segregation in public schools.[30] In order to defend public education as a white space, school districts took extraordinary measures, up to and including shelving public schools altogether.[31] This, in conjunction with other political and structural changes, led to the famous phrase "chocolate cities and vanilla suburbs," a succinct, if perhaps simplistic, representation of race and space over the last sixty years.[32]

Following an initial period of massive resistance, the late 1960s and early 1970s saw real progress toward school desegregation.[33] As researchers Jennifer Hochschild and Nathan Scovronick note in their study on education policy, school desegregation efforts "started slowly, but eventually transformed education throughout the south and in northern districts."[34] Thus, despite a widespread and multifaceted effort to maintain racial segregation—to preserve the white space—eventually, the weight of legal challenges, the momentum of the civil rights movement, and, to a lesser degree, the liberalization of white racial attitudes all combined to defeat this effort, leading to real and meaningful school desegregation.[35] As Jim Crow came crashing down, schools all over the country, but especially in the South, saw genuine racial integration. Unfortunately, in the decades following, a fierce and sustained white backlash emerged, which largely led to a pattern of school resegregation that exists to this very day.[36]

After several decades of continued progress, school desegregation efforts came under intense scrutiny.[37] For an increasing number of white Americans, both within and outside the Jim Crow South, federally mandated school integration had outgrown its usefulness. What was once hailed as a vital and virtuous fight for the rights of black children was, after decades of struggle, transformed into an unfair and unnecessary infringement on the rights of white children.[38] As a result, scores of white families migrated from diverse central cities to racially segregated suburbs, where they erected a network of private schools that were almost exclusive to white children from middle-class and affluent backgrounds.[39] What's more, in a number of communities from different parts of the country, white residents took to the streets en masse to vocally—and sometimes violently—protest the implementation of compulsory busing, which by that point had come to symbolize federal integration efforts as a whole.[40] Contextualizing everything, from successful school integration to backlash and retrenchment, was the conservative turn in American politics.[41] With the success of the southern strategy, large swaths of white and formerly Democratic voters shifted to the Republican Party, effectively causing the Democratic Party to rethink, and ultimately retreat from, the battle over civil rights.[42]

Other factors too contributed to contemporary school segregation and the social construction of urban schools as nonwhite spaces. Over the last forty-plus years, the US Supreme Court has issued a number of rulings that have inculcated and, according to some analyses, accelerated the resegregation of public schools.[43] Two cases stand out. The first, *Milliken v. Bradley* (1974), ruled that compulsory busing across district lines was not permissible if it could not be proven that specific school districts actively engaged in racial segregation.[44] That is, if school segregation within any given district occurred "organically," as a result of neighborhood segregation or the personal preferences of parents and families, then the school district in question *could not* be subjected to mandatory busing or any other federal desegregation efforts. The *Milliken* decision was groundbreaking because, following the collapse of Jim Crow, or de jure segregation, it provided legitimacy and constitutional cover for de facto segregation, a practice that remains commonplace today.[45]

The second case, *Parents Involved in Community Schools v. Seattle School District No. 1* (2007), considered the constitutionality of voluntary desegregation efforts.[46] *Parents Involved* consolidated two cases, one from Louisville, Kentucky, and the other from Seattle, Washington. At issue in *Parents Involved* was whether or not individual school districts could increase diversity and reduce isolation by voluntarily using racial classification in student assignments. In a rare 4–1–4 decision, the Supreme Court ruled that racial classification could be used in student assignments, but only if it was "narrowly tailored" to "compelling state interests." In this particular case, state interests included increased racial diversity and decreased racial isolation in public schools. Ultimately, the Supreme Court ruled that the voluntary desegregation plans in Louisville and Seattle were not sufficiently tailored to compelling state interests and were therefore unconstitutional.[47]

Though not the only Supreme Court decisions to consider the role of racial segregation in education, the *Milliken* and *Parents Involved* decisions— argued more than thirty years apart—rejected involuntary *and voluntary* efforts to desegregate our nation's schools.[48] In doing so, the Court not only legitimated and provided legal standing for de facto segregation but also set an incredibly high standard for challenging the constitutionality of racially separate schools. Absent evidence of intentional segregation, "separate but equal" schooling—what was once characterized as "inherently unequal"—is again the norm, legally protected by the highest court in the land.[49] Thus, in the contemporary United States, school segregation, no matter how pervasive or how damaging to black and brown children, is legally permissible when it is seen as the result of naturally occurring phenomena.[50]

Beyond Supreme Court jurisprudence and shifting (white) racial politics, school resegregation and the ossification of white versus nonwhite racialized space has been exacerbated by economic change. Casting a large shadow over the battle for, and against, school integration was a deindustrializing and rapidly changing economy.[51] Well-paying factory jobs that were commonplace throughout much of the twentieth century disappeared, replaced only by service sector and retail positions that offered a fraction of the pay and few of the benefits.[52] As manufacturing jobs fled urban centers for newly constructed suburbs, affluent and upwardly mobile African Americans did so as well, combining with white flight to produce a number of racially *and* economically segregated inner-city communities.[53] As these neighborhoods deteriorated and social dislocations such as poverty, joblessness, and crime rose sharply, a new term—*the urban underclass*—became a fixture in the American lexicon, casting a shadow over education policy that has remained in place for the last forty years.[54]

THE NEOLIBERAL TURN IN AMERICAN SCHOOLS

Since the late 1970s and early 1980s, urban schools have developed a negative reputation, stereotyped as dropout factories teeming with black and brown students who disregard, and even actively resist, educational achievement.[55] Often immersed within segregated neighborhoods, marked by concentrated poverty, single-parent households, and high levels of violent crime, these schools are seen as both a by-product and a genesis of the communities they serve. That is, on the one hand, educational failure is viewed as the inevitable result of an unfair and inequitable environment, while on the other hand, educational failure is regarded as one of the primary causes of disadvantaged or "dysfunctional" neighborhoods.[56] No matter the causal direction, "bad neighborhoods" and "bad schools" are now broadly constructed as symbiotic; they are so mutually reinforcing that, for a great number of people, their epistemological opposites—"good neighborhoods" and "good schools"—are automatically assumed to be white.[57] Therefore, questions of how best to fix so-called bad schools and boost black and brown educational achievement have been, and continue to be, of great concern to educators and researchers alike.

In the wake of growing concerns about urban schools, particularly concerns about lack of achievement, low standards, and future international competitiveness, America turned to the market.[58] A report commissioned by the Reagan administration, *A Nation at Risk* (1983), sounded the alarm about mediocrity in education and, from a policy perspective, ushered in an era of bipartisan neoliberalism.[59] Schools, once seen as a public good, became private commodities, turning students and their families into consumers who had to *compete* with others for the best possible product.[60] In lieu of segregation and unequal opportunity, government bureaucracies became the new villain, accused of stifling innovation, eschewing teacher accountability, and, in the words of former president George W. Bush, promoting "the soft bigotry of low expectations."[61] Therefore, the market, a keystone of neoliberal economic theory, was posited as the savior of American schools, one that would discard unnecessary regulatory burdens and ineffective teachers, boost pedagogical innovation, increase standardization for all K–12 students, and fortify American competitiveness in the international marketplace.[62]

Though it is sometimes only implied (see "good schools" versus "bad schools"), what stands at the heart of the discourse and debate surrounding schools, standards, accountability, and so on is race.[63] Compounded by economic isolation, race, in the form of neighborhoods, schools, and students, is deeply intertwined with our collective understanding of the purpose and promise of schools. For example, if schools are indeed the great equalizer, then in a material sense they are the great equalizer between the haves and have-nots, between poor black kids in the inner city and affluent white kids in nearby suburbs. With this in mind, the policy preferences of neoliberal regimes—including privatization, charter schools, and standardized tests—cannot be neatly separated from, and in some cases actively contribute to, the ongoing reality of racially separate and unequal schooling.[64] Thus, over time, the neoliberal turn in policy, with help from man-made and nonman-made disasters—such as Hurricane Katrina and the Great Recession—has reallocated space, reconfigured schools, and intensified the epistemological connection between race and geography.[65]

Despite being central to the material outcomes of people and society, neoliberalism transcends schools and other forms of social policy. Across the political spectrum, a significant fraction of the American public now views neoliberalism as a way of life: it has become a salient feature of their personal and political identities.[66] Constructed as a much-needed corrective to heavy-handed government regulation and the overly redistributive policies of the Great Society, neoliberalism has merged seamlessly, if not ahistorically, with other pillars of American ideology, namely colorblindness, meritocracy, and equal opportunity.[67] In addition to justifying the need for neoliberal policy, including privatization, gentrification, and an amplified surveillance state, neoliberal ideology also provides discursive cover for the disparate and seemingly inevitable outcomes that result from their passage.[68] All told, as the dominant ideological framework in many American cities, neoliberalism has given rise to a modern, spatialized, and predatory form of capitalism that, under the pretext of "market forces," leaves millions of people behind.[69] Brick City is no exception.

POVERTY IN THE BRICK CITY SCHOOL DISTRICT

The BCSD is located in one of the poorest cities in the country.[70] As of this writing, almost a third (30.5 percent) of Brick City residents live below the federal poverty line, which is only slightly better than the number of residents living in poverty (32.4 percent) during the time I was still conducting interviews. Compounding matters further, due to steady population decline, as well as entrenched layers of racial and economic segregation, Brick City is also home to elevated levels of concentrated poverty. This all but assures that individual families, regardless of their personal socioeconomic standing, are much more likely to live in impoverished communities with impoverished schools, subjecting them to the pervasive and often deleterious consequences of neighborhood effects.[71] For children, research has shown that living in chronically poor neighborhoods can increase criminal delinquency, expose them to environmental toxins, and adversely affect their mental health and physical well-being.[72] Unfortunately—but unsurprisingly—the same pattern of racial and economic segregation that characterizes Brick City generally is also reflected throughout Brick City schools.

According to the latest census data, 44 percent of Brick City children live below the poverty line, which is a noticeable improvement from the 50.2 percent of children who did so at the time of my fieldwork. While the general trend line may be positive, the fact remains that, even today, almost half the children of an entire city are grappling with poverty, being forced to navigate food and housing insecurity, in addition to other aspects of the modern neoliberal city, such as joblessness, increased police surveillance, and a gutted social safety net.[73] The city's child poverty rate itself is disconcerting, but again, due to segregation, the resulting effects are not dispersed evenly across Brick City schools. There are multiple schools that, both in terms of student demographics and physical structure, rival those of nearby, affluent suburbs, while many others, often close in geographical proximity, are home to entire student bodies that qualify for free and reduced-price lunch. Such an imbalance is reminiscent of the city—and the country—as a whole, where race, socioeconomic status, and access to opportunity are intimately connected to space.[74]

For its part, the BCSD has responded to student poverty in a number of ways. As with schooling in other neoliberal cities, however, elevating standardized test scores and improving skills—as opposed to combating poverty—are by far the highest priorities in the district.[75] In 2014, the BCSD identified seven of its lowest-performing schools and converted them to Innovation Area Schools. Each of the selected schools received an influx of financial resources and technology, saw its school day extended by seventy minutes, and was granted leeway to design and implement a new and "innovative" curriculum. Another program, Chasing Higher Education, is a collaborative partnership between the BCSD and numerous corporate and nonprofit organizations. Chasing Higher Education provides college scholarships to any BCSD student who (1) qualifies academically for participating schools and (2) spent all four years of high school in the district. Other corporate partnerships incentivize student achievement through professional internships, some offer five- and six-year programs that include a high school diploma and vocational training, and still others focus on parents, offering them classes and workshops to improve their own job marketability. The BCSD also provides after-school tutoring and weekend SAT prep courses, both of which have taken on greater importance since the arrival of multiple charter schools in the city.

For white teachers, then, many of whom subscribe to a neoliberal view of society, Brick City schools are far more than just schools: they are unique spaces where race takes place. With every building that is located in racially segregated, impoverished neighborhoods, with every classroom that is chock-full of low-income black and brown bodies, and with every policy response that is purportedly designed to raise standards and close the achievement gap, the intersection between racial identity, political ideology, and physical space gets stronger.[76] Today, over sixty years after the *Brown v. Board of Education* decision, a combination of factors has powerfully reinforced the racialization of urban schools. While it is difficult to pin down precise causal linkages between past and present, the aforementioned legal, residential, economic, and political changes have all but cemented urban schools as both racialized and problematized spaces.[77] Decades in the making, the discursive and ideological marriage of "urban" and "black" was reflected throughout my interview data when interview respondents clearly and consistently spoke of Brick City schools as black schools. That is, in stark contrast to the raceless identities they constructed for themselves, and far from anything resembling white space, white Brick City teachers constructed their classrooms and schools as explicitly racialized.

Everybody Knows I Teach at a Black School

That's funny, I only have to say Brick City and everybody knows what I mean. Everybody knows I teach at a black school. All my friends, my parents, my girlfriend, you know, they all look at me like I'm crazy, you know. Like, how can you work at a school like that?

—JAMES RHODES, 40

Brick City is a highly segregated city, which is subsequently reflected in the Brick City School District. Every teacher I interviewed worked in a school with a student population that was at least 60 percent black, with some working in schools with a student population that was 80 percent or even 90 percent black. Still, in order to examine the ways that racialized space *might* affect white racial identity, I first needed to ascertain whether or not white teachers actually thought of their workplaces as racialized. That is, did white teachers view Brick City schools as black schools? Without exception, the answer to this question was yes. Ms. Jarvis, a middle school health teacher, exemplified this particular construction when discussing her experiences at Gardener Middle School, a school with a student body that is over 90 percent black.

BELL: Do you consider Gardener Middle School to be a black school?

MS. JARVIS: Oh, yeah, absolutely. I mean, are you serious [*laughs*]? We only have a handful of, um, white students in the school, and, um, I think that, um, in my first couple of years, I've only had like four, maybe five white students. The rest of my kids come from more of an urban background, you know.

BELL: When you say "urban background," do you mean black or African American?

MS. JARVIS: Oh my god, does that sound bad [*laughs*]? I'm so sorry. I didn't mean it like, I didn't mean to be offensive or anything like that, I just meant, um, [*pause*].

BELL: No, no, no, I didn't get offended at all. I'm just trying to be as clear as possible, so when I go over my notes later, I'll know exactly what it was you were trying to say. This way I don't have to guess. It's all about clarification.

MS. JARVIS: Oh, OK. Well, that's a relief [*laughs*]. So, yeah, um, like I was saying: most of my kids, pretty much all of my kids, come from urban backgrounds. Um, and by that I mean they're black [*laughs*]. Like I said, this is my third year teaching, and I can pretty much count all of the white students I've had on one hand, you know. Some of our students are immigrants, you know, but they're like, they're black too, so, um, I would say yeah, Gardener is definitely a black school.

On multiple occasions throughout our interview, Mrs. Jarvis equated "urban" with "black," and the first time she was unsure as to whether she had broken some unwritten rule of racial discourse. When I asked a follow-up question, double-checking to see whether Ms. Jarvis was in fact referencing black students whenever she mentioned kids from "an urban background," her face turned red and she made a point to apologize for her ostensible faux pas. After I explained to her that my follow-up question was for the sole purpose of clarification, she resumed speaking about the racial composition of her students, including the fact that the majority of them, even those from immigrant backgrounds, were black. For Mrs. Jarvis, her overwhelmingly black student body was more than enough for her to conceptualize and describe Gardener Middle School as a black school.

In terms of black student population, Gardener was at the higher end of the spectrum. Still, teachers from schools with relatively more student diversity also constructed Brick City schools as black schools. Whether teaching at a school with a majority or, in cases like Gardener, almost exclusively black student population, the teachers I interviewed *all* constructed their workplaces as explicitly black spaces. Although culture and aesthetics played prominent roles here (see later discussion), two additional factors were nonblack student demographics and the surrounding community. Within a great number of Brick City schools, most of the nonblack students were also nonwhite, and the schools themselves were often located in racially segregated, predominantly black neighborhoods. Thus, the general lack of whiteness within schools, as well as the highly racialized geography around schools, helped bridge the gap between those with varying black student populations.

For other teachers, their construction of Brick City schools as black schools—as racialized spaces—went beyond student demographics; it also included student culture. A theme that emerged early and remained consistent throughout my data analysis was the idea that Brick City schools were dominated by a uniquely racialized, uniquely black culture. Speech patterns, modes of dress, student attitudes, student behavior, "school indifference," "bad values," and a "broken family structure" were all offered by white Brick City teachers as indicators of black culture. As Mrs. Edwards articulates in the following excerpt, her school was not only one with a predominantly black student body but also one that *acted black*.

MRS. EDWARDS: There's a certain, um, a certain culture at my school. I think the kids [*pause*], um, the kids and the type of neighborhoods that they live in and the type of families that they come from, um, I think it's more of, of what society might consider to be black culture. I mean, I don't want to come across as racist or anything, but if I'm being honest, there's a certain culture in the school that, um, I believe is a result of the students that go there.

BELL: You mentioned that society might consider your school's culture to be black culture. Is that how you see it personally?

MRS. EDWARDS: I do. I do. I mean, look, you'll have kids that don't show up to school for two weeks, but when they do come back, they have brand-new clothes, you know, brand-new sneakers. You'll have parents that will be front and center during the basketball game, but won't bother to show up to parent-teacher conferences, you know. You have kids sagging their pants every day, and if you say something to them, they cuss you out. Then you call their parents and they cuss you out, you know. So yeah, I think the culture of the school is, um, well [*pause*].

BELL: Black culture?

MRS. EDWARDS: Yeah. I think it's unfortunate, but it's the truth. Our students act a certain way, um, they act black almost in the stereotypical sense.

The idea that Brick City schools were permeated with black culture was itself laden with racial stereotypes. In a number of interviews, teachers recited many of the tropes that have come to be associated with black people and their commitment, or lack thereof, to educational achievement. Chief among them were the ideas that black students do not value education; that black people, as a whole, cannot delay gratification; and that black parents placed a higher premium on clothing, shoes, and sports than they did on the educational success of their children.[78] Real or imagined, these cultural practices weighed heavily on the minds of my interview participants. As one teacher said to me toward the end of our interview, "This is not the kind of school culture that I'm used to. Um, it's like, it's very different from the schools I went to as a kid. It's much more urban, and I don't always know how to respond to it."

While the negative stereotyping of black student attitudes, black student behavior, and black community values all contributed to racialization of Brick City schools, other cultural cues were less serious in nature. For example, numerous teachers remarked on how their black students dressed. From "sagging pants" to "bright-colored skinny jeans," black students were routinely characterized as having a unique style of dress that was visibly distinct from their nonblack peers. Even within those schools that required uniforms, white teachers, again conflating the terms "urban" and "black," described their black students as embodying an "urban style" or showcasing an "urban flair." Thus, while school uniforms were standardized, the various ways that students wore them were not. Some teachers saw black styles of dress as problematic, while others were more indifferent and saw them as harmless. A minority of teachers spoke of black styles of dress admiringly: one teacher openly admitted that she "wished she had their kind of style." However, no matter how they felt about or responded to the way their black students dressed, white teachers saw certain "urban dress codes" as embodying black culture, which made their respective workplaces all the more racialized.

In addition to the sheer number of black bodies and the numerous examples of "black culture," visual references to black historical icons draped the classroom and hallway walls of Brick City schools. Pictures of Martin Luther King Jr., Rosa Parks, Harriet Tubman, Malcolm X, Booker T. Washington, Frederick Douglass, and Thurgood Marshall, among many others, lined school hallways, and images of "Barack and Michelle" were "pretty much in every classroom." These visual references bolstered the racialization of Brick City schools, and for white teachers, the physical space of the school, with all its black iconography, came to embody blackness on an institutional scale. As one teacher, Mrs. Meredith, put it, "Every month seems to be Black History Month at my school. We're always celebrating somebody." Consequently, in conjunction with student demography, student culture, and surrounding neighborhood environment, openly celebrating blackness erased all doubt in the minds of white Brick City teachers; their school district, their school buildings, and even their individual classrooms represented black racialized spaces.

It should be noted here that, similar to their differing takes on black modes of dress, white Brick City teachers interpreted and reacted to the racial aesthetics of their individual schools in different ways. Although Mrs.

Martin—Malcolm X aside—was in favor of her school's position toward black historical and cultural iconography, other teachers were far less enthusiastic. Some teachers felt that highlighting race in such a selective manner was problematic because it elevated one race above others; or, as one teacher put it, "When you think about it, it's kinda racist." Other teachers did not feel strongly about what their schools should or should not do, but they did regard the entire debate over black iconography as a giant distraction, a "pointless exercise that had nothing to do with education." Still, whatever their individual takes on celebratory racial aesthetics, white Brick City teachers, collectively, saw the visual representation of African American history—and what they perceived to be African American culture—as an integral part of the racialization of Brick City schools. On the whole, while already impactful, this process was strengthened by the consistency and seeming normalness of explicitly racialized discourse.

They Love Calling Each Other the N-Word

I mean, just the way they talk to each other, you know. All you hear is "nigga" this and "nigga" that. Every day, day after day, "You my nigga," or "Shut up, nigga." I don't, um, I hate to say, you know, "nigga" in front of you. I personally hate that word, but that's pretty much all you hear some days. They love calling each other the n-word.—ALEXA BOYD, 43

Open and direct racialized discourse flooded the hallways and classrooms of Brick City schools. For white teachers, the relative ease with which their black students thought about, broached, and discussed the subject of race played a major role in how they conceptualized their particular workspaces. As employees of predominantly black schools, the same teachers who admitted to never having thought about race were suddenly inundated with "nothing but race." That is, in contrast to the seemingly nonracial discourse that permeated the predominantly, and sometimes exclusively, white spaces they were accustomed to, white Brick City teachers were exposed and reexposed to overtly racialized discourse by virtue of "just going to work." Whether directed at other students or at them as teachers, my research participants were not expecting, and were not prepared for, the constant barrage of racialized language that emanated from their students and their students' families.

Initially, the racialized discourse that grabbed the ear of white Brick City teachers was the discursive exchanges between black students and their peers. The way that black students spoke to one another, especially their nonchalant use of the word "nigga," caught many of my interview respondents off guard. For adults who had spent the vast majority of their lives in racially homogenous, ostensibly nonracialized spaces, exposure to this kind of discourse left many of them stunned, confused, and sometimes upset. In the following excerpt, Candice Satter, a middle school math teacher, describes the first time she heard her students using the word "nigga."

MS. SATTER: You wouldn't believe how much they use the n-word. Even the girls. I remember walking to my class, 7:30 in the morning, and out of nowhere I hear, "Fuck you, nigga." I mean, I'm sorry, I don't mean to say that word to you, but, you know, it was shocking. I hadn't even had my morning coffee and I'm already hearing racial slurs. I found myself getting really upset, you know. I mean, I don't get it. Why would students, black students, you know, why would they be using that word? I mean, I hate using it even now.

BELL: How did you respond to hearing that word for the first time?

MS. SATTER: Well, like I said, it was shocking. I turned around and it was a group of eleven- and twelve-year-old girls. As soon as they saw me, they all stopped talking and looked at me like I was crazy. I didn't know what to do. I had no idea what to say. So after a minute of standing there looking stupid, I just said, "Good morning" and walked away.

Ms. Satter described being shocked at hearing the word "nigga," a term that can be jarring in any context, but especially so within a school setting. Arguably one of the most loaded words in the English language,[79] "nigga" initially engendered feelings of anger and anxiety for Ms. Satter and other white Brick City teachers. Over time, however, she and many of her colleagues in the BCSD became desensitized to it, and with each passing day, they grew more and more accustomed to hearing "racial slurs." In fact, because the word "nigga" was so commonplace, white teachers focused more on policing the racial discourse within their own classrooms, as opposed to addressing every instance of problematic or inappropriate language throughout the school more broadly. Ms. Satter, for example, bars students from saying "nigga" in her classroom, but she often ignores it in other areas of the school. With the exception of her room, specifically, she now gives little more than a passing glance whenever she hears students calling each other "nigga." In her own words, "If you stop students in the hall every time you hear that word, it would take you an hour just to get to the bathroom."

The regularity with which black students called each other "nigga" was not the only type of discourse that challenged, or interrupted, the racial socialization of white Brick City teachers. On any given day, current events had the potential to spark a host of conversations about the salience of race and racism in the contemporary United States. And during these conversations, white teachers realized that they and their black students often disagreed about the relevance of race to the topic at hand. Time and again, white teachers found themselves at odds with their black students about the racial motivations for, and racial significance of, contemporaneous events. For example, when Trayvon Martin was killed by George Zimmerman in 2012, several teachers were surprised and eventually became frustrated by what they considered the unnecessary invocation of race into an "unfortunate situation."[80] Because these kinds of conversations always carried the potential to inflame passions and cause tension, white Brick City teachers did their best to avoid them. Eventually, though, as they would come to find out, discussing—and debating—the relevance of race to contemporaneous events was inevitable, leading to a patterned, yet powerful, form of racialized discourse.

Unfamiliar with the norms of racial debate, white teachers initially downplayed and tried to ignore conversations about racism and racial inequality within their respective classrooms. As one teacher put it, "I try not to go there with kids. It's a rabbit hole that's hard to come back from." With the passage of time, however, most teachers found it impossible to avoid their students on matters of race and reluctantly decided to engage them head-on. Mrs. Doyle, a high school language arts teacher, described an incident where she, after trying to ignore "so many cries of racism," decided to "take back" her classroom.

MRS. DOYLE: I wasn't used to talking about race so much, you know. In my family, we just didn't talk about it. It was never all that important. When I think about my students, I think it's crazy how much they bring up race, it's almost second nature to them. I mean, they see race in everything. I remember after the whole Trayvon Martin thing or whatever, um, the Zimmerman trial, for days on end, that's the only thing the kids talked about. They weren't interested in doing any work, they weren't interested in anything. It was just "Fuck George Zimmerman," "Fuck the police," "America is so racist," just racism, you know, everywhere. So many cries of racism. Finally, I just didn't want to deal with it anymore. I had to take back my classroom, so I just went for it.

BELL: What did you do?

MRS. DOYLE: Well, ignoring it didn't work [laughs]. I mean, you can only put your head in the sand for so long before you suffocate, you know. One day, there was a group of students in one of my classes that kept talking about Trayvon Martin. Every single day, that's all they talked about. So I just said something like, "Look, I agree, Zimmerman is a jerk, but that doesn't make him a racist. He had a fair trial and they found him not guilty. Stop making everything about race."

BELL: How did they respond?

MRS. DOYLE: Holy shit. You'd think I had just insulted their grandmother or something. The whole class just exploded at me. Every single one of them just lost it. They started yelling, I saw one boy crying. You know, it's something I'll never forget. After, I don't know, like twenty minutes or so, I finally got them to calm down. I told them I'd give them all a chance to speak. One of the girls, the ringleader I guess, she had these big, deep brown eyes and she looked right back at me. She said, "You know, Mrs. Doyle, why do white people pretend nothing is ever about race?" Something like that, you know.

BELL: Wow. So how did you respond?

MRS. DOYLE: Well, at that point, I knew the jig was up [*laughs*]. I could've tried to put my foot down, but this was a battle I probably wasn't going to win, you know. So from that point on, I knew I had to engage them. Whether I wanted to or not, whether I agreed with them or not, when they talked about race, I talked about race. I had no choice.

Mrs. Doyle's reluctant decision to discuss Trayvon Martin and George Zimmerman with her students was emblematic of the way white teachers, as a whole, transitioned from ignoring racialized discourse in their classrooms and schools to openly engaging their students in highly sensitive, explicit conversations about race. Initially, with the exception of the word "nigga" or other "racial slurs," teachers, to the best of their abilities, simply ignored racialized discourse. They would go about their daily routine, maintaining a discursive distance from any and all conversations about race, racism, or racial inequality. Eventually, however, in the face of what multiple teachers labeled an "obsession with race," the strategy of purposeful indifference proved inadequate, forcing teachers to engage their students directly. On doing so, white teachers quickly realized that they were outnumbered and, more often than not, distinctly outside their comfort zones. Whereas black students talked about race intentionally, white teachers did so only when coerced, when they felt they had no other choice. What's more, while black students were emotionally invested in conversations about race, white teachers viewed them as little more than an intellectual exercise. They were a nuisance or, at best, a necessary evil.

Regardless of how white teachers felt about racial conversations, they expected to have them on a regular basis. In spaces overflowing with black bodies, the presence of race loomed large, always ready to infiltrate, or even overtake, classrooms and schools at a moment's notice. Racial events, both within and outside the school, could animate black students to the point where teaching them became difficult, if not altogether impossible. For new and experienced teachers alike, even the most detailed of lesson plans could be waylaid, rendered obsolete by the always present, yet not always predictable, specter of race. As people who spent the majority of their lives publicly ignoring race, white Brick City teachers found explicitly racialized conversations at once unsettling and unavoidable. Combined with black bodies, as well as material, visual, and symbolic references to "black culture," the routineness of racialized discourse intensified the racialization of Brick City schools, making them unquestionably and unambiguously black in the minds of white Brick City teachers.

I'm Cool for a White Girl

Don't get me wrong, they still look at me as a white girl, but it's a little bit different. I'm cool for a white girl. That's what they always tell me: "Ms. J, I like coming to your class, you're cool for a white girl." At first I didn't know how to take it, but you know what, after working at Gardener for three years, hell yeah, I'll take it. —CYNTHIA JARVIS, 24

While significant, working in a hyper-racialized physical environment and being routinely exposed to racialized discourse composed only two aspects of the racialization of Brick City schools. A third and somewhat overlapping process involved the daily interactions between white teachers and their black student bodies. From the first day of class, black students left little doubt that they saw themselves as explicitly black and saw their teachers as explicitly white. In this particular environment, both teachers and students were racialized beings, and far from being an inconsequential demographic marker, one's racial status proved instrumental to a litany of experiential and interactive processes. Thus, the extent to which race shaped the worldviews and personal behaviors of black students, in tandem with their willingness to explicitly identify race, caused white teachers to view their respective workplaces as akin to what Eduardo Bonilla-Silva terms a *racialized social system*, an environment in which "economic, political, social, and ideological levels are partially structured by the placement of actors in racial categories or races."[81]

Alexa Boyd, a middle school math teacher, has spent her entire career working in urban schools. For the last twelve years, she has been at Jackson Middle School, a school with a student population that is close to 80 percent black. During our interview, Mrs. Boyd volunteered that she was "super progressive" and had been "committed to social justice" her entire adult life. For Mrs. Boyd, teaching racially and economically disadvantaged students was a calling, and the idea of teaching at an all-white, affluent suburban school was "never an option." Mrs. Boyd explained to me that she purposely enrolled in an urban education program and, accordingly, was well aware of the social problems that sometimes accompanied teaching in urban schools. Still, she was not prepared for the bombardment of how, and the bluntness with which, black students characterized and confronted her as a white teacher. As Mrs. Boyd herself put it, "I was prepared for the poverty, the single-parent homes, the academic and behavioral issues, you know, but I didn't think I'd have to defend being white every day. My social justice training didn't prepare me for that."

Similar to Mrs. Boyd, other teachers also spoke of being taken aback, or even feeling discriminated against, whenever one of their students called or referred to them as white. Unlike the racialized discourse between students (calling each other "nigga") or even engaging students in direct conversations about race (such as the death of Trayvon Martin), the teachers I interviewed, with several exceptions, could neither understand nor accept being explicitly and meaningfully referred to as white.[82] Socialized in racially segregated yet ostensibly colorblind environments, white Brick City teachers equated racial recognition with racial discrimination. Therefore, as Mrs. Martin explains below, getting called white in such an open and direct manner was analogous to African Americans getting called a "nigger in public."

MRS. MARTIN: Imagine that, um, you know, you had a group of black teachers teaching at a Grand Ledge school or whatever.[83] I mean, you know how it is out there, it's pretty much all white people out there. Now, if the students were running around calling their teachers nigger all the time, I'm sorry, but it would be front-page news. Nobody would allow that, you know.

BELL: So, when your students call or refer to you as white, you feel like you are being subjected to racial slurs, is that right?

MRS. MARTIN: Yeah, definitely. I mean, maybe it isn't the same as, um, you know, being called the n-word, but it's still a racial slur and it still hurts. And it doesn't go away. You don't get used to it. You think you will after a while, but you don't. It's emotionally draining and it has absolutely nothing to do with teaching. It's just, um, it's just something we have to deal with, I guess.

Mrs. Martin, like other white Brick City teachers, was not used to—and therefore not prepared to handle—the direct and intentional racial recognition that permeated her school. From her perspective, being called white by her black students was analogous to a group of black teachers being called nigger by white suburbanites. In this regard, recognizing whiteness was not merely a violation of ideological norms, it was an emotional shock to one's person, an insult and racialized form of belittling. As one teacher described it, to be outwardly addressed as white was to be "reduced to your skin color." Rhetorically, just as they had done when trying to discuss white racial identity, many teachers engaged in long bouts of silence, finding it difficult to describe how it felt to be openly recognized and addressed as white. Only this time, the pauses in question were not due to incoherence; they were the result of having to recall and talk about emotionally draining and sometimes painful memories.[84]

In the exchange that follows, Amanda Costa, a thirty-four-year-old social studies teacher who has taught in the Brick City School District for ten years and who, in her own words, "always wanted to be a teacher," goes into detail about an incident that almost caused her to leave teaching altogether.

MRS. COSTA: It can be really emotional at times. Um, it's like [pause], you put all this work into connecting with the kids. I mean, yeah, we're their teachers, but you want them to like you, you want them to appreciate all the hard work you put into helping them learn. And some of them do, you know. Some of them are appreciative, but they're few and far between. Most of my students just look at me as some white lady telling them what to do. That's all I am to them. It's pretty much the same thing every year. No matter how hard I work or, you know, how, um, how many years I've been at the school or whatever, I'm still white. No, let me take that back, I'm just a white girl. That's how they refer to me, you know. I'm thirty-four years old and I have a bunch of thirteen-year-olds calling me a white girl every day. And to be completely honest, as bad as the students are, the fucking parents are worse. I don't mean to swear at you, but oh my god. I can almost understand the students, at least to a degree, you know, they're kids. But the damn parents have no excuse. You're a fucking adult. Act like it.

BELL: Could you elaborate?

MRS. COSTA: Yeah, so I remember a time when, well, I have so many stories, but this one stands out. I was up for tenure and I was being observed. Perfect storm, you know. Things were actually going pretty well. I mean, I had a couple kids doing whatever the hell they wanted, but most of the kids were on their best behavior. I think they knew I was getting observed. So I'm right in the middle of a lesson when I had this parent, the parent of one of my worst students, you know, she fucking storms into the classroom. "Why the fuck are you picking on my son, he might get expelled." I couldn't believe what was going on, you know, she was just yelling at me, cussing me out in front of the entire class. So I look over to the VP [vice principal], you know, because he was the person observing me. He gets up and tries to intervene, saying, "Ma'am, ma'am, calm down." But at this point, she didn't care, she was out for blood. "I'm tired of you racist motherfuckers picking on my son." I mean it was just "white" this, "white" that. She pretty much accused me of being some kind of Nazi, just because I kicked her son out of my classroom. Her son, by the way, the reason I kicked him out is because just the day before he called me a "stupid white bitch," OK. It was [pause], it was pretty rough. I thought she was going to attack me. After it was over, I just got in my car and left. Didn't tell anybody, didn't say anything to anyone. I just left.

BELL: Wow. You just left the school?

MRS. COSTA: Yeah, I had to get out of there.

BELL: Did you get in trouble? Were you reprimanded by your school?

MRS. COSTA: Not really. I mean, my VP saw the entire thing. He saw how crazy she was. Besides, I didn't really care at that point. I was pretty sure that I was quitting. The thought of going back to that place literally made me sick. It made me physically ill. But here I am, close to ten years later, and I'm still there [laughs].

BELL: What changed?

MRS. COSTA: Well, I need the money [*laughs*]. It didn't take me long to realize that my bills weren't going to pay themselves, you know. Plus, that little fucker Jamal and his racist mom were banned from the school. So that helps.

Although Mrs. Costa recounted an experience that would have been harrowing in any context, she specifically connected it to race by attributing the anger and vitriol directed at her to, at least in part, the fact that she is white. As she would go on to explain, Mrs. Costa believed it was a "racist double standard" that she could be openly "berated for being white" and that "no white person could ever get away with a stunt like that." In this sense, from Mrs. Costa's perspective, the moment Jamal's mother uttered the word "white," she took an objectively painful, and perhaps embarrassing, episode and turned it into an overt act of racial discrimination. While this experience may have been an outlier in terms of severity, other white teachers too were able to provide examples of how, from their standpoint, racial categorization invariably led to their own mistreatment, particularly during interactions with black students and black families.[85] Thus, for white Brick City teachers, racial recognition—along with the interactional othering that followed—was directly linked to the physical, cultural, and discursive dynamics of their *black* work environments, fortifying them as uniquely racialized spaces.

CONCLUSION

Over the long arc of the twentieth century, a myriad of factors, including racial progress, racial backlash, policy changes, and legal precedent, led to a residential pattern of predominantly black inner cities surrounded by predominantly white suburbs. Such residential patterns are also reflected in our nation's schools, where even today the United States is home to separate and unequal schooling. Located in a city that is saturated with racial segregation, the BCSD is among the most segregated districts in the country, currently housing a number of schools with student populations that are predominantly, or almost exclusively, one-raced. This pattern was not lost on my interview respondents, as, contrary to how they failed to see themselves in racial terms, they *all* saw their schools as racialized spaces. From geography to aesthetics, from demographics to culture, and from discourse to interactions, blackness, as constructed by white teachers, permeated Brick City schools, making the racialization of these particular spaces all the more real. Taken together, white Brick City teachers and their socially constructed raceless identities crashed headfirst into the hypervisible and hyper-racialized spaces that are Brick City schools. As the remaining chapters will show, this collision had profound consequences, heightening white racial awareness, engendering white racial identity, and, to a lesser degree, altering white racial ideology.

3. BECOMING WHITE TEACHERS

Racial identifications are not merely individual achievements but are formed in relation to collective identities within racialized societies. . . . Understanding race relations, racial realities, and racial identities then requires that attention be paid to the specifics of various racial contexts.
—AMANDA E. LEWIS, *Race in the Schoolyard*

I just want to teach, OK? I wish everybody left all that race stuff out of it. I don't see what my race or your race or anybody's race has to do with teaching. Just let me do my job.—REBECCA DARLING, Brick City High School

Sometimes I just want to stand up and shout, Look, I'm white, OK, get over it! —REBECCA DARLING, Brick City High School

When Leah Thompson started teaching at Walnut Middle School, she believed she had landed her dream job. Since childhood, Ms. Thompson had wanted to be an art teacher, and she had long since decided that she could make a bigger difference working with students of color from poor inner-city backgrounds. Located in a predominantly black neighborhood, Walnut Middle School has a student population that is over 80 percent black. Although she knew that, as a physical space, Walnut Middle School was racially segregated, Ms. Thompson was not prepared for the highly racialized environment that Walnut represented, nor was she expecting the openness with which her new students—and their families—recognized race, including her own. Working in such an environment led to Ms. Thompson seeing and eventually accepting herself as white. Despite her lifelong desire to become a teacher and her commitment to her students, Ms. Thompson was quickly confronted with the reality that teaching black students, within a "black school," meant that she would have to navigate the personal and professional consequences of white racial identity. As she stated early in our interview, "It didn't take long for me to realize that I was in over my head. To them, I was not their teacher, I was just another white person bossing them around. That's it, I'm just white." Just white. She was not alone.

Ms. Thompson, like many white Americans, had been socialized not to see or recognize white racial identity.[1] For the majority of her life, she had equated whiteness with normalness, thinking of race as something that belonged only to people of color. As demonstrated in chapter 1, this particular view of race and identity, one that situates whiteness outside the realm of racial classification, was quite common among white Brick City teachers. Also, as demonstrated in chapter 2, such a broad—and privileged—construction of white racial identity left teachers surprised by, unprepared for, and ill-equipped to handle the extent to which their predominantly black student bodies saw and treated them as white. On an almost daily basis, white teachers could expect to have some form of racialized interaction with black students or their families. These interactions, already permeated with racial content, eventually led to the creation and adoption of new meaning. Through a series of symbolic interactions, white Brick City teachers begrudgingly came to adopt a spatially specific, localized form of white racial identity.

In this chapter I examine the process of white racialization. Using interview data, I deconstruct the interactional and iterative process through which white teachers adopted a localized racial identity. In three overlapping and mutually reinforcing steps—seeing white, feeling white, and being white—epistemologically raceless teachers transitioned to racialized white teachers as their own racial identities became visually and experientially meaningful to them. First I briefly review symbolic interactionism, one of the foundational theories of American sociology. Given the salience of interaction, particularly to racial socialization, I think it is important to outline the central components of this seminal theory. Next I examine the intersection of race, identity, and space. Several studies have advanced our understanding of white identity development by focusing on the localness of racial experience. In order to provide the proper context for my own study, I highlight some of their core theoretical and empirical findings. Finally, I break down the process of becoming white teachers. In a three-step, dialectical process, teachers first began to see whiteness, followed by negative feelings of whiteness, only to reluctantly make the conscious decision to be white, or *do whiteness*, on their own terms. These overlapping and interlocking steps, demonstrating the significance of local interactions, played out over and over within Brick City schools.

SYMBOLIC INTERACTIONISM

Symbolic interactionism is one of the most prominent and long-standing theoretical traditions in American sociology.[2] A micro-level theory, symbolic interactionism analyzes the interactive processes between people, as well as the various ways that interactions and symbols are used to create and recreate meaning.[3] Part of the interpretative tradition, symbolic interactionism disagrees with, and ultimately eschews, those all-encompassing theories of the social world that seek to mimic the natural sciences. In lieu of grand theoretical pronouncements, social scientists who utilize symbolic interactionism seek to understand the more intimate, routine, and face-to-face interactions that help people shape and understand their own lived realities.[4] Meaningful interactions are the heart of this theoretical framework. Meaning affects how people interact, and interactions between people create new meaning. For over a hundred years now, social scientists have used symbolic interactionism to analyze, understand, and discuss a multitude of social processes that affect, and are affected by, people as they go about their daily lives.[5]

Symbolic interactionists also examine the cyclical relationship between people and their various social environments.[6] Scholars working in this tradition believe that people shape society every bit as much as they are shaped by society. As one noted interactionist put it, the method is "simultaneously interpretive and analytic, structural and interactional," and "is both a theory of experience and a theory of social structure."[7] This is important because, despite being a micro-theory, symbolic interactionism does speak empirically to the salience of social structure. By focusing on the active role of people, however, symbolic interactionism challenges many top-down theoretical paradigms, those that give primacy to structure over the agency of individuals.[8] To be clear, symbolic interactionism does not ignore or discount the significance of structure, but it does challenge the notion that people are mere products of their environments. Rather than being completely at the mercy of larger institutional forces, symbolic interactionism holds that people, through interaction and other meaning-making processes, are instrumental in creating the very social worlds that shape their lives.[9]

Like most theoretical traditions, symbolic interactionism has a diverse and interdisciplinary background.[10] From the philosophical pragmatism of John Dewey to the urban ethnographic tradition of Robert E. Park, this analytical framework has been used in a variety of ways to study a variety of topics.[11] Still, despite its inherent variation, symbolic interactionism holds human interaction, and the meaning it produces, at the center of analysis. As the late Herbert Blumer noted, symbolic interactionism sees "meanings as social products, as creations that are formed in and through the defining activities of people as they interact."[12] Therefore, the meaning ascribed to any given thing—whiteness, for example—is intimately connected to the interpretations of, and interactions between, various people or even groups of people.[13] What's more, just as social meaning is formed through symbolic interactions, it can be re-formed, or changed, through subsequent interactions.[14] In fact, ascribing new meaning to symbols is precisely what took place within Brick City schools as white teachers, after repeated interactions with black students and black families, observed and adopted an explicit, yet local racial identity.

RACE, IDENTITY, AND SPACE

Although it remains undertheorized in the broader research literature, the intersection of race, identity, and space has been explored by a number of scholars.[15] Departing from the spatially neutral norm, these studies underscore the importance of racial context—including the importance of space—to the social construction of whiteness and the lived experiences of actual white people. In doing so, they place spatial variation on the same conceptual plane as class, gender, sexual orientation, age, and other demographic structures, highlighting the importance of the physical world and exploring the dramaturgical dimensions of white racial identity. Taken together, this scholarship takes a local approach to white identity development and, to varying degrees, paints a more nuanced, much more complex portrait of whiteness in America.[16] I highlight several core themes below.

Among its principal findings, research into the effects of space on white racial identity demonstrates that white Americans, within particular racial environments, can recognize and sometimes experience a temporary minority status.[17] To put it another way, on losing the veneer of racelessness, whiteness can be made visible through the formal and informal presence of people of color.[18] Formally, racial demographics and racialized interactions always carry the potential to heighten white racial awareness; informally, concerns over the loss of power and racial autonomy often lead to feelings of stigmatism, antiwhite bias, and even reverse discrimination.[19] Both processes, formal and informal, can affect how and where white Americans situate themselves within the broader racial hierarchy.[20] As sociologist Charles Gallagher notes in his study of white college students at an urban university, experiences with "momentary minority status and the anxiety often associated with this experience" color how white students see themselves "and their relationship to other racial groups."[21]

Relatedly, scholars have also shown that white racial identity varies between and within spaces that are themselves demographically and culturally dissimilar.[22] Pamela Perry, in her book *Shades of White: White Kids and Racial Identities in High School*, used ethnographic methods at two demographically different schools to examine the way white students viewed, understood, and experienced white racial identity.[23] The school (Valley Grove) in an affluent suburb housed a student population that was 83 percent white, while the other (Clavey), economically diverse and predominantly nonwhite, was home to a student population that was only 12 percent white.[24] For white students attending Valley Grove, white racial identity was constructed as meaningless, or, as Perry describes it, an "empty cultural category."[25] Conversely, for white students attending Clavey, white racial identity was constructed as a meaningful, or, as Perry describes it, a culturally relevant category. Complicating matters further was the fact that white students *within* each school constructed whiteness differently. That is, the contrasting constructions of white racial identity between schools were not monolithic within schools. Some kids at Valley Grove deviated from the general consensus of white normality, while at Clavey, some kids failed to adopt a meaningful racial identity.

Moving beyond identity construction as a process, several scholars have shown that the substance of white racial identity is also influenced by the interactional and intersectional dynamics of race and place.[26] For example, white privilege, often a function of demography, power, and prestige, can be epistemologically stripped away within particular spatial environments.[27] In this sense, white racial identity can be recognized, and ultimately developed, in a manner that dislodges whiteness from its perch atop the racial stratification system.[28] When married to space, factors such as lower socioeconomic status or physical proximity to people of color can impede the kinds of experiences that engender invisible racial identities.[29] Thus, white people who live in urban, predominantly nonwhite areas, or those who struggle with poverty, joblessness, and addiction, over time may develop racial identities that construct whiteness as disadvantageous rather than privileged.[30] I say more about this particular racial construction in chapter 4.

Finally, numerous studies have shown, empirically, that whiteness is a prompted identity, "one that becomes a topic of interest when respondents are directly asked to talk about it."[31] Accordingly, for a great number of white people in America, whiteness and white racial identity become relevant, or even visible, only through external provocation.[32] Given the interactive dimensions of white racialized spaces—namely, the socializing effects of white racelessness—it comes as no surprise that proximity to nonwhites, particularly in terms of physical space, cultural change, or actual people, directly influences how members of the racially dominant group come to see, or not see, their own racial identities. This pattern has been shown to hold true across a number of social locations, as demographic variations based on social class, gender, sexual orientation, and age, while instrumental to how white people experience and conceptualize whiteness, do little to blunt the significance of people of color in prompting white racial identity.[33] For many white Americans, regardless of exposure to momentary minority status, regardless of how often white racial identity is negotiated within and between spaces, and regardless of how strongly white privilege is mitigated by socioeconomic or other forms of disadvantage, whiteness itself becomes more visible and more salient when prompted by the formal, informal, and spatial presence of people of color.[34]

Departing from the norm of contextual overgeneralization, a number of scholars have taken physical space seriously, examining local constructions of race and racial identity. Although these studies have advanced our current understanding of space and the effects it has on white identity development, many unanswered questions remain. One of those questions is the one I seek to answer with this study: How do individual white Americans experience, navigate, and make sense of whiteness in and between spaces with different racial identities? To date, we are limited in what we know about the effects of space on white racial identity because most of the studies that examine it directly do so by focusing on *different* subsets of white people within different racial environments. While theoretically and empirically valuable, this type of research design makes it difficult to isolate the racializing effects of space. I overcome this limitation by examining the *same* subset of white people within different racial environments. Therefore, my research design allows me to compare how a specific group of white Americans construct white racial identity within, and between, disparately racialized spaces. Below, I delve deeper into this process, showing how, within the physical space of Brick City schools, white racelessness transformed into a hypervisible and hypermeaningful racial identity.

BECOMING WHITE

Becoming white teachers followed an identifiable, symbolic interactionist pattern. In three steps, teachers would go from never thinking about white racial identity to routinely doing so, particularly within their respective schools. First, white teachers began to *see* themselves as white. In contrast to the invisible norm, interview respondents started to see themselves in distinctly racialized terms. Second, white teachers started to *feel* white. Owing specifically to their race, as well as the overtly racialized environment that predominantly black schools represented for them, white teachers began to feel uncomfortable, especially whenever they found themselves to be the only white person in the room. Finally, white teachers began to, in their own words, *be* white. That is, they behaved in ways they believed would minimize the probability of them being accused of racism, and they also wanted to mitigate the largely negative effects of feeling white. These three steps—seeing white, feeling white, and being white—all intersected and worked in concert to racialize white teachers within Brick City schools.

I Started to See Myself as White

There's only so many times you can get yelled at for being white before you start to internalize it. Eventually you start to think of yourself as white first, and a person second. That's exactly what happened. I started to see myself as white. Once that happens, you have to look for those moments that remind you why you're there. Like, Oh yeah, I'm a teacher.
—AMANDA COSTA, 34

Working in predominantly black schools had a significant impact on how white teachers looked at themselves racially. Across interviews, the way teachers talked about being white in a general sense, versus how they talked about being white in predominantly black schools, stood out for its contrast, its clarity, and its consistency. When describing their experiences in Brick City schools, gone were the stutters and the bouts of nervous laughter, and not one teacher claimed to have "never thought about" what it means to be white. In stark contrast to how they spoke earlier in the interview, white Brick City teachers spoke clearly, and at times concisely, about the various ways that whiteness and white racial identity shaped their experiences within these particular spaces. Thus, both in terms of rhetorical clarity and thematic content, the responses to questions about being a white teacher in Brick City schools were more certain and more comprehensive than responses to questions about being white generally.

Jessi McCormick, a high school English teacher who struggled considerably when trying to discuss what it means to be white, became completely sure of herself and knew exactly what she wanted to say about teaching at a predominantly black school. Mrs. McCormick went on to describe being a white teacher as something she thought about "all the time."[35]

BELL: Earlier I asked you what it means for you to be white. Along those lines, can you tell me what it means for you to be white working in a predominantly black school?

MRS. McCORMICK: Well, this is something that I actually think about a lot. All the time, really. I feel like, that, um, as a white teacher, my kids are automatically suspicious of me, you know. I, I mean, building relationships is a big part of being an effective teacher. It's absolutely vital to build strong relationships with the students and their parents. But sometimes, you know, I think many of my students have a hard time trusting me. It can be very difficult. Not impossible, but harder than it needs to be.

BELL: You say that at times your students have a hard time trusting you?

MRS. McCORMICK: Correct.

BELL: And do you believe this is because of the racial variation between you and your students? Do you believe it's because you're white and they're black?

MRS. McCORMICK: Yeah, I mean that's a really big part of it. One thing I always tell my husband about my students is that they're not shy about expressing their opinions. Seriously. Through all the stress and frustration they cause me, at least they're honest. They'll flat-out say to me, "Look, Mrs. M, I don't really trust white people" or "Nobody in my family trusts white people," you know. So I'm like, Oh, well that's nice, we're going to have a great year [laughs].

BELL: How do you respond whenever one of your black students admits to not trusting white people?

MRS. McCORMICK: Well, I expect it now. It's no big shock when I hear it these days. But, um, to me, it simply means that I have to find a way in. Whether it's sports, music, the Obamas—that's a good one, they all love the Obamas—um, you have to be willing to put in the work. It's not easy, believe me it's not easy, but once a student drops their guard and decides to let you in, all the work you put in is worth it. Now you can teach.

Mrs. McCormick went on to describe some of the meaningful relationships she has formed with black students over the years. Considering them to be a necessary prerequisite to effective teaching, Mrs. McCormick attributes her success in forming these relationships to the herculean effort she undertakes to overcome the general distrust of white people. As she mentions, building relationships with her black students, although not impossible, is often made unnecessarily difficult because of racial mistrust. A latent consequence of this relationship-building process is that in breaking through the racially motivated barriers erected by her black students, Mrs. McCormick is forced to consider the various ways that whiteness has impacted—and continues to impact—their lives within and outside Brick City schools. Mrs. McCormick makes this point later in the interview when she rather concisely states, "It can't be a coincidence that so many of my kids don't trust white people. It's my job to figure out why."

Although Mrs. McCormick was somewhat unique in how she made sense of whiteness within predominantly black schools, the genesis of her seeing whiteness to begin with, student-teacher interactions, was consistent with other white Brick City teachers: like Mrs. McCormick, other teachers too began to notice their own racial identities through extensive interactions with black students. Ms. Livingston, a physical education teacher who works at a school that is close to 70 percent black, talked at length about seeing herself specifically as a white woman, as opposed to a raceless woman.

MS. LIVINGSTON: I've always taken pride in being a strong woman. I mean, come on, I'm a gym teacher. Not many students expect to walk into the gym and see me standing here. So being a woman, um, it's something I've always thought of as important to who I am. But, after working here for six years, it's a little more complicated now. I just don't see myself as a woman—I see myself as a white woman, you know. When you're standing in front of a gym full of black kids, um, it's impossible not to notice that you're not quite in the club [*laughs*]. It's like, Yep, I'm definitely white.

Constantly finding herself surrounded by black students, Ms. Livingston began to see whiteness as something bigger and more meaningful than simple demography. Thinking of herself specifically as a white woman, as opposed to a raceless woman, was the direct result of her experiences within nonwhite racialized spaces. That is, the racialization of predominantly black schools, including the students, the culture, and the physical space itself, caused Ms. Livingston to look at herself racially, to see herself as meaningfully white. Furthermore, by positioning herself outside the racial norm, as "not quite in the club," Ms. Livingston placed herself squarely in the realm of the racial other. Accordingly, within these spaces she is not only white but also different. She is demographically and experientially deviant. Thus, for Ms. Livingston, the overwhelming blackness of her student body, as well as the racial isolation it engendered, proved more than enough to facilitate her transition from a woman to a white woman, from the invisible norm to the racial other.

Other white Brick City teachers had a similar experience to Ms. Livingston's: the more they interacted with black students, the more they realized that black students ascribed specific meanings to whiteness, including racism, power, and privilege. As one teacher remarked about her nearly all black student body, "They think all white people are privileged snobs who don't know anything about struggle. They think we all have it easy." In this sense, no matter its gendered or classed dimensions, no matter its intraracial variation, whiteness was privileged in the black imagination, an assumption that many teachers found upsetting. Also, in addition to the seemingly universal assumption of white privilege, black students routinely conveyed their thoughts about white racism. Ms. Stacey, a twenty-nine-year-old health teacher, was surprised to learn that her black students, at least initially, saw her as racist. This revelation, while alarming, helped her to see whiteness in different, more meaningful ways.

MS. STACEY: Ivory, she's probably one of my favorite students, just flat-out told me one day that she was happy I wasn't a racist. And I'm like, "Why would you even think that?," you know. She looks me right in the eyes and casually says, "Because you're white." Then she just walks off like it was no big deal. Meanwhile, I'm standing there shocked. I mean, is this how she sees white people? Is this how they all see white people? I don't know, it just got me thinking a lot, you know, like, how am I supposed to respond? What am I supposed to do?

Even though Mrs. McCormick, Ms. Livingston, and Ms. Stacey reacted somewhat differently to seeing themselves as white, the process by which whiteness was revealed to them was largely the same. Before working in predominantly black schools, not one of them looked at herself in racial terms. For all three teachers, whiteness symbolized normalness, and white racial identity remained invisible. Once they began interacting with black students, however, they soon realized that whiteness, in the eyes of those very students, was not only visible but also carried a specific and deleterious meaning. To a significant number of their black students, whiteness symbolized a combination of racial advantage and racial bigotry; it was the marker for racial oppression. This particular construction of whiteness, both visible and dangerous, was diametrically opposed to that of white teachers, who, as documented previously, largely saw themselves as raceless or "just normal." Ultimately, whiteness, interpreted in disparate ways, shaped the interactions between black students and white teachers, which, for the latter, made white racial identity a lot easier to see.

It Really Sucks Being the Only White Person in the Room

I've wanted to be a teacher since I was in the fourth grade. . . . People look at you funny when you're a boy bragging about wanting to be a teacher. So I'm used to being uncomfortable, I'm used to being different, you know. I think it's hard to make me feel uncomfortable or like the odd man out, but somehow, a group of fourteen-year-old boys, um, black boys, did it by the second month of school [*laughs*]. I laugh now, but man, let me tell you, sometimes it really sucks being the only white person in the room.

—CLAY DAVIDSON, 36

Seeing whiteness was only the first, and most benign, step in the three-step process of becoming a white teacher. Although the realization that black students looked at them in racial terms was itself jarring, it was the way these white teachers felt after seeing whiteness that forced many of them to adopt a locally specific racial identity. It should also be noted that seeing white and feeling white were not mutually exclusive processes. Seeing white influenced how white teachers felt, and feeling white helped white teachers recognize their racial identities on a more consistent basis. After recognizing themselves racially, white teachers started to notice their surroundings more; they began connecting physical space, racial status, and racial experience in a much more conscious and explicit manner. Even though racial context was instrumental to them seeing whiteness to begin with, now they started to *feel* white, particularly in that they were racially out of place. Thus, feeling white, while overlapping and intersecting with seeing white, was far more consequential, as it often led to feelings of dread, sadness, frustration, and anger.

Mrs. Gray, a high school music teacher, recalled an incident that epitomizes the process of feeling white. I asked her if she had ever felt uncomfortable or out of place at work because of her race, and she immediately answered in the affirmative. Mrs. Gray told the story of how, during a rehearsal for a Black History Month celebration, one of her black colleagues started speaking openly and negatively about white people. Stunned and left speechless, Mrs. Gray remarked on how she felt both disgusted and guilty, not because of anything she had done personally, but simply because she was white.

BELL: During your time at Baldwin High, have you ever felt uncomfortable or out of place due to your race?

MRS. GRAY: Yes, I have. I've felt, um, there's been plenty of times. I mean, it happens pretty often, not like it used to, but it definitely still happens.

BELL: Do you have any specific examples?

MRS. GRAY: Um, yeah. So normally every Monday we do community forum where we all get together as a community and kids perform and do things. . . . And normally during Black History Month, a lot of the music teachers always focus on, um, black heroes and black musicians that have affected our history in some way, you know, highlight them. The kids do speeches and learn their music and all that other stuff. Well, um, after a while I started to feel uncomfortable. Um, at first, I never felt uncomfortable in the building, I always felt a part of them, a part of the school, a part of the community, and, um, more and more, I just didn't. It started feeling like I was an outsider or like an imposter. One year about three years ago, we had a new music teacher, um, who was black. She was young, she had just got out of college, and she, she was up there, she spoke for like twenty-five minutes and I felt disgusting [*pause*]. She, she made me feel like a horrible person. She just, made me feel horrible by what she was saying about white people and how we all are.

BELL: What was she saying?

MRS. GRAY: She, um, she was like, she was kind of, and I guess, maybe this was my philosophy 'cause I look at people, I try to look at people and the fact that, you know, there are good and bad people no matter what color you are, you're a good seed or a bad seed. And she was kind of making the assumption that white people are just bad seeds. And, um, she was talking about white and black and was basically kind of like, Don't believe what they say, you don't need to embrace them or embrace their lies. . . . She talked about white people in such nasty generalizations and, um, I remember that people were nodding their head as she spoke. Right in front of me, you know. I, it just made me feel so uncomfortable, like I didn't belong there. I felt really guilty, like I almost needed to apologize for being white.

Mrs. Gray's experience of feeling white—of feeling like the racial other—typified the experiences of other teachers who similarly attributed their feelings of discomfort to the way that white people were symbolized and stigmatized within Brick City schools. Already having recognized themselves as white, and often finding themselves the only white person in any given space, white teachers went into great detail about feeling "disgusting," like "an outsider," and how they otherwise "didn't belong." For Mrs. Gray, these feelings of racial otherness were sparked by antiwhite "nasty generalizations" that were openly broadcast by one of her black colleagues. Making matters worse was her observation that other adults in the room, the majority of whom were black, evidenced their support for what was being said by nodding their heads in agreement. This behavior, according to Mrs. Gray, showed zero regard for her feelings or even her presence, which only served to intensify the negative feelings associated with being white.

Beyond their black students, white Brick City teachers also had much to say about black parents. Although they spent considerably more time with the former, the latter were just as likely to engender feelings of racialized discomfort. For black parents, of particular concern was what they perceived to be a cultural mismatch between the predominantly white teaching staffs and predominantly black student bodies at Brick City schools.[36] More specifically, in the eyes of many black parents, whiteness—personified by white teachers—suffered a fundamental lack of understanding; it was incompatible with black students, black communities, and black culture as a whole. Compounding matters further was the willingness of black parents to express this sentiment at inopportune times, such as in front of their own children, other students, or even entire classrooms. According to multiple teachers, the racial and cultural incongruity between themselves and their students, as openly expressed by black parents, made them feel not only insecure as educators but also, more to the point, racially stigmatized as people.

Kate Meredith, a middle school English teacher, epitomized this process by recalling a litany of experiences that had accumulated over nearly three decades of teaching in predominantly black schools. At this point in her career, Mrs. Meredith was starting to give serious consideration to retirement. Still, even after all this time, she remembers, in vivid detail, the very first time a parent questioned her ability to effectively teach black students. I recount our discussion at length.

BELL: You mentioned that parents have made you feel uncomfortable because of your race. Do you have any specific examples?

MRS. MEREDITH: Oh, god, yes [*laughs*]. I don't know how much time you got, but I can talk about parents for hours. I mean, they're the worst. Well, I probably shouldn't say that, some are amazing and very helpful, but some are hell-bent on tearing down anybody that upsets their kid, especially if you're white.

BELL: Can you elaborate?

MRS. MEREDITH: Yeah, um, I remember my first year as a teacher. Here I am, fresh out of college, bright-eyed and ready to change the world, and by the end of the first week I was ready to quit and do something else. I'm pretty sure I went home crying every day for almost a month. It was that bad. Um, I remember this boy, Michael, he always gave me shit for no reason at all. I'm talking 8:30 in the morning and he already has an attitude. So one day, we're like twenty minutes into class and he just starts being a jerk. He won't let me take attendance, he's yelling at me, yelling at his classmates, so I just lost it. I yell at the top of my lungs, "Get out of my classroom and don't come back," you know. I didn't want to be that teacher, I hate teachers like that, you know, yellers, but I was over it. So he gets up, flips over his desk, and storms out of the classroom. I knew in the moment that I didn't really handle it well, but I just didn't care, I was happy to see him go. A few of my kids helped me clean up the mess and we got on with the day [*long pause*].

BELL: Are you OK?

MRS. MEREDITH: Yeah, I just, um, I should've known it wasn't over, but I was brand-new to teaching, what the hell did I know? So, um, later in the day, I'm sitting with my kids, setting them up in small groups, then all of a sudden, boom, this woman, this grown woman who I'd never seen before just burst into my classroom. She slams the door behind her and starts screaming at me in front of the entire class. "Why did you kick my son out of class?" I was in shock. I froze. My mind went completely blank until I saw Michael standing behind her. So now I know it's about to get crazy, and she just starts yelling all of these racist things, you know. Just god-awful things.

BELL: Wow.

MRS. MEREDITH: Yeah, I know. This was all in front of the kids. She was pretty much screaming at the top of her lungs, telling her son, "Don't listen to this white lady, she doesn't know what she's talking about," you know. It seemed like this went on forever, but, um, finally the teacher in the class next to me, a black woman, she heard what was going on and came in the class and got her out of there. I looked at my kids and I just broke down. I completely fell apart. We have a bathroom in my class, so I just ran inside the bathroom and shut the door behind me. I didn't even turn on the lights, I just sat there crying. I was completely humiliated.

At this point, Mrs. Meredith's voice cracked and she had tears in her eyes. I could see that she was visibly upset, so I asked her if she wanted to take a break. I also reminded her that if need be, we could stop the interview altogether. Mrs. Meredith shook her head and said it was OK to continue. Still, as she wiped tears from her eyes, it was clear that she was grappling with painful memories. Mrs. Meredith recounted a number of stories, detailing the ups and downs of a career in education that spanned three decades. With this retelling, however, the trauma she experienced as a first-year teacher came rushing back in real time, causing her to become emotional for the only time during our entire interview (which ended up being one of my longest). As we explored this experience further, Mrs. Meredith posited that race—more specifically, whiteness—was the "real reason" for her treatment. From her perspective, the repeated use of the word "white," interspersed with invective, was clear evidence that she was being targeted because of her race, not because of her actions. Therefore—and, again, after thirty years as a teacher—Mrs. Meredith explicitly connected one of the most traumatic experiences of her career to white racial identity.

This example captures the pattern by which white teachers came to feel uncomfortable, or in this case "humiliated," because of their racial identities. Whenever a black student or black parent specifically invoked whiteness while objecting to student-teacher interactions, it indicated to white teachers that they were being singled out because of their race. This process consistently led to feelings of frustration, humiliation, sadness, anger, and even guilt. Overwhelmingly negative and specifically tethered to whiteness, these emotions had the power to disrupt relationships and destroy confidence. They also served as a powerful reminder that whiteness, as a social category, occupied a more precarious position within these particular spaces.[37] That is, within Brick City schools, to feel white was to feel mistreated, to feel stigmatized, to feel marked as the racialized other.

I Do Everything as a White Teacher

How can I be an effective teacher if I'm constantly looking over my shoulder? How do I know one of my students won't misinterpret something I say and I get labeled a racist or that teacher that hates black people? You just never know for sure, so you have to be extremely careful. So I keep that in the back of my mind, you know. You're not just a teacher, you're a white teacher. . . . I do everything as a white teacher.
—LEAH THOMPSON, 33

Seeing white and feeling white were both highly salient steps in the process of becoming white teachers. The third step—*being white*—moves beyond racial recognition and feelings of discomfort and crosses into the realm of behavior, performance, and any manner of doing whiteness.[38] For the teachers I interviewed, white racial identity was never an explicit process before they started working in predominantly black schools. In fact, in a general sense, reinforcing the invisibility of whiteness through personal behavior is a crucial, if not always conscious, characteristic of being white in a white-dominated society. As John T. Warren notes, "Whiteness, while a systemic historical process that is diffuse and abstract, is also located through embodiment—through a repetition of mundane and extraordinary acts that continually make and remake whiteness, all while eluding scrutiny and detection."[39] Within Brick City schools, though, making and remaking whiteness while "eluding scrutiny and detection" was virtually impossible, as whiteness, in the form of white teachers, was easily detected and outwardly scrutinized via symbolic interactions.

On the lighter side of such scrutiny, teachers were accused of dressing "like a white boy" or talking "like a white girl." As one teacher put it, "The kids get a kick out of the way I dress, they always make fun of me for dressing like a white boy." Conversely, on the more serious side, teachers endured "racially charged insults," they were accused of discriminating against black students, and they were often criticized for being insufficiently attuned to, and culturally incompatible with, the behavioral patterns and learning styles of their predominantly black student bodies. With their racial visibility in mind, white teachers were well aware that any aspect of their behavior, from interacting with students to pedagogical praxis, ran the risk of being interpreted racially, meaning that their actions could be attributed to their racial identity. Thus, they took steps to perform whiteness, to be white in ways that presented more amenable, more racially compatible versions of themselves.

If, throughout the country more broadly, the performance of whiteness typically comprises unrecognizable and unintentional acts, the context of Brick City schools rendered such acts recognizable and intentional. After seeing themselves as white, and subsequently experiencing the discomfort, sadness, and anger that accompanied feeling white, white teachers sought ways to accept the former while reducing the later. They made peace with that fact that their own racial identities were suddenly visible to them, but they actively strategized and consciously acted in ways that minimized the likelihood of them feeling like the racial other. Also, as professionals, they wanted to find an "in" with black students, a process they believed was far more difficult than it needed to be. Finally, white teachers wanted to insulate themselves from charges of racism, and they found that particular kinds of white racial identity were more effective than others in doing so. Thus, in order to best reach out to their black students, as well as to avoid any racialized confusion or confrontation, white Brick City teachers performed compensatory and protectionary versions of white racial identity. Next I break down each process.

Compensatory forms of white racial identity involved behaviors that sought to compensate for the racial and cultural mismatch between white teachers and black students.[40] Teachers engaging in this type of performance did so with the intention of reassuring their students that they accepted, if not embraced, black culture. Whether authentic or inauthentic, spontaneous or staged, white Brick City teachers routinely described scenarios in which they lionized black celebrities, familiarized themselves with black music, and, in some cases, even integrated "black vernacular" or "black slang" into their own speech patterns. None of this was meant to be mocking or condescending toward black students, but as one teacher, Mr. Davidson, put it, "You want the kids to know that you understand them and you're not judging them. Even if you have to fake it, you want them to think what's important to them is important to you. Otherwise you're just some ignorant, bland-ass white person."

For Mrs. Scott, her compensatory behavior started off as purely strategic, but after multiple years of teaching in Brick City schools, it became something more. Looking for a better way to connect in the classroom, Mrs. Scott enlisted her students to teach her "their lingo," thereby facilitating better communication between herself and her various classes. As time went by, she came to appreciate the way her black students talked to each other, and she found herself repeating their speech habits outside of school. While Mrs. Scott initially adapted to the linguistic styles of her black students in order to become a better teacher to them, she eventually "saw the complexity in how they spoke to each other" and realized that "their communication style makes more sense when you see it up close." As a result, Mrs. Scott, in her own words, sometimes speaks "like a fourteen-year-old black girl." When asked to provide an example, she replied, "I always find myself saying, 'Now I'm Gucci' whenever I'm in a good mood. I got that from the kids, you know. 'I'm Gucci' means 'I'm good.' My husband thinks I'm crazy."

After performing a compensatory form of white racial identity at school, Mrs. Scott subconsciously integrated parts of her performance into her personal life. For other teachers, though, their compensatory performances started off strategic and stayed that way. For example, a central goal of this strategy was to convince skeptical black parents that whiteness, or being white, was not some insurmountable obstacle to reaching and successfully teaching black students. Therefore, in order to accomplish this goal, white teachers performed their racial identities in ways that reassured black parents that they did, in fact, possess the requisite cultural competency to not only educate but also care for their children. These performances ranged from the playful, such as secret handshakes with individual black students, to the profound, such as openly celebrating and promoting Black Lives Matter.[41] Ultimately, through various ways of being white, white Brick City teachers sought to bridge the cultural gap between black students and themselves and, in the process, to become more effective teachers and reassure skeptical black parents.

The other, and in some respects more serious, way of performing white racial identity was protectionary. To protect themselves against accusations of racism—to avoid being branded a racist—white teachers closely monitored their behavior, always accounting for the racialized ways it could be received and interpreted by black students and their families. Protectionary performances were not immediate. Teachers did not come into Brick City schools expecting to be seen as white, nor did they expect their pedagogy to be scrutinized through an explicitly racialized lens. After being spatially socialized, however, formerly "normal" teachers internalized their new roles as white teachers, eventually adjusting their performances to avoid any and all forms of racialized stress. This form of white racial identity—this way of being white—was much less about teaching and much more about peace of mind and self-preservation.

For Mrs. Weaver, a middle school science teacher, the need to adopt protectionary performances of white racial identity resulted from a traumatic experience that took place early in her career. In her third year of teaching, Mrs. Weaver, in a bout of frustration, scolded her students for not working hard and asked whether they wanted to spend their adult lives on welfare. Initially unaware that she had done anything untoward, let alone discriminatory, Mrs. Weaver would quickly learn just how controversial her remarks were, particularly considering that they were directed at a room full of black children. As she explained, the incident in question quickly grew out of control, and it forever altered the way she performs white racial identity in the classroom.

> MRS. WEAVER: I had 130 kids, only African American kids, and we had them for ninety-minute blocks. . . . I remember that I was like, oh my god, it was the hardest thing I ever done in my entire life. . . . Just to make my year kind of really tough, they were really being bad for me and I was very frustrated, and I think I was reading them a riot act or something . . . and I said, you know, you need to get to college and get a good job, you don't want to spend your entire life on welfare or something like that. I was trying to be, like, motivational, but I, they didn't take it that way and they pounced on me. . . . They started, like, saying I was being racist and being, you know . . . they kind of turned the tables. Sort of a mutiny.

Looking for a way to simultaneously motivate her students, address their behavior, and quell her own frustration, Mrs. Weaver blurted out words that, intentionally or not, included a reference to the decades-old stereotype about African Americans and welfare dependency.[42] Although she claimed to be oblivious to the racialized significance of her words, her black students recognized it immediately and responded by "turn[ing] the tables" on her and staging a "mutiny." Unfortunately for Mrs. Weaver, as she goes on to explain, the backlash to her comments would only get worse.

MRS. WEAVER: So I got very frustrated, and after class I go down and talk to Florence, like, Oh my god, that was just an absolute nightmare. . . . The kids mutinied me. . . . She was a, you know, a black principal, so I thought, OK, she can help me. And she did. She was like, "Listen, go get a coffee, relax, this happens." . . . So I come back the next day and she goes, "You have to leave the school, you can't be here." So I go, Can I go to my room and get stuff? And she says, "No, you have to leave." . . . And she never really told me why. . . . So all of a sudden, Nelly Fisher . . . she wrote me a letter and said . . . the kids had kind of said that I said all black people are on welfare, and I'm like, What, where would I have even gotten that in my entire life? I never would've even known that statistic. . . . So I was like twisted all around and then I got suspended for six weeks. . . . And I realized from that day on, you got to be super careful, super clever, and super, you know kind of like, leveled off, and that's what I've done ever since then.[43]

Despite her claims to the contrary, invoking "welfare" while chastising black students was seen as racially insensitive at best, and explicitly racist as worst. As a result, Mrs. Weaver developed a negative reputation, one that painted her as a teacher who harbored racial animosity toward her black students. She was not seen as an inexperienced teacher who, under immense pressure, made a thoughtless and racially insensitive remark; rather, she was seen as a white teacher who openly trafficked in racial stereotypes. This latter construction was especially prevalent among her black student body, and to her surprise—and frustration—it was quite common among her black coworkers as well. As Mrs. Weaver would go on to explain, this "unfortunate incident" soured her relationships with her black colleagues for years to come.

MRS. WEAVER: Probably for two or three years, the black teachers in the building didn't talk to me. They kind of shunned me, they didn't look at me, they didn't invite me to little luncheons or picnics or anything like that. We were very separate for a long time and, um, really it was, I almost had to pretend to be someone I'm not. . . . And, um, after they sort of got to know me and knew that I was not the evil one or whatever, they were like, Wait, maybe she wasn't being racist. So after a while they started, their eyes got a little bit more opened and they were fine, you know, I got them on my side.

BELL: You say you had to pretend to be someone else. What exactly do you mean by that?

MRS. WEAVER: Sure. Well, now I watch every word that comes out of my mouth, and sometimes I slip up, I have to admit. . . . But when I do and they still kind of pounce on me and call me a racist or whatever, um, I find that I tend to play up racism more, you know, against blacks. I mean, I do think there's still racism against blacks, but there's racism by blacks too, you know. So I tend to play that up more, especially with black teachers.

After becoming a teacher at an almost exclusively black school, it did not take long for Mrs. Weaver to develop protectionary performances of white racial identity. Her story was not unique, and it demonstrates why white Brick City teachers saw the need to perform whiteness, to consciously be a specific kind of white person. Resulting from symbolic interactions that were interpreted along racial lines, protectionary forms of white racial identity, at their core, were designed to protect white teachers against charges of racism. Anytime race became the focal point of student-teacher interactions, white teachers believed they were willfully misinterpreted, knowingly misrepresented, and unfairly mistreated, all under the guise of accountability. They also found that any one incident could linger, sometimes for years, affecting their relationships with students, parents, and even their colleagues. Because the stakes were so high, many teachers decided to be white, or *do* whiteness, on their own terms, ultimately taking control of their newly discovered racial identities.[44]

Protective performances of white racial identity, for Mrs. Weaver and other teachers, included the careful monitoring of discourse and behavior, and the presentation of an artificial or "politically correct" self.[45] Any actions that could be perceived as racist were to be avoided at all costs, and any words that could be connected to racial stereotypes were to be struck from the lexicon. Also, as the educators of black children, white Brick City teachers knew that any disagreement, no matter how benign, ran the risk of taking on a more ominous, more hostile racial significance. Thus, through spatially specific behaviors, they learned to distance themselves from whiteness, particularly from the negative ways it could be constructed and weaponized within Brick City schools. Combined with compensatory performances, interview respondents found that protectionary forms of white racial identity bolstered their chances to be successful teachers, all while protecting them from unfair criticism and unnecessary stress.

Brick City schools, a far cry from the racially segregated, ostensibly nonra-cialized environments that normalize whiteness, had a clarifying effect, mak-ing the contours of white racial identity both visible and meaningful to white Brick City teachers. Based on repeated symbolic interactions, white teachers over time constructed new, spatially specific identities for themselves. After first seeing themselves in racialized terms, they then started to feel like racial outsiders, a status that could manifest itself at any time within their respec-tive schools. Finally, following what could be painful and emotional experi-ences, white Brick City teachers strategically embraced whiteness, negotiating with themselves about when, where, and how to deploy their nascent racial identities. Furthermore, discursively, once centered on predominantly black schools, rhetorical incoherence gave way to a more precise and determined fluency, and white deflection transformed into a concerted focus on white ra-cial identity. In a stark departure from their inability to connect race to their lives outside Brick City schools, white teachers within Brick City schools could easily enumerate the myriad ways that being white affected their daily expe-riences. Ultimately—and in the span of a single interview—the very teach-ers who previously epitomized white racelessness spoke forcefully to the local process of racial socialization.[46]

4. THE WHITE RACE CARD

Considerable research has illuminated the ways historical, political, and/or economic processes constitute and alter the meanings and ideologies of race and white domination, but much less has been done with respect to the more intimate, everyday processes that link the self to the racial order.—PAMELA PERRY, *Shades of White*

I just get tired of people playing the race card all the time. I mean, yeah, we still have problems with race, but there has never been a better time to be black in America. Stop making excuses.—DAN RADKE, Sexton High School

Not to make excuses or anything, but the racism at Sexton almost makes it impossible to do your job. I'm sorry, that's just the truth. —DAN RADKE, Sexton High School

The race card. It is a term that is often used, but rarely defined.[1] For some, the race card is a canard, a myth employed by those looking to make excuses and blame others for their personal, cultural, and even moral failings.[2] For others, the very term "race card" is nothing more than a tool used to minimize the impact of institutional racism and delegitimize the legitimate grievances of people of color.³ References to the race card can be heard in a variety of places, ranging from casual conversations to cable news television.⁴ They can be heard in political ads, on talk radio, and even on college campuses.⁵ Across the ideological spectrum, you can read about the alleged motivations for "the race card" in both online and print publications, including conservative outlets such as the *Daily Caller*, the *Federalist*, and the *National Review*, as well as more liberal journals such as the *Atlantic*, the *New Yorker*, and the *New Republic*.⁶

In addition to political and lay commentaries, social scientists too have spent considerable time analyzing the various constructions of, and subsequent responses to, the race card.⁷ Of particular interest is the extent to which Americans still believe in the existence and relevance of interpersonal and institutional racism.⁸ While not always framed in the specific "race card" language, countless empirical studies have assessed the general public's belief, or lack thereof, in ongoing issues of race and racism.⁹ That is, to what extent do Americans feel that racial discrimination affects or makes a discernable difference today in the lived experiences and life outcomes of white people vis-à-vis nonwhite people? Also, to what extent are charges of racism real, and to what extent are they fabricated?¹⁰ An often unstated yet consistent theme permeating the many debates and controversies surrounding the proverbial race card is that the very term almost always refers to people of color.¹¹

Broken down to its most basic level, the race card is about racial victimization, or, more specifically, the lack of it. Accusations that people of color—and their white allies—play the race card are, in essence, accusations of fraud.¹² In this line of thinking, accusing individuals of playing the race card is the equivalent of accusing them of lying, or, at best, exaggerating the impact that racial discrimination has on, and in, their respective lives. It is a way to question or outright reject someone's claim of racial victimization. Central to this entire process is the broader, more general belief that the United States is no longer marred by racism, at least not beyond the fringes of society.¹³ Unsurprisingly, the extent to which people believe in or question the reality of racism in the contemporary United States is in large part predicated on their racialized experiences.¹⁴ Therefore, for white teachers, their various perspectives on the legitimacy of racial victimization corresponded directly to their lived experiences within and outside Brick City schools.

Race and, to a lesser degree, space were both relevant factors in the social construction of racial victimization. Above and beyond any one specific claim was the question of which racial group was making it. That is, for many of my interviewees, white teachers told the truth about racial discrimination, but black people played the race card. Throughout my fieldwork, white teachers repeatedly accused people of color of fabricating excuses for individual and collective failures, while simultaneously claiming to be victims of racial discrimination within predominantly black schools. In one sentence, they would chastise African American students and families for being "too focused on race," then, sometimes only moments later, they themselves would focus on race, describing it as a legitimate concern and genuine impediment to professional success. The spatial and demographic bifurcation of legitimate versus illegitimate claims of racial victimization is part of a discursive and ideological process that I term *the white race card*.

In this chapter I show how, as with the spatial conditionality of racial awareness, white teachers' belief in the authenticity of racial victimization fluctuated between white and nonwhite racialized spaces. In the former, most claims of racial victimization, particularly those made by people of color, were almost instantly rejected and dismissed out of hand. As a whole, white teachers did not give much currency to the idea that people of color experience much racial discrimination today.[15] Conversely, in the latter, almost any claim of racial victimization made by white teachers was unreflexively accepted as legitimate. In fact, for the teachers I interviewed, general claims of white racial victimization were made all the more real by their own experiences within Brick City schools. Thus, even though they expressed great skepticism about nonwhite claims of racial victimization, white Brick City teachers had no problem accepting white claims of racial victimization, nor did they hesitate to make similar claims themselves. Ultimately, the data presented in this chapter highlight the degree to which racial victimization, though real in its effect, remains socially constructed.

THE RACE CARD

With few exceptions, white Brick City teachers were highly skeptical of general claims of racial victimization. Some teachers went beyond skepticism and dismissed outright the idea that racism plays a meaningful role in the contemporary United States. The race card, according to my interview respondents, was a multistep tool that people of color used to shield themselves from personal responsibility and, in the process, make white people feel guilty about being successful.[16] Step 1 is rampant, out-of-control political correctness. Each of the teachers I interviewed, to varying degrees, described political correctness as a problem, one mostly perpetrated by people of color. Step 2 consisted of making excuses for personal failures. As opposed to taking personal responsibility for their lives, the theory went, too many people of color choose to make excuses or, in the words of one teacher, "blame the white man for their own fuckups." In the eyes of white Brick City teachers, out-of-control political correctness and the incessant need for people of color to play the victim, today only served to exacerbate the already tense race relations between white Americans and nonwhite Americans.

I Just Hate How Politically Correct We've Become

You can't really say or do anything anymore without somebody somewhere being offended, you know. It's like every day now. Oh, somebody over here said something that was racist or somebody over there did something that was racially insensitive. Like what does that even mean, racially insensitive? I don't know, I just hate how politically correct we've become. It's out of control and I think it's a way for people to avoid dealing with their own lives. —ALLISON HALL, 44

Dan Radke has been teaching at Sexton High School for six years. Described as a "straight shooter" and someone I "should definitely talk to," Mr. Radke was referred to me by more than one teacher in my snowball sample. True to form, one of the first things he said to me during our interview was "Look, I don't know what you expect to hear from me, but I'm not the type to pull punches, I tell it like it is. That's just who I am." In "tell[ing] it like is," Mr. Radke made it clear that he believed racism in the contemporary United States was all but extinct. While acknowledging those "neo-Nazi types" who apparently live beyond the fringes of polite society, Mr. Radke lamented the "much bigger problem" of political correctness. As he repeatedly opined over the course of our interview, Mr. Radke saw political correctness as the new, sophisticated way to "blame white people for everything wrong in society." In other words, political correctness was just a more complex, more contemporary way of playing the race card.

Other teachers had similar takes on the purportedly "new world of out-of-control political correctness." Teacher after teacher expressed anger and frustration about always having to watch what they say—up to and including telling jokes—lest they be accused of being a racist. Tellingly, as with Mr. Radke's, other complaints about political correctness were explicitly conceptualized as attacks on white people, as another way to blame them for the problems associated with communities of color. Denise Bradley, a middle school teacher of nine years, was among those who made this point:

MRS. BRADLEY: I mean, it's gotten to the point where you can't even make a joke anymore. A simple, harmless joke on Facebook can get you fired from your job. Seriously, that happened to close friend of mine. She told a harmless joke on Facebook, and all of a sudden she was a racist. Somebody reported her, and she ended up getting suspended and eventually quit. I mean, to be honest, it's like, um, political correctness is a way to get back at white people, you know.

BELL: Could you elaborate on that last point?

MRS. BRADLEY: What, about being against white people?

BELL: Yes.

MRS. BRADLEY: Yeah, OK, um. Well, um, I hope I don't sound racist or politically incorrect [*laughs*], but I think the people who complain the most about being hurt or offended or whatever, um, they're not white. And not just that, but, um, it's white people who are always getting in trouble, you know, like my friend. So look, I think most of the people who complain about being offended are not white and they, um, they're always complaining about white people. They never complain about each other, it's always white people.

In this brief exchange, Mrs. Bradley made explicit that which is often only implied: political correctness is a way for people of color to police the discourse and collective behavior of their white counterparts. She had "noticed," she said, that it was people of color who "complain the most," and the complaints themselves always seemed to be directed at white people, never at each other. Also, whether regarding "innocent jokes" or "hard truths," Mrs. Bradley believed that political correctness entailed people of color, in conjunction with "overly sensitive whites," using faux outrage and public shaming to silence anyone—especially anyone who "happens to be white"—who ever criticized them, even when such criticism was warranted. Other teachers conceptualized and spoke of political correctness in much the same way, but they contextualized it within the veil of meritocracy. In this sense, political correctness was less about addressing authentic claims of racial victimization and more about (1) policing white behavior and discourse, and (2) punishing white people for their success relative to people of color. As one teacher stated rather defiantly, "We're not living in the Jim Crow South here. I'm not going to apologize for having money."

While these examples explicitly connect political correctness to attacks on, and accusations against, white Americans, interview respondents also considered the very existence of political correctness a well-intentioned yet blatant form of affirmative action. According to this logic, because of the misguided belief that "white people are always the bad guys," often, in an effort to be politically correct, African Americans and other people of color are given opportunities and rewards that they have not earned. For example, Mrs. Gray, a high school music teacher, conceptualized political correctness as accepting the fact that "things aren't really going to be fair" and that sometimes "diversity takes the place of merit." As such, her biggest objection to "PC culture" amounted to an objection to affirmative action. When I asked Mrs. Gray if she could provide any examples of more-qualified whites being passed over by less-qualified nonwhites, she was unable to do so. Still, she remained resolute, claiming that one only had to "look around" to find necessary proof. Thus, despite her inability to provide specific examples, Mrs. Gray maintained that greater parity between whites and nonwhites resulted, at least in part, from our new, ostensibly antiwhite, politically correct culture.

While defining political correctness as an attack against white Americans or a covert form of affirmative action was common across interviews, white Brick City teachers saved their harshest criticisms of political correctness for how it was allegedly used by their students and their students' families. Complaints about political correctness in Brick City schools were plenty in number and sometimes malicious in content. Because of the way it intersected with white Brick City teachers' professional lives, political correctness in the classroom was personal, and for this reason they spoke of it with passionate disdain. Mrs. Nelson, a high school math teacher, exemplifies such disdain when she discusses the proverbial "PC game."

> MRS. NELSON: You can't work where I work and not see political correctness [*laughs*]. If you want to keep your job, you absolutely have to play the PC game.
>
> BELL: Can you provide specific examples of playing the PC game?
>
> MRS. NELSON: Um, OK, so, like we have this new program, computer software that is supposed help the students learn Spanish. We had this whole PD [professional development] series . . . and I freaking teach math, so I didn't understand why I had to be there. But the part that bothered me the most was most of our students can't even speak English. Why don't we teach them what a noun and a verb is before we

try to move to another language? Now this is something I could never say. None of us could. We were all thinking it, we all wanted to say it, but I guarantee you if just one of us dared to criticize Ebonics or whatever it's called these days, we'd all be called racists. Parents who can't be bothered enough to show up to parent-teacher conferences or send their kid to school with clean clothes will be all over you if you say anything remotely critical of black people or culture, you know.

Mrs. Nelson not only spoke about her students and her students' parents negatively; she did so in a particularly harsh tone. She was not merely angry at what she believed to be nonsensical school policy—using software to help students learn Spanish—or even the fact that she, a math teacher, was forced to attend a professional development series that focused on language arts. For Mrs. Nelson, her frustration was rooted in the low skill level of black students, the misguided priorities of black parents, and the politically correct school culture, which prevented her or any of her white colleagues from voicing criticism of either circumstance. To do so, according to Mrs. Nelson, was to subject oneself to accusations of racism and thereby put one's job in jeopardy. The possibility of losing her job, all in the name of political correctness, has worn on Mrs. Nelson over the course of her career. This, along with a host of negative interactions with black students and families, has long since engendered a racialized form of resentment that, in both content and in form, spills out whenever she talks about her experiences in Brick City schools.

Though variously defined, white Brick City, either implicitly or—as in the case of Mrs. Nelson—explicitly, connected political correctness to race. More specifically, political correctness was described as a political, economic, and social device that, once utilized, was advantageous to people of color and disadvantageous to anyone racially designated as white. Furthermore, in the eyes of white Brick City teachers, political correctness was fraudulent. It was based on little more than hurt feelings and a wrongheaded desire to see people of color succeed, even at the expense of better-prepared and more qualified whites. In our new, collective consciousness, it was argued, political correctness is a way for people of color and their white allies to eschew personal responsibility and ignore their own culpability in the maintenance and reproduction of racial inequality. Political correctness, then, was constructed as a modern-day version of the race card.

At Some Point You Have to Stop Making Excuses

It's always something, you know. "We don't have any money, my mom had to work, my dad is in jail." Oh, and racism. Racism, racism, racism. I'm not saying we don't have problems, that racism is entirely gone, but the civil rights movement was a long time ago. At some point you have to stop making excuses. Just get it done. —STEPHEN HAYES, 28

Lamenting political correctness was only one way that white Brick City teachers responded to claims of nonwhite racial victimization. The second, and in some ways more visceral, reaction was to almost reflexively equate any charge of racial discrimination with making excuses or "being a victim." Throughout my time in the field, the word "victim" was always used pejoratively. According to white Brick City teachers, to complain about racism in modern America was to be a victim, and to blame your problems on racial discrimination was to harbor a "victim mentality." Although unfortunate, and perhaps uncomfortable, for the majority of my interview respondents, if racial inequality seemed endemic, then black people and other people of color needed to look inward, not outward. Contemporary racial disparities were better explained by cultural pathologies and personal failings. Any suggestion otherwise was determined to be a counterproductive and outdated excuse.

A VICTIM MENTALITY

Collectively, white Brick City teachers were highly skeptical of nonwhite claims of racial victimization. This held true in a general sense, as well as for the predominantly black students and families that populated their schools. Such broad skepticism led most teachers to delegitimize accusations of racism, dismissing them as evidence of a "victim mentality." From their perspective, a victim mentality is a self-defeating mindset, one that comes with "ready-made" excuses and predetermines that other people are responsible for your negative life outcomes. No matter its veracity, any complaint about racism or racial discrimination was tantamount to a pretext for personal failure, and it was this mentality—*not racism*—that prevented people of color from being successful. Alexa Boyd, a middle school math teacher, was one teacher who expressed this sentiment:

BELL: I want to go back to this idea of a victim mentality. What exactly do you mean by that term?

MRS. BOYD: Well, it's like, um, it's like this. If you always see yourself as a victim, if you think white people are always out to get you, then you're setting yourself up for failure, you know. It's almost like you have a ready-made excuse for every time something doesn't go your way, and as long as that's in the back of your mind—Oh, I didn't get the job because I'm black—then you're never going to be successful. You're never going to make anything of yourself.

BELL: Do you believe that having a victim mentality is more of a barrier to people of color than racial discrimination?

MRS. BOYD: Absolutely. If you're looking for an excuse to fail, you're probably going to fail. You don't need any help from me or any other white person.

Mrs. Boyd not only laments what she considers to be a self-defeating mentality; she also argues that the mentality itself is more consequential, and more real, than actual racism. To be clear, Mrs. Boyd did not discount the existence of racial discrimination, she just, in an ideological defense of American meritocracy, placed the onus of racial inequality squarely on the shoulders of nonwhite groups. On this point, she was abundantly clear. When asked about the salience of racial inequality today, Mrs. Boyd readily admitted that it was "still a problem," but that did not mitigate her belief that people of color needed to dispense with the mentality that they were mistreated and/or "owed anything" by the country as a whole. In this sense, any one example of racial discrimination, no matter how blatant or consequential, paled in comparison to the abundance of opportunity currently available throughout the country and was dwarfed by the debilitating and destructive power of a victim mentality.

A similar dynamic was evident when it came to assigning blame for the social problems that currently exist in the inner city. White Brick City teachers scoffed at the notion that they, or any other white person, were responsible for the negative conditions—such as urban blight, poverty, and crime—that are commonly associated with inner-city communities.[17] As such, their denials of responsibility were more than mere racial ideology: they were personal. Historically, racism in America has been associated with the white majority, and for white Brick City teachers, the modern world was no different.[18] Transitively, then, nonwhite claims of racial victimization, past and present, are synonymous with claims of white racism. Therefore, if African Americans and other people of color truly experience racism in the contemporary

United States, then by definition white people, including white teachers, are implicated in an unfair, inegalitarian system. For white Brick City teachers, as with many white Americans throughout the broader United States, their vehement rejection of nonwhite racial victimization was in part fueled by their desire to defend themselves against charges of racism.[19]

Today an extensive research literature demonstrates the extent to which white Americans hold a particular aversion to being labeled racist.[20] Not only do they see it as an unfair slander, but as advocates of postracial politics, they recoil at the notion that they are somehow culpable in the maintenance and reproduction of racial inequality.[21] This pattern held true for my interview respondents: to a teacher, they rejected overt forms of racism. Resultingly, because they saw themselves as defenders and practitioners of the colorblind tradition, white Brick City teachers outwardly expressed anger and hostility toward nonwhite claims of racial victimization, particularly those that pertained to urban education. Paige Vincent, for example, has been teaching in Brick City schools for thirteen years, and to this day she struggles with the fact that many of her students, as well as their families, think of her as someone who dislikes black people.

> MRS. VINCENT: I do this work because I want to do this work. I've always wanted to do this work. Being an educator is a big part of who I am. So when, um, you invest in kids—not money, but almost like yourself—you put yourself into these kids and you want them to be successful, but then out of nowhere, almost without warning, *bam*, you're a racist. A kid gets suspended, you're a racist. A kid fails a test, you're a racist. I've had kids show up after missing an entire month of school, a month, only to have their mom call me a racist because I tell her how far he's behind. It's very hurtful, especially when you think you have a great relationship with a kid and he calls you a racist. I mean, most of the time they're just looking for an excuse, but getting called racist by kids you care about never gets easy to hear. It hurts every time [*long pause*].

After teaching in a predominantly black school for over a decade, Mrs. Vincent still finds it "very hurtful" to be labeled a racist by her students. Even though she describes such accusations as nothing more than excuses, she nonetheless considers them an attack on her character. Other interview respondents too equated claims of white racism to racially based excuses, but in lieu of sadness, they responded with anger and condemnation. Multiple teachers became visibly angry during this portion of the interview, chastising their black students and their students' families as "unserious," "lazy," and "always looking to pass the buck." On more than one occasion, white teachers described African Americans who made claims of racial victimization, including their own students, as "race hustlers" or "the real racists." For these teachers, claims of white racism were more than mere accusations: they were racist overgeneralizations that were themselves discriminatory against whites. In this sense, the very people complaining about racism were the ones perpetuating racism, which, according to white Brick City teachers, was a feature—not a bug—of playing the race card.

During my interviews, "playing the race card," which included a combination of rampant political correctness, harboring a victim mentality, and making excuses for personal failure, was routinely characterized as both unfounded and counterproductive. In the eyes of white Brick City teachers, nonwhite claims of racial victimization, outside of the most obvious and extreme examples, were simply not credible. Furthermore, because they understood charges of racial discrimination to be accusations against whites *as whites*, a number of teachers took such charges personally, interpreting them as an attack on their professionalism and overall character. Thus, not only were nonwhite claims of racial victimization seen as fraudulent, but the claims themselves were seen as inherently unfair and even racist toward whites. Although several respondents expressed sympathetic views toward the economic conditions faced by many of their black students, they gave little consideration to the idea that racism was all that relevant to their overall chances for success.[22] As a whole, nonwhite claims of racial victimization were not taken seriously by white Brick City teachers, including those made by black students and black families.

THE WHITE RACE CARD

Although they took a negative and dismissive tone toward nonwhite claims of racial victimization, white Brick City teachers saw white racial victimization as a raw and authentic portrayal of modern American life. For the teachers I interviewed, whereas African Americans and other people of color "played the race card," whites who complained about racism were the unfortunate purveyors of "uncomfortable truths." That is, claims of racial victimization were interpreted differently when they originated from the mouths of white teachers and spoke to the lives of white people. As long as white Americans were the supposed target of racial discrimination, then racism, whether institutional or interpersonal, was a harsh reality that needed to be openly and honestly confronted. Likewise, whenever people of color were the alleged perpetrators of racial discrimination, the skepticism that accompanied charges of white racism was minimal; in most cases it disappeared altogether. Within the majority of my interviews—and often in the span of a few questions—claims of racial victimization transformed from fiction to nonfiction, from fantasy to reality, and from evidence of a victim mentality to bold truth-telling about a deepening racial divide.

The disparate construction of white versus nonwhite claims of racial victimization is part of a phenomenon I term *the white race card*. Unlike the race card, which was described as an untrue and unfair slander, the white race card was real, an authentic characterization of racialized experience. On the one hand, the white race card entails making explicit claims of racial victimization. White teachers repeatedly named racial discrimination as a significant impediment to them and others like them. On the other hand, the white race card is validation, particularly validation through personal experience. Across interviews, teachers were eager to provide examples of what they considered to be "racism against whites." Some examples were general, some were specific; others were not so much examples as ideological statements. Still, because they perceived antiwhite animus to be ubiquitous within Brick City schools, white teachers accepted any claims of white racial victimization, even those they had not directly experienced.

The white race card was also an exception, a spatial exception. Contextualizing these purportedly authentic claims of racial victimization were schools where black bodies were the racial norm and white bodies were the racial exception. In this regard, the legitimacy afforded to white versus nonwhite claims of racial victimization was contextualized by the incongruent racial dynamics of physical space. Generally speaking, nonwhite claims of racial victimization situated whites as the numerically, politically, and socially dominant group, whereas for white Brick City teachers—particularly within Brick City schools—their claims of racial victimization situated whites as numerically, politically, and socially subordinate. Therefore, the white race card was more than a mere accounting and authentication of white racial victimization; it was also a confluence of race and space, one that affected both racial experience and racial ideology. Specifically developed and deployed within the physical space of Brick City schools, the white race card, as articulated by white teachers, constituted a form of spatial victimization, the concept I turn to now.

Spatial victimization is a spatially specific claim of racial victimization. It involves accusations of racial discrimination that are all predicated on being of a particular race within a particular space. For my interviewees, being a white teacher alone was not sufficient to engender feelings of victimization; it was being a white teacher within a predominantly black school that caused them to feel like the maligned and mistreated racial other. Another feature of spatial victimization is that it did not follow teachers outside of nonwhite racialized spaces, at least not to the same degree or with the same level of specificity. White claims of racial victimization were rarely made in reference to the United States writ large; rather, they were made specifically in reference to Brick City schools. Thus, in many ways the most salient aspect of spatial victimization is space. Space—or, to be more precise, nonwhite racialized space—caused white teachers to become more aware of, and subsequently believe in, the authenticity of racial victimization, even in what they routinely described as a colorblind, postracial society.[23]

Spatial victimization consists of three overlapping and interconnected processes. The first, reverse discrimination, is based on the idea that whiteness acts as a badge of inferiority within predominantly black schools. As such, due to their status as white teachers, my interview respondents claimed to be victims of reverse discrimination at every level of their respective workplaces. The second process, collective whiteness, is the idea that whiteness is a collective identity, essentially rendering all white people the same. For white Brick City teachers, it came as a shock that before all else, their students and their students' families saw them as white, subsuming their individual identities under a broad and stigmatized racial collective. Finally, the third process, black privilege, is based on the idea that black teachers have an advantage with black students and black parents. If whiteness is a badge of inferiority within Brick City schools, then blackness, by contrast, is a badge of superiority. Together, reverse discrimination, collective whiteness, and black privilege prompted a reliable, yet spatially specific, belief in white racial victimization.

It's Like It's Racism against Whites, It's Everywhere

I hate to use this phrase, I really do. But it's almost like reverse discrimination, you know. I never thought I would say anything like that, but I look around and, um, it's like it's racism against whites, it's everywhere. I'm not saying that happens every single day, but it happens often enough to be noticeable. —CANDICE SATTER, 35

On the whole, white teachers believed in the realness and salience of reverse discrimination within Brick City schools. During my time in the field, the term "reverse discrimination" appeared in all but two of my interviews. There was considerable variation, however, in how teachers described reverse discrimination. That is, though it was a constant theme across interviews, some teachers were more vocal than others in detailing their claims of racial victimization, labeling any perceived slight as an example of antiwhite racism. Other teachers, though, were more deliberate in their assessment of racialized experience. These teachers took the time to consider nonracial explanations for their alleged mistreatment, only attributing it to reverse discrimination when, from their perspective, nothing else made sense. Still, to varying degrees, almost all the teachers I interviewed believed that Brick City schools exposed them to some form of antiwhite hostility and antiwhite praxis.

Reverse discrimination came from three primary sources: black teachers, black students, and black parents. To their surprise, white Brick City teachers first felt the sting of racial hostility at the hands of their black colleagues, often before the school year had formally begun. For example, Mrs. Meredith recalled feeling like an outsider in a series of pre–school year professional developments (PDS) that were required by the district. As the only white teacher on her eighth-grade team, she felt as though her black colleagues purposefully kept her at a distance, leaving her out of much of the planning and decision-making processes.

> MRS. MEREDITH: Every year before the kids come, before the year starts, we have this whole series of PDS. They're mostly useless, but some of them are helpful, you know. But the team, my eighth-grade team, we all agreed to meet afterwards to set up a basic framework to start the year. Um, we have to deal with the same students, so we all wanted to be on the same page in terms of expectations, discipline, you know, stuff like that. Well, from the very beginning I felt like I was an outsider, like they looked at me differently.

BELL: Were these teachers black?

MRS. MEREDITH: Oh, yeah, I'm sorry. Yeah, my team was very unique. Out of all the teachers in the school, only six or seven of them were black and three of them were on my team. We had four-teacher teams, and of the four of us, it was three black teachers and me, you know, the white lady [*laughs*]. So, like I was saying, I was excited to get a game plan for the year because those first couple of weeks are absolutely crucial. But they didn't include me. They wouldn't listen to any of my ideas, they kept talking over me. Then, like a week or two after the year started, I come to find out they had met several times without me. I mean, I know if three white teachers did that to a black teacher, she'd yell racism, and she might even be right. So the only reason I think they treated me like that was because I'm white, you know. I wasn't one of them.

Unable to think of a plausible reason for her mistreatment by her black colleagues, Mrs. Meredith concluded that she was being excluded simply because she was white. That she was ignored, overlooked, and all but treated as an "uninvited guest" by her fellow team members eventually caused Mrs. Meredith to connect various work experiences to her social status as a racial minority. Interestingly, though, despite her contention that black teachers were sometimes prone to reverse discrimination, Mrs. Meredith also emphasized that "at the end of the day, it was no big deal." Other teachers followed a similar pattern. After providing an example of reverse discrimination that allegedly occurred at the hands of black coworkers, white Brick City teachers would immediately mitigate its severity by laughing it off or describing it as not "that big of a deal." Mrs. Thompson exemplifies this process when talking about the kitchen staff at her school.

MRS. THOMPSON: OK, so I don't know if this is that big of a deal, but I was thinking of cliques in my school. The, um, kitchen staff, all black women, they're hilarious, they're so much fun, but they have this, their own little clique, and they only let people in that are black. They don't let, um, I honestly think they don't like white people. They'll give free food to the black teachers, they'll do all this stuff, but I'll go ask for change and they won't give it to me, they like won't. I have to go ask my friend Anthony if he can go get me change for five dollars and he goes and gets it right away [*laughs*]. But it's like, they have their own little clique downstairs and they're very, um, very evident in their likings, I guess, of other staff members, and it's not white people. So, yeah, I mean, I like them. Like I said, they're really funny, but they might just be a tad bit racist against whites [*laughs*]. That's fine. I just wanted to make sure I brought that up.

Here, by laughing while recalling her inability to get change from her school's all-black cafeteria staff, Mrs. Thompson displayed a bit of levity, even as she depicted what she believed was racially discriminatory behavior. Discursively, Mrs. Thompson wanted to convey the idea that many of her black colleagues engaged in reverse discrimination, and she also intimated, somewhat paradoxically, that reverse discrimination by those colleagues was not all that serious. She even went so far as to describe the cafeteria staff from her story as just "a tad bit racist." Overall, while Mrs. Meredith, Mrs. Thompson, and others dismissed or laughed about racially discriminatory behavior when it came from black colleagues and building staff, they took a decidedly different tone when it came from black students and black families. In these retellings, all levity and lightheartedness disappeared, as this form of reverse discrimination was more serious and consequential.

Ms. Western, a veteran high school teacher, recounted two stories, one that had happened recently, and another that had happened over twenty years ago in one of her first years of teaching. Each story involved negative interactions with black students, and in both cases, Ms. Western attributed to her treatment to reverse discrimination. In the first story—the more recent of the two—Ms. Western describes finding a racially discriminatory message carved into one of the desks in her classroom.

MS. WESTERN: You want to hear about what it's like to be white at Northside, let me tell you about something that happened fairly recently. It just happened like a month or so ago. I was in a pretty good mood. It was Friday, we were done with testing for the year, and I was just, I don't know, I was happy. . . . So I'm cleaning up my room, you know, that's always the last thing I do before I go home. . . . I'm walking around the class clearing everything off of the students' desks. . . . There was this one desk with a huge stack of papers on it. I'm not going to say who it was, but, um, this student always leaves stuff behind, but at the same time, he is one of my favorite students. When I grab the papers off of his desk, I see that, um, carved into the desk, it says, "I hate white people." And, um, I was shocked. I know exactly who it was, you know. He had his head down the whole time, he was distant and not himself. And I know for a fact it wasn't there before, and just like that my good mood was gone. So much for being happy. It pretty much ruined my entire weekend.

Ms. Western went on to describe how "awful" seeing the words "I hate white people" carved into a desk in her classroom made her feel. She talked about feeling both sad and anxious: sad because, given that the desk was in her room, the message was probably directed at her, and anxious because she felt helpless to do anything about it. Even if she were to report the student in question to the school principal or vice principal, she did not feel that anything of consequence would come of it, because "he would just deny it was him." Also, as she pointed out, the accused student was someone she admired. Ms. Western felt as though she had a strong relationship with this student, and up to that point, she had counted him among her favorites. That this particular message came from him, which she later confirmed, "added insult to injury," and it caused Ms. Western to take it more personally than she otherwise would have.

The second story happened over two decades ago when Ms. Western was a new teacher fresh out of college. It involved a both a student and a parent. According to Ms. Western, one of her students was disruptive to the point where it was "impossible to teach," and when she called the student's home, she was subjected to a "racist onslaught" by the kid's mom. This one incident affected Ms. Western so deeply that it still impacts her decision-making processes. Today calling home to report student behavior is something she is reluctant to do, even under the most stressful and strenuous of circumstances.

MRS. WESTERN: I stayed up all night working on my lesson plans, and I had about three or four hours of sleep. I was literally exhausted. Three weeks into teaching and things were not going well at all. I felt totally unprepared to do my job. . . . And this kid, I will never forget him for as long as I live. . . . He's just disrupting the class all over the place. I tried to ignore him, just let him do his own thing, but he flipped over a desk and slapped a pencil out of another student's hand. So I'm like, OK, I have a decision to make. I can send him to the office or try to handle it myself. I tried to handle it myself by calling [his] mom, you know. Big mistake. As soon as she picks up the phone, she just lays into me with this racist onslaught. . . . Why can't you white people leave me alone? Why are you even there, you know? I'm like, Look, lady, your kid is out of control, then she blows up at me. You know, swearing at me and calling me names. I actually ended up hanging up on her. I'm not going to sit there and listen to some uninvolved parent bitch about how awful white people are just because her kid is a disaster. So she ends up calling the school demanding to speak to the principal, and she said I was being racist against her. Excuse me, how was I being racist? She literally called me a white bitch, and I never once mentioned race. Not once. If anything, this was reverse discrimination. And you know the worst part is that people automatically believed her. . . . People looked at me differently after that. So now I hardly ever call home. Somebody's life literally has to be in danger for me to even consider picking up that phone.

Ms. Western, in retelling her personal stories, demonstrated how many teachers interpreted and talked about their experiences with reverse discrimination. When it came to students and families, teachers repeatedly recalled having been treated unfairly due to their race and subsequently feeling powerless to do anything about it. They recounted experiences in which, after being subjected to racialized slurs—such as "cracker" or "white bitch"—they themselves were somehow branded as racists or, as one teacher put it, "turned into the bad guy." They also talked about being mistreated by superiors for doing their jobs, which sometimes included "holding black students accountable." From their perspective, being white prevented them from teaching to the best of their ability, because *as white teachers*, their interactions with black students were always scrutinized through the lens of race, a lens that assumes white racism as a matter of course. Thus, for white Brick City teachers, the combination of racial insults, racial powerlessness, and racially motivated performance limitations constituted the most common form of reverse discrimination in their respective schools. But there were others as well.

Another claim of reverse discrimination, one that went beyond racial slurs and racialized criticisms of job performance, was the alleged existence of a racialized glass ceiling on career advancement. Although only a handful of respondents made such claims, those who did became angry, striking a more aggressive tone and lashing out at what one teacher called a "bullshit system." At the heart of this form of reverse discrimination was the claim that white teachers were sometimes passed over for promotions by less qualified black teachers and, in one case, a less qualified white teacher who "pandered to blatant PC culture." For example, Mrs. Edwards, an almost thirty-year veteran of the Brick City School District, had recently applied for a vice-principal opening at her school. Despite being "eminently qualified," she believes she was "screwed out of the job" because of (1) her skin color, and (2) her refusal to compromise her standards for the sake of racial politics.

MRS. EDWARDS: It's weird, it's not as simple as, Oh I'm white so I didn't get the promotion, I could've gotten the promotion. The thing is, because I am white, I have to go about it a certain way, I can't really be who I am or the type of teacher I've been.

BELL: What do you mean by that? Could you elaborate further?

MRS. EDWARDS: Here, let me give you an example. My entire career, I've been a no-nonsense type of teacher. I have a reputation for being one and done, you get one warning and then you're out of my class-room. But when I was interviewing for VP, they kept asking me about my position on suspensions, like suspending black kids. I don't know what they expected me to say, but I told the truth. If your behavior warrants suspension, you should be suspended. If you're constantly disrupting the class, if you threaten or assault a teacher or another stu-dent, you have to go. . . . I don't care what color you are. Later I come to find out that I didn't get the job because of my position on suspend-ing black kids. Mrs. Johnson, you know, the teacher who became VP, apparently she was the right type of white lady. She pandered to bla-tant PC culture and I didn't. She agreed to show favoritism to black students and I didn't. . . . How is that not reverse discrimination?

Mrs. Edwards's story, and her subsequent interpretation of why she was passed over for vice principal, adds more complexity to the concept of re-verse discrimination. Namely, it indicates that white teachers could mitigate the effects of racial victimization by doing whiteness a certain way or being the "right type of white lady."[24] Even though it was not as straightforward as simply hating white people, forcing white teachers to alter their behavior and pander to racial politics, all for the sake of job advancement, was a transpar-ent, if not indirect, form of reverse discrimination. Teachers should be evalu-ated, it was argued, only on their ability to teach, and vacancies for principal, vice principal, or any other administrative position should be filled by the most qualified applicants. Using race—or racial politics—in any way while assessing job applicants was, according to multiple teachers, inherently dis-criminatory against whites.

Reverse discrimination was a central feature of spatial victimization. Though conceptualized differently at times, reverse discrimination included a combination of racial exclusion, racial insults, racial pandering, racialized criticisms of job performance, and the intersection of racial politics and oc-cupational advancement. Without regard to age, gender, professional, and political differences, every teacher I interviewed claimed firsthand experience with, and offered numerous examples of, white racial victimization within Brick City schools. Still, while ubiquitous across interviews, reverse discrimination was but one aspect of this spatialized process. A second component, collective whiteness, also played a prominent role in how white Brick City teachers experienced white racial identity and made sense of racial victimization.

Now He Just Hates White People, All White People

Sometimes I would go home and rack my brain trying to figure out what I did wrong. Like, Why is this kid so angry with me, you know? Come to find out, he had a run-in with the police a year or two back and it went very badly. Now he just hates white people, all white people. I've known this kid for less than a month and he thinks I'm the devil reincarnate. Just because I'm white.—BRYAN PALMER, 45

Using herself as a conduit to explore the advantages of being white in the contemporary United States, educator and critical whiteness scholar Robin DiAngelo writes about what she terms *psychic freedom*, defined as the freedom to see oneself as an individual.[25] DiAngelo notes, "Because I have not been socialized to see myself, or to be seen by other whites as having a race, I don't carry the psychic burden of race." She continues, "I don't have to worry about how others *feel* about my race. I don't have to worry that my race will be held against me."[26] Psychic freedom, then, affords whites an advantage not readily available to nonwhites. Whereas people of color are often held accountable for the words and actions of other people of color, in a white-dominated society such as the United States, whites are individual people, each beholden only to their own words, actions, or deeds.[27]

DiAngelo's theory of psychic freedom is born out in my interview data, but only those data that pertain to white racialized spaces. When speaking in general terms, white teachers presented themselves as individual people, unbothered by the words or actions of other whites. When the topic shifted to Brick City schools, however, the privilege of psychic freedom did not hold. Surrounded by black bodies and openly recognized as white, white teachers lost their sense of individuality and instead felt subsumed under a stigmatized racial collective. Within their respective classrooms and schools, gone were individual teachers who just happened to be white; they were replaced by white people who just happened to be teachers. Whites, as discussed previously, are often not seen as individuals in the black imagination, meaning that, at least symbolically, any one white person could be held responsible for the behavior and discourse of *all white people.*[28] Thus, within the physical space of Brick City schools, white teachers lost the racial privilege of psychic freedom. They were, in effect, burdened by race.[29]

The loss of psychic freedom, or what I term *collective whiteness*, was facilitated by meaningful and consistent symbolic interactions with black students and black families within Brick City schools. Collective whiteness is when individual white teachers felt blamed, singled out, or otherwise held accountable for something another white teacher—or even another white person—said or did in another classroom or in another place. On any given day, individual white teachers could face anger and hostility from black students, all because of negative interactions between the students in question and other white teachers. After repeated occurrences of "paying for somebody else's fuckup," white Brick City teachers became cognizant of the reality that they were judged, and ultimately treated, as a group, one constructed with little substantive variation among group members. Therefore, collective whiteness, the conceptual and experiential opposite of psychic freedom, quickly became a function of spatial victimization.

Mrs. DeYoung spent the first twelve years of her career teaching at an exclusively white school in rural West Virginia. When her husband was relocated to Upstate New York for work, she followed and eventually made her way to the Brick City School District. After spending her whole life in white racialized spaces, spaces she conceptualized as "normal," Mrs. DeYoung was aghast and, at least initially, confused by the hostility she faced from her black students. As a teacher new to the district, she had expected some student pushback, but it did not take long for Mrs. DeYoung to notice a pattern in the resistance she received from her black student body. To them, "everything was racist," a charge that caught Mrs. DeYoung off guard and eventually caused her to ask her team leader for advice.

MRS. DEYOUNG: Um, uh, and, like, I can't tell you how many times, like in the first couple of weeks, if I told a kid that, you know, they need to sit down or they need to leave my room because they called me a name or whatever, I was called a racist. Here I am, new to the city, you know, new to the district, and suddenly I'm a racist. I hadn't even learned half their names yet, but they were already convinced that anything I said to them was because, you know, they're black and I'm white. I was really confused: like, What did I do? Finally, I had to ask my team leader if it was normal for so many students to call me racist, and he laughed. He said something like, Yeah, of course it's normal; they think all white people are racists.

BELL: At the time, was your team leader white as well?

MRS. DEYOUNG: Yes. Mr. Ball, he's white.[30] He's actually a principal now.

BELL: Oh, OK. So, do your black students still call you racist today?

MRS. DEYOUNG: Oh, yeah. All the time. I'm called racist all the time.

BELL: Does it still bother you?

MRS. DEYOUNG: Sometimes it does, but not really. They love to pull that crap, so I just try to ignore it.

On arriving in the Brick City School District, Mrs. DeYoung was immediately exposed to, and informed about, collective whiteness. Baffled by the consistency in which her black students labeled her a racist, Mrs. DeYoung sought clarification from one of her superiors. In her mind, nothing she had said or done came close to constituting racist behavior, so the repeated charges of such were both hurtful and confusing. Unaccustomed to working with black students, it did not occur to Mrs. DeYoung that they were making a general assumption about her because of her racial identity. Conversely, Mr. Ball, an educator who had spent years in the Brick City School District, found it humorous that Mrs. DeYoung was attempting to find fault in her own individual behavior. By asserting that "they think all white people are racists," Mr. Ball was alluding to collective whiteness, the idea that all white people, including white teachers, are essentially the same. Mrs. DeYoung's somewhat dismissive attitude toward collective whiteness today, after a dozen years in the district, indicates that satiation may have taken effect.

Collective whiteness within Brick City schools was bigger than hurtful and confusing generalizations; it also affected relationships. According to multiple teachers, being thought of as a racist, particularly for, as one teacher put it, "shit somebody else did," compromised their ability to form effective relationships with black students and black families. If, as was often the case, a black student or a black parent had any negative experiences with white teachers—or white people in general—white Brick City teachers found that the resulting generalizations were not only held against them but also taken out on them. That is, the personal characteristics and pedagogical practices of any one white teacher, while important, were always competing with the status and stigma of a collective white racial identity. Consequently, in trying to form bonds with their students, white Brick City teachers were often held accountable for, and were affected by, the beliefs and behaviors of other white people, both within and outside Brick City schools.

Ms. Stacey, for example, spent a considerable amount of time talking about the "absolute need" to form meaningful relationships with students. Like the majority of teachers I interviewed, Ms. Stacey believed that both teacher and student benefited from a trusting, mutually appreciative relationship. Also like the majority of teachers I interviewed, Ms. Stacey believed that, regardless of her individual behavior, she was routinely held responsible for the actions of other white teachers, forcing her to compensate for people and processes that were beyond her control.

MS. STACEY: Yeah, a lot of the students keep you at a distance, especially at first. It's like they see you as something you're not. It's like you're a racist until proven not racist [*laughs*]. When I look back on my life, I can't think of anything I've ever said or done that's racist, but the kids, the black kids, some of them look at me like I called them the n-word. They just don't want to let you in. It's like enjoying the company of a white person is out of bounds. Like they'll lose street cred or something. You just have to stay at it, you know. Keep at them, keep showing them who you are, be true to yourself, and eventually they come around. Well, most of them come around, until the next year, where you have to do it all over again.

BELL: Is it the same or similar with black parents or guardians?

MS. STACEY: Yeah, parents are suspicious of you, I think. They tend to think, um, sometimes I think that they didn't have a very good experience at school or maybe with a white person, so, like, they're suspicious right away, no matter who you are or even how you treat their kids. White is white, and like I said with the kids, if you're white, you're racist. Even when you call them on the phone to say something to them, you know, something nice, like calling to let them know their son or daughter is having a good day. A lot of the time, they just don't want to deal with you. So I have to choose my words wisely when I call them.

Ms. Stacey went on to describe the process of having to prove she was not a racist as "demeaning and incredibly frustrating." She repeatedly complained about how unnecessarily difficult her job could be, primarily because of the racial mistrust that many black students and black parents harbored toward white teachers as a whole. Making matters worse, according to Ms. Stacey, was that the entire basis for mistrust was a stereotype-laden caricature of white people, as opposed to her as an individual teacher. Even though Ms. Stacey, for the most part, has successfully navigated racial mistrust in her classroom, she sometimes feels that defending herself against charges of racism is pointless, because no matter what she says or does, she can never fully account for the attitudes and behaviors of other white teachers. As she stated later in our interview, "Most days, I'm fine, you know, but sometimes I wanna just throw my hands up and say, You know what, screw it. Yeah, whatever, we're all racist, now will you please sit down and let me teach."

Collective whiteness, while a crucial component of the white race card, also complicated the social construction of the race card. Remember, for white Brick City teachers, the race card was a myth, a ruse used by African Americans and other nonwhites to excuse their personal failures. This framework is challenged, however, by white teachers' own words, particularly when trying to disassociate themselves from white coworkers who do harbor racial animus toward black students and black families. For example, Mr. Palmer wanted to make it absolutely clear that he, unlike several of his colleagues, treats all of his students fairly, regardless of their racial background.

MR. PALMER: Look, I'm not going to sit here and pretend that there aren't any, um, racist teachers at Pattengill, OK? Of course there are. We have a lot of white teachers in that building, and a couple of them probably shouldn't be working there. But what does that have to do with me? Why should I be held responsible for somebody else's bullshit? In my classroom, everybody gets a fair shake. I don't care what color you are, I don't care where you come from, what your parents do or don't do, everybody gets the same treatment in Room 228. But if some other teacher did something to piss you off or said something that they shouldn't have, somehow that's my fault, right? I just, I [pause], I don't think I should be punished for stuff other teachers do. Yeah, some of them might be racist or whatever, but we're not all like that. If you want to be treated like an individual, then you gotta give me the same consideration. Otherwise it's just a racist double standard.

While criticizing the practice of lumping all white teachers together, Mr. Palmer acknowledged that there was indeed white racism in Brick City schools. To this very point, when addressing whether or not there were racist teachers at Pattengill Middle School, he directly replied, "Of course there are." Mr. Palmer was so focused on defending himself against collective whiteness that he failed to realize he was providing corroboration for black students who claimed that some of their white teachers were racist. By admitting that several of his white colleagues sometimes said or did things "that they shouldn't have," Mr. Palmer was actively lending credence to nonwhite racial victimization, a process that he previously described as fraudulent and "completely made up." He was not alone. Other teachers too, in their eagerness to distance themselves from collective whiteness, acknowledged the existence of white racism within their respective schools, directly contradicting their previous construction of white racism as a nonwhite fiction and evidence of a "victim mentality."

Even though the majority of teachers I interviewed found ways to work around racial mistrust, collective whiteness was never far from their minds. The construction of white teachers as a single, and often racist, collective was interpreted not as some momentary obstacle to be overcome but, rather, as an ongoing process that always carried the potential to shape interactions and disrupt student-teacher relationships. Furthermore, for white teachers, collective whiteness was yet another example of the reverse discriminatory practices that permeated Brick City schools. While numerous teachers did admit to having white colleagues who occasionally engaged in racist behavior, they recoiled at the notion that said colleagues or such behavior should be held against them personally. Because they were socialized as individuals and accustomed to psychic freedom, exposure to collective whiteness caused white Brick City teachers great trepidation, ultimately contributing to, and at times complicating, their disparate constructions of white versus nonwhite racial victimization.[31]

Black Teachers Have It Easier. They Really Do.

It gets so frustrating sometimes. I work and I work to build these relationships and I make glacial progress. I spend years working my ass off just to be accepted, you know, to get them to look at me as a professional, then a black twenty-something, fresh out of college, can just stroll in and automatically have everybody's trust. I would kill for an advantage like that. And that's what it is, an advantage. Black teachers have it easier. They really do.
—DENISE BRADLEY, 31

In addition to reverse discrimination and collective whiteness, there is a third component to spatial victimization; black privilege. It was not lost on white teachers that if whiteness served as a disadvantage within Brick City schools, then blackness, by contrast, served as an advantage. Acutely aware of how white racial identity was conceptualized by many of their black students, white Brick City teachers paid special attention to how their black colleagues were treated by, and interacted with, those same students. The same was true for black parents. Interview respondents took notice of how black parents responded to black teachers, juxtaposing the respect and trust shown to them with the disrespect and mistrust that they themselves received on an almost daily basis. Whether discussing their interactions with black students or their relationships with black parents, white Brick City teachers expressed a strident belief in, and provided what they considered to be relevant examples of, black privilege.

Black privilege fell along three intersecting lines. First, there were teachers who focused more on the physical embodiment of racial similarity. These teachers felt that their black colleagues were privileged because they reminded black students of a parent, an aunt, an uncle, or even a grandparent. Second, there were teachers who focused more on the cultural embodiment of racial similarity. These teachers felt that their black colleagues were privileged because they could leverage similar cultural backgrounds to build trust and maintain effective relationships with black students and black families. Finally, there were teachers who focused on antiwhiteness. These teachers felt that black teachers were privileged simply by virtue of not being white. In this sense, blackness was the archetypical representation of antiwhiteness, and that fact alone established blackness as a privileged category. These separate formulations of black privilege, while conceptually different, were not mutually exclusive: there was considerable overlap among them.

Black privilege in the form of physical similarities was mentioned in all but four of my interviews. The idea that black students possibly saw black teachers as surrogate relatives, or relatives by proxy, was the most prevalent form of black privilege articulated during my time in the field. According to white teachers, the privilege of blackness, of sharing the physical traits and phenotypical characteristics of black students and their loved ones, was as immediate as it was pervasive. That is, *all black teachers*, but particularly black women, reminded black students of someone in their lives, thus *all black teachers* enjoyed some form of advantage. Mrs. Martin demonstrated this line of thinking when imagining what it would be like to remind black students of "their mother or grandmother."

BELL: Do you feel that your job teaching in predominantly black schools would be easier if you were black?

MRS. MARTIN: Yeah. I mean, think about it. I think my voice would carry a lot more weight, um, I would have a lot more authority with certain kids if I looked like their mother or grandmother. Can you imagine that, that every time you see your teacher, every time she tells you to stop misbehaving and do your work, she reminded you of your mom? The black teachers in my school can do that; it's not a hypothetical for them. I think it's an advantage, a big advantage. I don't mean to imply that it's a bad thing. It can be, but it can be a good thing too, for the students, I mean. But to answer your question, yeah, if I were able to remind my students of their mom or someone they're close to, my job would be a hell of a lot easier.

As indicated here, black privilege in the form of physical similarities was constructed as relatively benign. While white Brick City teachers did regard phenotype as an advantage that only black teachers enjoyed, they also believed it could be pedagogically useful. Reminding black students of authority figures from their immediate and extended families "could be a good thing" if it contributed to the individual and collective benefit of those very students. To put it differently, in the hands of quality teachers, black privilege predicated on physical characteristics was an effective pedagogical tool in the effort to increase student achievement and enhance student success. That being said, privilege is still privilege. As white teachers, my interview respondents were excluded from possessing or utilizing any advantages derived from physical similarities with black students. Thus, despite its potential usefulness, this form of privilege was still an unfair advantage for black teachers, meaning it still contributed to the process of spatial victimization.

The cultural embodiment of black privilege is somewhat unique because, unlike its physical counterpart, culture can be learned by anyone.[32] As discussed in chapter 3, one of the ways that white teachers performed whiteness was by embracing what they perceived to be black culture, actively incorporating it into their pedagogical toolkits. In doing so, they not only sought to protect themselves from the negative effects of feeling white; they also wanted a stake in culturally based privilege. Although several teachers found this approach effective, the interactional benefits of culturally sensitive whiteness paled in comparison to actually "being of black culture."[33] Black teachers, especially those from similar backgrounds as black students, understood black culture on a visceral level, speaking the same language and sharing the same worldview.[34] If leveraged correctly, the thinking went, black teachers could utilize black culture in a manner that white teachers, even at their best, simply could not match. While they had to strategize and pretend, black teachers could simply be themselves, an authenticity that black students recognized, respected, and, more times than not, responded to in favorable and prosocial ways. Thus, for white Brick City teachers, despite their best efforts to learn and make use of black culture, the real and authentic cultural similarities between black students and black teachers was yet another source of black racial advantage.[35]

The third form of black privilege, antiwhiteness, was the one most explicitly associated with racism and white victimization. It was one thing for black teachers to benefit from reminding black students of loved ones or from sharing cultural dispositions, but it was something else altogether for black teachers to benefit from simply not being white. Whereas black privilege in the form of physical and cultural similarities was about the positive traits of black teachers, black privilege in the form of antiwhiteness was about the negative traits of white teachers. Although there is no neat or clear dividing line between antiwhiteness and other forms of black privilege, there is a discernable difference in how white teachers described and reacted to what they perceived to be a problack manifestation of antiwhite hostility. Ultimately, for white teachers, black privilege that emanated from antiwhite racism was a great source of frustration, as it was found to be the most hurtful, most harmful, and most indicative of white racial victimization within Brick City schools.

When the advantages enjoyed by their black colleagues stemmed from antiwhite sentiment, it was difficult for white Brick City teachers not to personalize and internalize them. Teaching is a social and, at times, intimate vocation. Therefore, this particular form of black privilege became personal, causing a number of white Brick City teachers to become highly critical of themselves, both as educators and as people. For example, after teaching in the Brick City School District for close to fifteen years, Mrs. Clark now considers the antiwhite manifestation of black privilege to be an indictment of her personal character.

MRS. CLARK: When I look at Carol and how the kids respond to her, I can't help but think I'm the problem. I know she's black and that, um, she has certain advantages that I don't, but maybe it's simpler than that. Maybe it's me.

BELL: Why do you say that?

MRS. CLARK: Because, um, [pause], I think, um, so take my school, for example. There are a lot of white teachers who manage to do just fine, you know. I mean, they deal with the same hostility. Some of their students hate white people too, but they still have really good relationships with their kids. At that point, the only reasonable explanation is me. What is it about me that—how can I put this? Um, what is it about me that makes being white worse? Does that make sense?

Mrs. Clark struggled to understand why she has had such a difficult time connecting with her black students. In her attempts to reconcile the complexity of race with her experiences as a teacher, Mrs. Clark took notice of her black *and* white colleagues. She acknowledged that Carol, a black teacher, was advantaged because she was not white, but she also noticed that many of her white colleagues had successfully bridged the demographic gap between white teachers and black students. For Mrs. Clark, then, the presence of successful white teachers complicated the idea that white racial identity alone accounted for her struggles within Brick City schools. Seeing no other explanations, she looked inward and eventually came to the conclusion that being white combined with her personal character flaws to limit her effectiveness as an educator of black students. Other teachers went through a similar process, personalizing the antiwhite form of black privilege to such a degree that it essentially became an impeachment of them as people.

Black privilege as antiwhiteness also affected the way white teachers talked about teaching as a profession. Mrs. Edwards, fifty-one, has been teaching in urban schools for over twenty years. A lifelong reader, Mrs. Edwards teaches language arts at Emerson Middle School, a school with a student population that is over 80 percent black. During our interview, Mrs. Edwards repeatedly lamented black privilege, describing it as "the racial sorting of teachers." To be clear, Mrs. Edwards was not inherently opposed to sorting teachers into different categories, but she believed the sorting in question should be based on talent and overall ability. In her estimation, "making it about race" undermined public education and made a mockery of professional standards.

MRS. EDWARDS: I'm a good teacher, a damn good teacher. I've worked extremely hard to become one. I was completely lost my first year, but I never gave up and I've never even considered quitting. I just worked that much harder to become what my students needed me to be, and I've been at the same school for close to twelve years, while so many other teachers don't even make it through the year, you know. I know it sounds, I don't know, cocky or whatever, but I'm good at what I do, and as a white teacher that's not always easy. There are so many students that are determined to make your life harder. They just don't like white people. Then I meet their parents and I see why. They just think all white people are bad, all white people are racist, you know. You can tell right away, like on the first day: Oh, this kid has a problem with white people.

BELL: Do you think your job would be easier if you were black?

MRS. EDWARDS: That's not even a question. Are you kidding me? I've watched so many black teachers get ahead and they weren't very good at all. I don't want to come across as racist or anything, but this is my career, I take it seriously. So just like students give me trouble just because I'm white, they'll suck up to black teachers just because they're black. They have it much easier, and I think it affects their teaching. Shit, it affects my teaching too. The more we make racial exceptions for bad teaching, the less serious teaching becomes. That's something that really pisses me off.

Mrs. Edwards, more so than others, was highly protective of teaching as a vocation. For her, black privilege, in addition to being discriminatory against whites, was a direct assault on the profession because it undermined the painstaking process of becoming an effective teacher. In her opinion, the judgment of who is—or is not—a high-quality educator should be based on one's ability to teach children. Everything else, including race, should be excluded as a relevant factor. Still, despite her personal desire to see teaching become a meritocracy, Mrs. Edwards believed that black teachers had an inherent advantage over white teachers, an advantage that was primarily fueled by antiwhite racism.[36] Accordingly, when asked whether her job would be easier if she were black, Mrs. Edwards replied that it would, going so far as to assert, "That's not even a question." All told, from her perspective, black privilege not only masked the shortcomings of some of her black colleagues but also undermined the profession of teaching as a whole.

Whether based on physical similarities, cultural similarities, or antiwhiteness, black privilege was a real phenomenon in the minds of white Brick City teachers. Within predominantly black schools, they felt inherently disadvantaged by white racial identity, which, by contrast, meant that their black colleagues were inherently advantaged by black racial identity. In the case of physical and cultural similarities, black privilege was described as relatively benign or even pedagogically useful, but in the case of antiwhiteness, it was described as racialized mistreatment or outright racism. No matter how it was constructed—and despite its potential benefits to black students—black privilege was still considered a racially discriminatory process, one that made teaching in the Brick City School District easier for black teachers and more difficult for white teachers. In conjunction with reverse discrimination and collective whiteness, black privilege completed the conceptual and experiential process of spatial victimization, and spatial victimization, both personal and communal, provided the evidentiary foundation for the white race card.

CONCLUSION

"Playing the race card" is a common phrase in the contemporary American lexicon. It is meant to undermine claims of racial victimization, and typically it is deployed by white Americans in response to specific claims made by people of color.[37] This pattern permeated my interview data, specifically when white teachers shared their general thoughts about racism and racial inequality. Almost reflexively, white Brick City teachers scoffed at the notion that nonwhites in general, and African Americans in particular, were exposed to "real racism" in their lives, today. Any claim that racial discrimination prevented people of color from being successful was, according to white Brick City teachers, an excuse for personal failure and the inevitable outgrowth of a hypersensitive, politically correct culture. In lieu of "blaming the white man for all their problems," people of color needed to take personal responsibility for their lives and, as more than one teacher put it, dispense with the destructive and counterproductive "victim mentality." Once the topic shifted to white racial victimization, however, everything changed.

Brick City schools, just as they had done with racial awareness, elevated racial victimization by making it more visible, and more salient, to white teachers as they navigated the spatialized contours of white racial identity. In stark contrast to their construction of nonwhite racial victimization, white Brick City teachers found white racial victimization much more credible, particularly when it affected them personally. Within the physical space of Brick City schools, white teachers saw themselves as the racialized other, which allowed them, at least numerically, to experience racial identity from the perspective of racial minorities.[38] As a result, the teachers I interviewed not only felt excluded and ostracized by the racial majority but also believed that their ability to become effective educators and move up the professional ladder was unfairly limited by racial discrimination. Looked at holistically, in a very real sense, the specter of racial victimization became valid only under specific racial and environmental conditions.

The data in this chapter demonstrate the degree to which racial victimization, like race itself, is a social construction. Although often appearing to be self-evident—chattel slavery and Jim Crow segregation, for example—racial victimization is always in the eye of the beholder. In their broader, more general construction, white Brick City teachers constructed racial victimization as little more than a farcical attempt to make excuses for personal failures (*the race card*). In their personal, spatially specific construction, these same teachers treated racial victimization as an obvious and overt process that negatively affected them as people and undermined them as professionals (*the white race card*). Whether in the form of reverse discrimination, collective whiteness, or black privilege, white racial victimization was as real in the minds of white Brick City teachers as nonwhite racial victimization was imagined. Next I contextualize these competing notions of racial victimization within a purported culture of postracialism, one that posits colorblindness as its normative racial ideology.

5. COLORBLIND

National survey data suggest that a majority of whites view race relations through the lens of color-blindness. . . . The new color-blind ideology does not, however, ignore race; it acknowledges race while disregarding racial hierarchy.—CHARLES GALLAGHER, *Color-Blind Privilege*

I was raised not to see color, and that's exactly how I've lived my life. I think we'd be in a much better place if we really were colorblind, you know, if we stopped making everything about race.—AMANDA COSTA, East Genesee Middle School

Race can't escape this place. You'd have to be blind not to see it. —AMANDA COSTA, East Genesee Middle School

In the landmark *Plessy v. Ferguson* case of 1896, the United States Supreme Court, in a 7–1 ruling, upheld the doctrine of "separate but equal," thereby providing constitutional legitimacy for Jim Crow segregation.[1] Justice John Marshall Harlan, in the lone dissenting opinion, famously wrote, "In view of the constitution, in the eye of the law, there is in this country no superior, dominant, ruling class of citizens. . . . Our constitution is colorblind, and neither knows nor tolerates classes among citizens."[2] Thus, as far back as the nineteenth century, only three decades removed from chattel slavery and the American Civil War, colorblindness was being promoted from one of the highest levels of government.[3] Today, in the contemporary United States, a majority of whites, as well as many people of color, subscribe to the racial ideology of colorblindness.[4] Distilled down to its most basic level, racial colorblindness seeks to omit racial classification as a meaningful determinant of both personal identity and institutional functioning.[5] Therefore, it is argued, individual people, groups, the law, employers, schools, universities, and especially social policy should adhere to a strict code of colorblindness, eschewing race-consciousness in every aspect of society.[6]

Related to, and in many ways undergirding, the idea of colorblindness, is the widespread belief that the country as a whole has formally entered a state of postracialism.[7] Since the conclusion of the civil rights movement, but particularly over the last three to four decades, a broad swath of the American public has proudly proclaimed that America, rising above its white supremacist and discriminatory past, is now best characterized by racial egalitarianism.[8] Ostensibly no longer burdened or bolstered by race, the logic goes, all Americans now have the freedom and opportunity to pursue their dreams unencumbered.[9] As such, claims of racial discrimination, especially those made by people of color, are questioned, treated with skepticism, and, in many instances, dismissed altogether.[10] This particular belief only grew stronger after the election of Barack Obama as the first African American president of the United States.[11]

In this chapter I examine the intersection between ideology, experience, and discourse. More specifically, I compare the racial ideologies of white Brick City teachers with their own racialized experiences within predominantly black schools. In the majority of cases, I found that the racial ideology of colorblindness and the assertion that we are beyond race were both contradicted by repeated claims of white racial victimization. Also, without being specifically pointed out, this particular contradiction was unrecognizable to white teachers. When confronted with their ideological and experiential contradictions, interview respondents struggled to make sense of their own words, a process that triggered a range of defense mechanisms. Ultimately, white Brick City teachers found creative ways to distance themselves from their own contradictions, negotiating a compromise between their normative racial ideologies and their spatially specific racialized experiences.

This chapter proceeds in two parts. The first focuses on what sociologist Joe Feagin calls the *white racial frame*, a framing of society that minimizes, rationalizes, and justifies racial inequality.[12] Central to the white racial frame is ideology, a set of ideas and ideals that filter the way white Americans view issues of race, racism, and racial inequality.[13] More than anything else, white Brick City teachers expressed their belief in the racial ideology of colorblindness, principally supported by the sincere fiction of a postracial America.[14] The second part of this chapter looks beyond racial ideology and analyzes the way it intersects with, and is contradicted by, actual experience. This section juxtaposes the ideological premise of a colorblind, postracial America with the experiential reality of color-conscious, hyper-racialized experiences. With few exceptions, white teachers held strong to their belief systems, even in the face of contradictory evidence. In this section I also introduce the concept of spatial negotiation, the process by which white teachers rationalized and made sense of their ideological and experiential contradictions.[15] Ultimately, I show that nonwhite racialized space and highly racialized interactions, while consequential, have an uneven effect on white racial ideology.

THE WHITE RACIAL FRAME

Joe Feagin defines the white racial frame as the "broad, persisting, and dominant racial frame that has rationalized racial oppression and inequality and thus impacted all U.S. institutions."[16] He continues, "The white racial frame is a centuries-old worldview and has constantly involved a *racial construction of reality* by white and other Americans, an emotion-laden construction process that shapes everyday relationships and institutions in fundamental and racialized ways."[17] Feagin conceptualizes the white racial frame in a multifaceted and multidimensional way, accounting not only for institutional and interpersonal arrangements but also for emotions and other affective dimensions. In this sense, the white racial frame moves beyond cognitive or ideological processes and explicitly addresses the visceral and emotional aspects of white supremacy. Finally, according to Feagin, the white racial framing of society includes an expansive rationalization of racial inequality, one that is often used to reconcile white social, political, and economic dominance within a presumably colorblind, egalitarian society.

Throughout my fieldwork, white Brick City teachers routinely spoke in ways that reflected a white racial framing of society. Not only did they construct whiteness as normal, as a category devoid of racial significance, but they also rejected—except in the most extreme and obvious of cases—all nonwhite claims of racial victimization.[18] By positioning whiteness as a meaningless physical characteristic, white Brick City teachers were able to chastise and lament people of color for giving too much primacy to their own racial identities. Furthermore, by rejecting all, or most, nonwhite claims of racial victimization, white Brick City teachers were also able to attribute any ongoing racial disparities between whites and nonwhites to the cultural and personal pathologies of the latter, as opposed to the systemic structural advantage of the former. In short, white teachers framed race in a way that denied the salience of white racial identity and rationalized the causes and consequences of contemporary racial inequality.[19] Central to this framing was the racial ideology of colorblindness.

COLORBLINDNESS: IDENTITY AND IDEOLOGY

In his highly acclaimed book *Racism without Racists: Color-Blind Racism and the Persistence of Racial Inequality in the United States*, sociologist Eduardo Bonilla-Silva offers a comprehensive theory of colorblind racism.[20] Describing the utility of his theory, Bonilla-Silva writes, "The United States does not depend on Archie Bunkers to defend white supremacy. . . . Modern racial ideology does not thrive on the ugliness of the past or on the language and tropes typical of slavery and Jim Crow." He continues, "Today, there is a sanitized, color-blind way of calling minorities niggers, Spics, or Chinks. Today most whites justify keeping minorities from having the good things of life with the language of liberalism."[21] According to Bonilla-Silva, the ideology of colorblindness has changed since the end of the civil rights movement. Whereas colorblindness was once regarded as the cure for white supremacy, today it is one of the chief mechanisms perpetuating it.[22]

Colorblind racism entails four interconnected frames: *abstract liberalism, naturalization, cultural racism*, and the *minimization of racism*.[23] Here I focus on two, abstract liberalism and minimization. According to Bonilla-Silva, abstract liberalism is "using ideas associated with political liberalism . . . and economic liberalism in an abstract way to explain racial matters."[24] So whereas civil rights activists promoted colorblindness as a means of toppling Jim Crow, today colorblindness is used to attack affirmative action and other ameliorative forms of race-consciousness. The second frame, minimization, minimizes the significance, and at times the very existence, of racism in the contemporary United States. Whether interpersonal or institutional, the minimization frame all but erases racial discrimination today, paving the way for biological or culture-based explanations for racial inequality.[25] While the other two frames were certainly present in my interview data, abstract liberalism and the minimization of racism both played outsized roles in shaping the way white Brick City teachers looked at the world racially.

Other scholars have also theorized about colorblindness in modern society.[26] In a number of institutions, colorblindness has been shown to hamper racial progress and reproduce racial inequality, all while appearing to be a fair and just approach to the social world.[27] A powerful ideological framework, colorblindness is a way to distort reality and is often used to deny the overwhelming evidence of racial stratification.[28] In addition, by benefiting from the moral weight of history, colorblindness has now become an identity.[29] That is, many white Americans today wear colorblindness as a badge of honor, as a public display of their enlightenment and racial liberalism.[30] Despite this construction, particularly given the ongoing reality of racial segregation and other examples of race-consciousness, colorblindness has functioned more as an interactive "now you see race, now you don't" process, not a hardened philosophy to live by.[31] Materially, the ideological and experiential interplay between colorblindness and color-consciousness provides context for the data presented in this chapter. Despite their ostensible commitment to colorblindness, white Brick City teachers displayed a remarkable tendency to look at their schools, their students, and themselves in highly racialized ways.

I Don't Understand Why We Can't Be Colorblind

I'm not crazy, I know that there're still racists out there, on both sides, you know, but I really am confused about why that is. I mean, if we just saw each other as people, living, breathing people with feelings and emotions, we'd be a lot better off. We wouldn't have so much hate. I don't get why that's a bad thing, I don't understand why we can't be colorblind. It's 2015, you know. If we can't get past race now, then we probably never will. It's kind of heartbreaking. —JESSI MCCORMICK, 42

As a group, white Brick City teachers were highly supportive of, and rhetorically committed to, the racial ideology of colorblindness. Across nearly all interviews, teachers expressed their fidelity to the idea that people should be treated as individuals, judged not by their racial classification but, as so many of them repeated, by the "content of their character."[32] Framing it cyclically, white Brick City teachers described colorblindness as something that everybody should be afforded, as well as a principle that everyone should adhere to, thereby ensuring that no individual person, of any race, would ever feel the sting of racial prejudice or the stigma of racial discrimination. Also, colorblindness was not constructed as mere ideology; rather, it was a moral imperative, integral to the overall functioning and well-being of a multiracial, egalitarian society. Therefore, in ideology and in practice, colorblindness was good not only for individual people but also for society as a whole.

Ms. Livingston, a high school teacher with eight years of experience, spent a considerable amount of time expressing her belief in colorblindness. Just under thirty, Ms. Livingston was proud to be a member of a younger, "more tolerant" generation of people who refuse to "constantly focus on race." Speaking at length about her personal ideology, Mrs. Livingston went on to describe racial colorblindness as a solution to past, present, and future forms of racial conflict. In response to a general question about the potential effects of race or racism on her life, Ms. Livingston went on a mini-tangent, imploring America to finally "get past race."

MS. LIVINGSTON: [*Pause*] Um, I can't think of anything right now, but I can't say for sure, you know. Maybe, like, affirmative action. I didn't get into every school that I applied to, so who knows, but I think it's funny you ask that question because we're like so focused on race in this country. We're obsessed with it. Which is unfortunate because it can really hold us back, all of us, you know. I don't want to sound like some naive white girl, but I think we should really do our best to be colorblind. Think about all the bullshit we've been through, you know, as Americans. Like, enough already. Let's start treating each other as people and get past black, white, green or whatever. . . . To be honest, and, um, this might come across as rude or mean, but I think some people like to use race as a crutch. Like, it's just easier to blame something on race. I don't know. I'm not saying it happens all the time, maybe it does, but I wouldn't know.

Speaking about her life in general, Ms. Livingston was unable to recall a specific experience that she believed was affected by race or racism. After sitting quietly for several moments, she spoke about the possibility of being a victim of race-based affirmative action, but then she went on to discuss the dangers of our collective "obsession" with race and the need to finally move past it. What was telling about her response, though, was that it was unclear just how Ms. Livingston constructed colorblindness. Was colorblindness the solution to racial discrimination ("think about all the bullshit we've been through"), or was it a way to disincentivize people of color from playing the race card ("some people like to use race as a crutch")? Also of note, Ms. Livingston described past forms of racial discrimination in a very passive, almost laissez-faire manner. In her telling, Native American genocide, chattel slavery, Japanese internment, and other manifestations of racial oppression were all things that happened to the country, as opposed to varying examples of systematic white racial domination.[33]

After several follow-up questions, Ms. Livingston clarified that she believed colorblindness to be a solution to poor race relations. If we, as a country, were ever to move past race, then color-consciousness—including antiracism—needed to be abandoned. Other teachers also discussed colorblindness in this manner. Several of them claimed that whites and nonwhites alike were guilty of violating the normative ideology of colorblindness and therefore were guilty of exacerbating racial strife. Mrs. Nelson used the 2014 riots in Ferguson, Missouri, as a prime example of how "both sides" spent too much time thinking about race.[34]

MRS. NELSON: When you look at the riots that happened last year, it was absolutely terrifying. The whole time, I kind of felt like both sides were looking past each other. Nobody wanted to sit down and try to understand where the other side was coming from. Nobody saw the other side as people, you know. Unfortunately, I think, um, I think this is the natural outcome when the only thing you see is race. When you see everything through the lens of race, there's no room for nuance, you know, there's no such thing as subtlety. If you're a cop, you're a racist, and if you're black, you're a criminal. I was horrified seeing those images on TV every night . . . but I can't say that I was surprised.

For Mrs. Nelson, seeing predominantly black protestors clash with predominantly white law enforcement officials was the horrifying, yet completely unsurprising, outcome of a society that "see[s] everything through the lens of race." Much like Ms. Livingston, Mrs. Nelson viewed the violation of colorblind norms as an issue that "both sides" needed to confront. The two of them, consistent with other white teachers, ideologically conflated the charge of racism with racism itself. That is, while racial discrimination was bad, claiming to be a victim of racial discrimination was equally bad, as they both were examples of explicit color-consciousness. Tellingly, in a number of interviews, the more that white Brick City teachers voiced their support for racial colorblindness, the more they directed their ire at those who sought to combat racial discrimination, or, as one teacher put it, "hucksters who fixate on racism."

Intentionally or not, white Brick City teachers routinely practiced colorblind racism.[35] Using multiple ideological frames—particularly abstract liberalism and the minimization of racism—they repeatedly described contemporary racial inequality in ways that absolved institutional or interpersonal racism of any meaningful responsibility. Furthermore, given their nonracist construction of racial stratification, interview respondents took a skeptical and sometimes harsh view of antiracism. Pejoratively labeled "social justice warriors," antiracist activists were deemed politically redundant and racially divisive. According to a number of teachers, antiracist violations of colorblindness ran the risk of alienating the broader white majority, a process that would effectively undermine race relations throughout the country as a whole. Thus, with several notable exceptions, white Brick City teachers dismissed racism as a major cause of contemporary inequality, and they described antiracist activism as both unnecessary and counterproductive.[36]

You Can't Call Someone a Racist and Expect Them to Take Your Side

You know, it's bigger than, um, racism or the possibility of discrimination, it's also about how things stand between the races, you know. That might sound bad when I say it like that, but what I mean is, um, I don't know the exact term, um, race relations or whatever, they've gotten a lot worse over the last couple of years. All these protests and riots and stuff, they've made things worse for everybody. I think that, um, if we continue to see color in everything, race relations will only get worse. You can't call someone a racist and expect them to take your side.—JENNIFER WESTERN, 48

Though not to the same degree, all but five teachers expressed a variation of the same theme: that violations of colorblindness did lasting damage to race relations between white people and people of color writ large, and between white people and black people in particular. White Brick City teachers described antiracist activists such as Al Sharpton, Jesse Jackson, and "that guy from Black Lives Matters"[37] as racially divisive figures who, through their activism, today contribute to the deterioration of race relations. Political figures too, such as Barack Obama, Eric Holder, and Susan Rice, were identified as people who engaged in "divisive identity politics." It should be noted, though, that the belief in, and expression of, this particular sentiment was not uniform across interviews. Instead, it tended to fall along a continuum. On one end, you had teachers who believed racism against people of color was successfully eradicated in the 1960s, and on the other hand, you had teachers who thought of themselves as potential allies. Still, twenty-seven out of thirty-two teachers, regardless of how they felt about racial inequality, expressed their belief that color-consciousness, however well-intentioned, was a blight on contemporary race relations.

For example, on one end of the spectrum, Mrs. Martin, a teacher who often spoke of her students in empathetic terms, talked about how frustrating it was to have to "always deal with race" in her classroom. While Mrs. Martin did acknowledge the barriers and social problems that are commonly associated with poverty, she did not feel that white people in general, and white teachers in particular, should be blamed for the "unfortunate" economic conditions faced by many students of color. According to Mrs. Martin, her black students' penchant for "injecting race where it doesn't belong" was counterproductive because it had the potential to make enemies out of allies. She herself put it, "I'm not one of these people who pretends we've reached some racial utopia, but if your first instinct is to blame racism for all your problems, then at some point I'll stop listening to you. I just get tired of it." Thus, even as someone who was attentive to the economic conditions of her black student body, Mrs. Martin became disillusioned by students who "focused entirely too much on race."

Opposite Mrs. Martin were those teachers who held zero sympathy for race-consciousness. Teachers on this end of the spectrum saw racism as a thing of the past, making colorblindness—in discourse, identity, and policy— the appropriate, fair, and moral racial ideology. These teachers were more than disillusioned by color-consciousness; they believed it was doing "irreversible damage" to the country. Mr. Radke, for example, had a very strong reaction to color-consciousness. In his mind, any claim that race was somehow relevant in the contemporary United States was not only factually incorrect but also, as he described it, a "racist way to make white people look bad."

BELL: Why do you feel that talking about racism is inherently racist against whites?

MR. RADKE: Oh, come on, this one should be obvious. If I say the word "racist" right now, you would probably think of a white guy, wouldn't you? I bet I could go up to a hundred black people on the street, random strangers and people I don't even know, and ask them to describe what a racist is, and I'd bet my house that every last one of them would say a white person. I bet they would even look at me as racist. Now you tell me, how is that not racism? Treating all white people like we're the KKK is treating us a certain way because of our race. That's literally the definition of racism, and I'm sorry, but when we talk about racism today, blacks need to look at themselves. They do more to perpetuate racism than anybody else. And then they turn around and wonder why race relations are the way they are.

BELL: How would you describe race relations?

MR. RADKE: They're horrible. And you know what, they're only going to get worse. I don't mean to keep going back to this, but you can't
keep talking about racism this and racism that and expect race relations to be good. You can't keep bringing up race all the time. . . . You
can only blame us for so much before we say, You know what, we'll
live our lives and you can live yours. Quite frankly, we'll see who does
better. Don't call me a racist and expect me to like you.

Mr. Radke emphatically voiced his belief that color-consciousness, especially antiracism, was harmful to race relations. Any suggestion that, in the
contemporary United States, African Americans and other people of color
were subjected to racial discrimination was, according to Mr. Radke, equivalent to calling white people "a bunch of racists." As a result, this specific form
of color-consciousness was one that he took personally, making him feel targeted and unfairly accused of racism by folks he considered "race hustlers."
Race relations, then, were never going to improve unless African Americans
and other people of color stopped talking about racism, unless they adopted
colorblindness as their prevailing way of looking at the world. As it stands,
currently, for Mr. Radke and other white Brick City teachers, constantly accusing white people of racism, directly or indirectly, is a surefire way to turn
them against you, and it severely diminishes the likelihood of building multiracial communities and sharing national prosperity.

The contrast between Mrs. Martin and Mr. Radke, while significant,
should not obscure the fact that they both regarded color-consciousness—
including antiracist activism—as detrimental to race relations between white
and nonwhite Americans. Although these particular teachers were on opposite ends of the ideological spectrum, others fell somewhere in between.
Some teachers agreed more with Mrs. Martin, while some leaned closer to
Mr. Radke. Again, though, twenty-seven of thirty-two teachers expressed the
belief that explicit color-consciousness in any form was racially divisive, and
many of them equated antiracism with antiwhiteness. Whether individual
teachers agreed with Mrs. Martin or Mr. Radke, or fell somewhere else along
the spectrum, central to this entire framework was the belief that, despite its
ugly racial history, the United States had done its part to "finally move past
race." That is, in the eyes of most white Brick City teachers, America has either come close to or has actually entered a formal state of postracialism.

How Real Can Racism Be in a Country
with a Black President?

I find it funny that people still complain about race in this day and age. Have they noticed the president of the United States? How real can racism be in a country with a black president? It just seems foolish to say we're racist as a country when the face of the country is black. Don't get me wrong, I love the Obamas, but doesn't the fact that the First Family is black kind of disprove racism? —PAIGE VINCENT, 36

Undergirding white Brick City teachers' support for colorblindness was their related belief that America had officially become a postracial state. Even those teachers who admitted that racial discrimination had not been completely relegated to the past still believed that enough progress had been made to alleviate the charge that the country, as a whole, is fundamentally a racist one. In order to "prove" American postracialism, white teachers drew attention to a number of indicators. Some pointed to the litany of black celebrities now firmly entrenched in our popular culture. Some pointed to black professional athletes who now serve as role models for children of all colors, and still others highlighted the emergence of a black middle class and the rise and acceptance of interracial relationships. Multiple teachers even invoked Asian Americans and the model minority myth as proof of America's new, postracial culture.[38] But there was no greater "evidence" of America's interpersonal and institutional egalitarianism than the election and reelection of Barack Obama as president of the United States.

Mrs. Edwards, without prompting from me, proudly proclaimed that she was a "traditional American" with "strong conservative values." After spending a good deal of time criticizing President Obama for being "racially divisive" and "always playing the race card," Mrs. Edwards then used his presidency as an example of "just how far we've come as a country." Even though a majority of white voters voted against President Obama in both the 2008 and 2012 presidential elections, Mrs. Edwards was adamant that the existence of a black president negated the assertion that the United States was still a country marred by antiblack racism.[39]

MRS. EDWARDS: I'm sorry, I don't mean to go on and on about the president, I don't want to get too political, I know that's not what this interview is about, but the last time I checked, he is black, isn't he? I may not like him or what he stands for, his policies and all that, but I, I think he does symbolize something important about the country.

If we can elect a black person as president, you know, to the highest, most important office in the land, then people can't really use race as an excuse anymore. Like, if Obama can become president, then maybe you can't blame racism for why you didn't finish school or why you don't have a job, you know. The whole race thing is over.

Even though Mrs. Edwards disapproved of President Obama—and did so in harsh and hyperbolic terms[40]—she still believed his presidency reflected positively on the United States and its commitment to racial equality. Having an African American president, according to Mrs. Edwards, officially rendered the charge of racism obsolete. Neither dropping out of school nor being unemployed, to name two examples, could be attributed to racial discrimination in a country with a black head of state. While Mrs. Edwards did not specifically use the term "postracial," she spoke of the United States as a (white) racism-free state, and for her, the election of a black president was the ultimate proof. A number of other teachers also presented President Obama as evidence of American postracialism, including those teachers who were broadly supportive of him and his agenda.

In answering some of my background questions about what influenced him to go into education, Mr. Rhodes, whom I was interviewing in his own home, pointed to a picture of an elderly woman hanging on the wall. With tears in his eyes, he looked at me and replied, "Because of her, my mother. Everything good in me I got from her. . . . She passed away last year." Mr. Rhodes went on to describe growing up with a single mom and how she, owing to her deep faith, instilled in him a commitment to public service. This type of upbringing led Mr. Rhodes into education, and it also engendered in him a deep sense of progressivism. As such, he was a huge fan of President Obama. Still, although his feelings about the former president were the exact opposite of those held by Mrs. Edwards, Mr. Rhodes by and large reached a similar conclusion about the racial significance of his electoral success. As he put it, "I think we're just about past race now or we wouldn't have Barack. We should focus more on poverty. That's the much bigger problem, I think."

Even though Mrs. Edwards and Mr. Rhodes held competing and contrasting political beliefs, they both—perhaps for different reasons—saw the election of an African American president as the death knell for racism in America. For the former, President Obama symbolized the end of legitimacy for race-based excuses; for the latter, he symbolized the need for a heightened focus on poverty and a decreased emphasis on race. Other prominent African Americans were also offered as examples of American postracialism.

Oprah Winfrey and LeBron James were specifically mentioned in a majority of my interviews, while Jay Z, Beyoncé, and Will Smith were mentioned in slightly less than half. Still, despite the regularity with which white Brick City teachers broached the subject of black celebrities, next to President Obama and the First Family, nothing was cited more as evidence than the aggregate educational and economic success of Asian Americans, the so-called model minority.[41]

In twenty-four out of thirty-two interviews, white Brick City teachers used Asian American educational and occupational success as an example of expansive racial opportunity in the United States. Repeatedly, interview respondents held up the "model minority" as proof that anyone, regardless of race, had the chance to make something of themselves, essentially proving that the United States had truly become a postracial nation. Mrs. Hall, a high school history teacher, went into great detail about the history of racial discrimination faced by Asian Americans and how, despite this discrimination, they are "the most successful racial group in the country."

MRS. HALL: Look, I've been teaching history for a very long time and I've studied it even longer. Anyone who pretends America wasn't a profoundly racist country is either blinded by political bias or too stupid to take seriously. We have an ugly, truly horrific racial past in this country, but if you look around, you can clearly see that that's no longer the case. So, um, the idea that blacks are the only group that faced racism is laughable to me. Seriously, whenever I hear somebody blame slavery for their problems today, I laugh. You can't take them seriously. Asian Americans faced just as much discrimination as blacks, but look at where they are today. I mean, um, they were brutalized too. They were lynched in the West. They were detained during World War II, and they were even excluded from coming to America for a very long time. Yet somehow Asians have the most education, you know. They have the best jobs, and they make the most money, even more than whites. So it doesn't bother me at all to talk about racism in the past, because that's just it, it's in the past. Today I think race is irrelevant. If you can't make it today, then I suggest you take a good hard look in the mirror before crying racism. It doesn't work that way anymore.

As a history teacher, Mrs. Hall was well aware of, and had no problem referencing, past acts of racial discrimination. In fact, even though most teachers cited Asian Americans in their respective interviews, Mrs. Hall was one of the only participants to specifically mention Japanese American internment during World War II or Chinese exclusion during the nineteenth century.[42] In doing so, however, she engaged in what sociologists Matthew Desmond and Mustafa Emirbayer term *the fallacy of undifferentiating difference*, "a fallacy that takes hold of all the extremely diverse histories and social experiences of nonwhite groups and flattens them."[43] Using the fallacy in this way allowed Mrs. Hall to bolster her claim that the United States had successfully transitioned from a racist society to a postracial state. After all, if Asian Americans and Asian immigrants can be exposed to discrimination, exclusion, and internment, and nonetheless become one of the most educated and economically successful groups in the country, then the country itself has solved "the race problem."[44]

Postracialism, despite the frequency with which it was invoked, was never fully interrogated by white Brick City teachers. According to *Merriam-Webster's*, the prefix "post-" means "after, subsequent to, or later than."[45] Within the context of "postracial" discourse, then, one must ask, What does it mean to be "subsequent to" or "later than" race? Who gets to determine that we are "after" race, and if that is truly the case, what comes next? Furthermore, whom does a world "after race" benefit, and whom does it harm? These are empirical questions, and the answers to them may vary, but one thing they all have in common is that they reflect the "master frame" of racial progress.[46] That is, inherent to any discourse on postracialism, particularly the one articulated by white Brick City teachers, is that getting to a time after race means getting to a time of desirability. The result of an inevitable, and seemingly linear, progression, postracial temporality is constructed as a universal good, indicative of a society that is "meliorative—gradually moving towards perfection—through incremental reforms or social action."[47] Despite its universality, writ large—and ubiquity throughout my interview data—the progress narrative is far from warranted, and, beyond ideology, it speaks more to temporal inequality than it does to the empirical reality of race in America.[48]

Whether admonishing people of color for focusing too much on race, or asserting that the United States has moved beyond race, white Brick City teachers consistently utilized the white racial frame and, intentionally or not, engaged in colorblind racism. The teachers I interviewed professed an unyielding fidelity to colorblindness, doing so, in large part, because they sincerely believed that America had officially become a postracial nation. Using the election of an African American president, the prominence and visibility of black celebrities and athletes, the emergence of a black middle class, the rise and acceptance of miscegenation, and the relative success of Asian Americans, interview respondents offered "proof" that state-sanctioned racial discrimination had finally and firmly been relegated to the past. In the discussion to come, I juxtapose this particular ideological framing with actual racialized experience. Interview data will show that white teachers' commitment to colorblindness and their stated belief in postracialism were both challenged by the way they talked about and described their own experiences within Brick City schools. This ideological and experiential contradiction led to a discursive impasse of sorts, one that was eventually overcome by a multistep process that I term *spatial negotiation*.

SPATIAL NEGOTIATION

Here I move beyond racial ideology alone and highlight the various ways it intersects with, and is contradicted by, actual racial experience. As detailed earlier, bolstered by their belief in a postracial America, white Brick City teachers were highly supportive of the racial ideology of colorblindness. In lived experience, however, as detailed in chapters 3 and 4, these same teachers were extremely color-conscious, as race, for them, was a salient feature of teaching in the Brick City School District. Looked at comparatively, the ideology of white Brick City teachers belied the experiences of white Brick City teachers, specifically those experiences that took place within Brick City schools. Indeed, absent any external provocation—and similar to white racial identity—this particular contradiction was completely invisible to the teachers themselves. Once it was brought to their attention, however, most teachers struggled to make sense of their disparate positions and eventually negotiated a compromise between their postracial, colorblind ideology and their hyper-racial, color-conscious reality.

Spatial negotiation—the cognitive reconciliation of racial ideology, situated experience, and discourse—is composed of four primary themes: (1) *rhetorical incoherence*, (2) *racial rationalization*, (3) *authentic grievance*, and (4) *reluctant recognition*. Rhetorical incoherence is identical to the rhetorical incoherence discussed in chapter 1. When questioned directly, white Brick City teachers found it very difficult to make sense of and talk about their ideological and experiential contradictions. Racial rationalization is the process of reconciling contradictory statements by attributing the discrepancies to Brick City schools as opposed to any personal or internal conflict: that is, interview respondents blamed black students and black families for "forcing" them to broach the subject of race. Authentic grievance is the process of allocating legitimacy to claims of racial victimization. By treating some claims as authentic and others as fraudulent, white Brick City teachers were able to justify their skepticism of, and simultaneous belief in, the existence of racial discrimination. Finally, reluctant recognition is the realization that racial status matters. After comparing their localized experiences to those of racial minorities throughout the country more broadly, several teachers reluctantly came to the conclusion that race and racism are more salient to contemporary American life than they had previously cared to admit. Next I discuss each theme in greater detail.

What Am I Saying, Is This Making Any Sense?

I, um, well, maybe it might be different, I think, but why would it be different, you know? Well, it's not so much that I didn't think, that, um, I didn't think that racism was real, it's just that, when you think about my job and what I do, I'm an outsider. But then again, what if, you know, outside of school, maybe I'm not an outsider, so it can even out some, at least, sometimes. What am I saying, is this making any sense? I have to be honest with you, this, um, this is a little eye-opening.

—CHELSEA CLARK, 34

Once exposed to their divergent ideological and experiential stances on racial identity and racial discrimination, white Brick City teachers relapsed into rhetorical incoherence, again finding it difficult to speak in comprehensible sentences. After they had spent the bulk of their interviews speaking lucidly about their experiences within Brick City schools, questions about racial ideology versus racial experiences caused white teachers to revert to stuttering, stammering, and speaking in ways that were hard to understand. Furthermore, the content of the answers often made little sense. That is, the substance of their answers was as incoherent as the structure of their answers. The same false starts, long pauses, nervous laughter, and nonsensical responses that characterized my general questions about whiteness all returned toward the end of the interview as I and my interview respondents mutually explored their patterned contradictions. In a very real way, the return of rhetorical incoherence signaled that many of my interviews had come full circle.

White Brick City teachers found it extremely difficult to make sense of how they could possibly violate their own deeply held beliefs about colorblindness and postracialism. For nearly all of them, the contradiction in the ways they discussed race in society versus how they discussed race in Brick City schools was, at least initially, invisible to them. Without explicit prompting from me, the teachers I interviewed saw no inherent conflict in proclaiming that the United States had effectively moved beyond race while simultaneously asserting that race shaped their workplaces and work experiences. Similarly, white teachers saw no inherent conflict in chastising people of color for "playing the race card" while simultaneously internalizing and subsequently describing whiteness as a racial disadvantage within predominantly black schools. My task, then, was to make these contradictions visible, and I did so by asking white teachers about them directly.

Bryan Palmer, a social studies teacher, has taught at Pattengill Middle School for thirteen years. Pattengill has a student population that is close to 90 percent black. Mr. Palmer was adamant that, "for the good of the country," America needed to "finally move past race." Unlike those teachers who refused to even consider the possibility that racial discrimination was still a prominent feature of society, Mr. Palmer believed that even if claims of nonwhite racial victimization were true, people needed to deal with them in their own way without "dragging the country through the mud."

MR. PALMER: I think, with social media and everything, like when you see some of the things police officers are doing, that, um, it's, at least it's clear to me, that, yeah, some of the stories are true. You know what I mean?

BELL: Could you elaborate further?

MR. PALMER: Yeah, so to be perfectly clear, um, I don't think racism as a whole is that big of a deal. People like to play that card a lot, but at the same time, I think certain individuals can still experience racism. Um, I think that, OK, yeah, sometimes a cop can be racist against a black guy or any one black person, but that's not the same as saying that all cops are racist, you know. I think people who go through something like that should find a way to deal with it in their own way. We don't need a new civil rights movement. We don't need protests or riots, you know. Um, we don't need all these groups dragging the country through the mud every time a cop does something racist. It's the exception, not the rule.

Although Mr. Palmer was willing to admit that cops could at times act in racist ways, he felt that such acts were the exception to the rule and that protests, riots, and the emergence of a "new civil rights movement" were unwarranted. I noted many of these themes during the exchange, and I had them ready to use later in the interview when, in talking about being discriminated against by black parents, Mr. Palmer stated that "something needs to be done" and "it should be national news" what he and other white teachers go through. Reading his own words back to him, I asked Mr. Palmer about his contradictory statements, causing him to become rhetorically incoherent.

BELL: Earlier in the interview, when you were talking about police officers and how sometimes some of them can do something racist . . .

MR. PALMER: Yeah, I remember.

BELL: You said that victims of racist actions by police officers should deal with it in their own way, but now, when talking about your own experiences with racial discrimination, you said it should be national news. Do you feel that those two statements contradict one another?

MR. PALMER: Um, well, no, not really. I think that, when we're talking about cops and what they do, it can be a very dangerous job, you know. But, um, actually, I don't know how that's relevant [*laughs*]. Um, so, I think more people know about police officers, but maybe not enough people know about us, but then again, I hate when people fall back on race. So maybe, I think, um, maybe it's somewhat consistent in that, uh, race and what it means for teachers can be misinterpreted, you know, and sometimes with cops, you, you, um, I, this is kind of hard [*laughs*]. Um, I don't even know, you know what, yeah, those are contradictory statements [*laughs*]. Damn, how did I not see that?

In his disjointed and convoluted response, Mr. Palmer made the valid point that while many people are aware of the problems with race and policing, far fewer are cognizant of the problems with race and teaching. As quickly as he approached this (quite reasonable) justification for his contradictory statements, he immediately backpedaled, stating, "I hate when people fall back on race." Tellingly, Mr. Palmer, after trying—and failing—to clarify his reasoning, ended the exchange with a question directed at himself: "How did I not see that?" Other teachers had similar reactions upon realizing they had made contradictory statements. Mrs. Meredith, a staunch advocate of colorblindness, was visibly and discursively taken aback when I made her aware of her own color-consciousness. As she tried to make sense of her own words, she lapsed into rhetorical incoherence.

BELL: Earlier in the interview, you suggested that African Americans who complain about racism were too focused on race and that they should be colorblind. But you also said that, I want to get this right, that being white "was a curse" at your school, and that you face racial discrimination on a daily basis. Do you think or feel that you are focusing too much on race at your particular school? Should you just be colorblind at work?

MRS. MEREDITH: Um, no, no, no. When I talk about being a white teacher, I'm not talking about race per se, but, um, it's more about, um, wait, that doesn't make any sense, does it [*laughs*]? Um, maybe I could let it go, you know, be colorblind or whatever, but what would that prove? Who would, um, believe that I get called a white bitch fifty times a week? So to be colorblind, to see race, I mean to not see race, it's hard because, um, it's right there, you know. I think it's virtually impossible not to see race, I mean, again it's literally right there. I'm white, they're not, everybody sees it, but I, I still just wish we didn't have to focus on race so much. It's bad. It's bad for everyone. Nothing good can come out of it, you know.

BELL: Right, but if everyone is seeing it, including you, does that mean that you, as well as your students, are focusing too much on race?

MRS. MEREDITH: [*Long pause*] I guess it kind of does. I mean, I don't think I've ever looked at it that way. I just, um, but thinking about it now, whenever I'm at work I do focus on race a lot. Hell, when I talk about work I focus on race a lot. That's funny to think about. That's kind of surprising, startling even. I never saw that before.

The realization that she herself could be highly color-conscious was something that Mrs. Meredith found at once "funny," "surprising," and "startling." Like Mr. Palmer, she was shocked to discover that, in describing white racial victimization, she was violating the norms of colorblindness. For Mrs. Meredith, this discovery was extremely difficult to talk about, as even pausing to collect her thoughts was not enough to prevent her from becoming rhetorically incoherent. At one point during this exchange, she appeared to justify the need for color-consciousness ("maybe I could let it go . . . but what would that prove"), only to reaffirm her belief in racial colorblindness a few seconds later ("I still just wish we didn't have to focus on race so much"). Even here, in answering a question about discursive contradictions, Mrs. Meredith contradicted herself, signaling support for both color-consciousness and colorblindness within the span of a few seconds.

As I outlined before, the rhetorical incoherence presented here was caused by external forces. Whether prompted by general questions about white racial identity or by me questioning their ideological and experiential contradictions, for long stretches of time white teachers lost the ability to speak in clear and complete sentences. The straightforward nature and simplicity of "moving past race" became a lot less straightforward and a lot more complex when it was white teachers describing their own racialized experiences. Furthermore, the ideological bankruptcy of "playing the race card" gave way to the courageous and moral currency of naming white racial victimization as an experiential reality. For white Brick City teachers, proclaiming to be colorblind while actively planning to perform white racial identity, and insisting on American postracialism while explicitly decrying antiwhite racism, were blatant contradictions that they simply could not see. Once they were made aware of them, however, all discursive fluency stopped, as once again, educated and articulate professionals fell victim to rhetorical incoherence.

Believe Me, I Would Much Rather Not Talk about Race

The only reason race is relevant to me is because of where I work. That's it. I don't go around bragging about being white, you know. And I really don't go around complaining about racism. I'm not a victim. Believe me, I would much rather not talk about race, but it is what it is, you know. I didn't teach my students to hate white people, but some of them do. Am I supposed to pretend they don't? Should I just be OK with that? So, no, I don't think it's a contradiction at all. I really don't see it that way.—TIFFANY EDWARDS, 51

Although rhetorical incoherence at times made thematic coding somewhat difficult, there were still numerous themes that emerged from the data. One such theme, racial rationalization, is the tendency of white Brick City teachers to justify their ideological and experiential contradictions by blaming them on black students, black parents, and black schools. Rather than grapple with the reasons for, or meanings of, their ideological and experiential contradictions, many of the teachers I interviewed simply explained them away without accepting any responsibility. If they focused on race too much, then it was because of the racialized environments in which they worked. Similarly, if they asserted that racism was salient in any real or meaningful way, then it was because black students and black parents made it so by consistently acting in a racist and discriminatory manner. Next I show how, in the face of their own ideological and experiential contradictions, some white Brick City teachers rationalized their newfound color-consciousness in an attempt to restore ideological purity and get back to what heretofore was racially familiar.[49]

Mr. Radke was a harsh and vocal critic of nonwhite racial victimization. At one point during our interview, he defiantly stated, "I have no sympathy for people who play the race card. None." Mr. Radke was a firm believer in colorblindness, and he was quite insistent that the United States had become a postracial state. As such, from education to employment, from voting to criminal justice, there was no claim of nonwhite racial victimization that he found to be credible. When it came to white racial victimization, however, Mr. Radke had a decidedly different take. On more than one occasion, he admonished Sexton High School for its allegedly antiwhite, racially discriminatory culture. When I questioned him about his contradictory stances, Mr. Radke was incredulous, sticking to the postracial script and shifting the blame to his black students.

BELL: Earlier in the interview, you suggested that your black students and their families should spend less time focusing on race, but you also said that you yourself spend a great deal of time thinking about race at Sexton. Would you say that those are contradictory statements?

MR. RADKE: Absolutely not. Not at all.

BELL: How do you differentiate between the two?

MR. RADKE: I just don't think that it is, that they are. I, I, um, when you look at all the chances for success in this country, then you can't say race is a factor. You simply can't. There're so many opportunities out there, and black people or anybody else, um, they can do anything they want. Blaming everything on race is a cop-out. It's just an excuse to make everything about race. It's time to move on. Not everything has to be a race thing.

BELL: I understand. But my question is that if you feel that it is time to move on from race, how do you justify thinking and talking about race in regards to your job?

MR. RADKE: [*Long pause*] I think it's different. Um, I would never think about race if I didn't work at Sexton. If I didn't have to deal with getting called white all the time, race would never cross my mind. I never talked about race before I started working at that school. Never. I treat people as people, how they deserve to be treated. I take them as they come, and everybody's the same until I know otherwise. You can't have that, um, that type of mentality—you can't do that at Sexton. Race is everywhere. And I'm not blind, deaf, or dumb, so I have to adapt. I have to swim with the sharks sometimes, you know. Understand, I'm still a teacher. I have a job to do.

Initially Mr. Radke saw no contradiction in admonishing students for focusing on race while he himself spent a great deal of time thinking about being a white teacher at a predominantly black school. Without any hesitation, he rejected the idea that he was acting in ways that were similar to the people he had previously described as "race hustlers." Only after a specific follow-up question from me did Mr. Radke realize the color-consciousness that permeated his own discourse. Once he had this realization, though, Mr. Radke found it difficult to cope with the resulting interruption of his normative racial ideology. Rather than grappling with the potential implications of his ideological and experiential contradictions, he simply rationalized them by blaming his students and his school. Thus, for Mr. Radke, when it came to the violation of colorblindness, he bore no personal responsibility. He was merely "swim[ming] with the sharks" and trying to do his job.

When confronted with their discursive contradictions, other teachers too engaged in racial rationalization. Ms. Livingston, who lamented our country's obsession with race, easily provided examples of her own racial victimization within Brick City schools. Furthermore, as a dedicated teacher, Ms. Livingston spent a significant amount of time devising ways to perform whiteness so as to better reach, and ultimately teach, her predominantly black student body. Therefore, whether describing her personal experiences with racial victimization or thinking about how best to use white racial identity as a pedagogical tool, Ms. Livingston, despite her previous objection to "obsessing over race," herself spent a considerable amount of time thinking about it. I detail Ms. Livingston's racial rationalization in the following exchange.

BELL: Earlier you described the country as being obsessed with race, yet you also say that you think about race a lot too. Does this mean that you're also obsessed with race? I mean, are you also implicated in our collective obsession with race?

MS. LIVINGSTON: [*Pause*] Um, I don't know. This sounds weird, but I've never really thought about, um, I haven't thought about thinking about race [*laughs*]. I guess, like I said earlier, I just was, um, the way I was raised was to treat everybody equally. I know it's kinda cliché, but I honestly don't have a racist bone in my body. My parents would be ashamed if I did, you know. So I just see people, I don't see race.

It's kind of like, um, whenever I'm at work, maybe I might sometimes, but in all honesty, it's about the person for me. I don't care what race they are.

BELL: To be clear, you're saying that you try to be colorblind in your own dealings and interactions with people, correct?

MS. LIVINGSTON: Yeah, that's exactly right.

BELL: What about when it comes to teaching black students? You said that you have to find the best way to be white. How do you reconcile a statement like that with your commitment to not focusing on race?

MS. LIVINGSTON: Um, well [*long pause*]. That's, I don't know, that's a good question. Damn, I don't think I know how to answer that. Like, I feel like, um, wow [*pause*], that's kind of tough. I don't really know what to say. I mean, um, I don't want to come across as a hypocrite or anything [*long pause*]. I just don't think of myself as one of those people, you know. They make everything about race and I don't. I guess I would say that, that they're the same, but they're not the same, you know. So, whenever I think about race it's because I have to, you know. I don't even mean to or really want to, but, um, like I said, I have to figure out a way to reach my students. A lot of them have their guards up—they don't trust white people at all. So I wouldn't be a good teacher if I didn't think about race, at least when it comes to being better for my students. But, um, I wanted to say that, um, I think it's one thing to think about race, you know, when you have to. When the situation calls for it. But I still think too many people use race too much. They do it just to do it, and that's certainly not what I do.

When I asked Ms. Livingston to reconcile her contradictory positions regarding colorblindness and color-consciousness, her normative racial ideology was challenged by her own words. The disruption of her racial equilibrium—fidelity to colorblindness and opposition to color consciousness—caused Ms. Livingston to engage in rhetorical incoherence, and it left her puzzled about how best to account for her discursive contradictions. After taking a few minutes to compose her thoughts, Ms. Livingston pivoted to racial rationalization, justifying her own preoccupation with race as an essential feature of high-quality teaching. Unlike "one of those people" who think about or "use race too much," Ms. Livingston claimed only to do so when her job called for it, meaning that, if not for her particular line of work, she would have little reason to, and therefore would not, ever focus on race. From her perspective, being an effective teacher to black students all but necessitated color-consciousness, and as a committed educator, she acted accordingly.

Before moving on to authentic grievance, I think it is important to emphasize that the term "racial rationalization" is not meant to undermine or question the veracity of how white Brick City teachers described their racial experiences. Each of the teachers I interviewed, from Mr. Radke to Ms. Livingston, can speak to their own thoughts, feelings, and experiences better than I can; therefore, it is not my responsibility, or my intention, to invalidate how they interpret and make sense of their own lives. My purpose in labeling these responses as rationalizations is to highlight the various motives for making contradictory statements. That is, using personal experience as a justification for explicit color-consciousness was not a consideration that white Brick City teachers afforded African Americans and other people of color. In lieu of considering the experiential reasons for why racial minorities might "obsess over race," white teachers simply assigned them nefarious motives, neatly summarized by accusations of "playing the race card." In their own lives, however, excuses gave way to legitimate justifications, thereby making the acknowledgment of race and racism experientially valid.

When I Talk about Racism, It's Because It's Real

Yeah, it may come across as contradictory or maybe seem hypocritical, but here's the thing, when I talk about racism, it's because it's real. I don't make things up to make myself look good. I don't want people to feel sorry for me, you know. I don't want to be seen as a victim, OK. But when it happens, it happens. If I, um, whenever I feel like there's reverse discrimination at play, I point it out. But it's not the same. If I say it was racism, then it was racism.—MR. MARSH, 54

Although racial rationalization was the most common response to ideological and discursive contradictions, authentic grievance was by far the most visceral. In a number of interviews, white teachers expressed authentic grievance in seemingly instinctual and exceedingly aggressive terms. Authentic grievance is the subjective legitimizing of racial victimization. It assigns legitimacy or illegitimacy to racial victimization claims based on who is making them and the substance of the claims themselves. Many interview respondents, once confronted with their own contradictory statements, responded by separating real or "authentic" claims of racial victimization from fictitious or "fraudulent" ones. In the overwhelming majority of cases, racial victimization neatly corresponded to the racial classification of the person making the claim. White racial victimization was largely treated as authentic, while nonwhite racial victimization, with few exceptions, was treated as inauthentic. This pattern was consistent across most interviews.

Authentic grievance can be broken down into three categories; the latter two overlap yet remain conceptually distinct. The first category is *acceptance*. Acceptance was the nearly unconditional legitimacy granted to claims of racial victimization, and, for the most part, it was reserved for whites. Categories 2 and 3, *skepticism* and *aggression*, were reserved for nonwhite claims of racial victimization. The teachers displayed skepticism when, while doubtful of the veracity of nonwhite claims of racial victimization, they nevertheless remained open to the possibility of authenticity. Even though they were skeptical of widespread, or systemic, racial discrimination, some teachers—typically younger and politically liberal—were open to situational or sporadic instances of racism against nonwhites. Aggression, on the other hand, was more emotional than skepticism, and teachers became angry at nonwhite claims of racial victimization. These teachers—older and politically conservative—maintained their fidelity to postracialism, only deviating when accepting the legitimacy of white racial victimization. I provide examples of each category below.

White racial victimization was almost unanimously granted legitimacy. While it was unsurprising that teachers believed their own experiences, it was somewhat remarkable that they so readily accepted the victimization claims of other white teachers. Given their stated belief in colorblindness, as well as the consistency with which they admonished people of color for "playing the race card," I expected at least a modicum of pushback against white, nonpersonal claims of racial victimization.[50] This was not the case. Mrs. Darling typified this process. When I asked her about her disparate interpretations of white versus nonwhite racial victimization, she replied as follows.

MRS. DARLING: It's probably because, well, all I can say is what I go through and what I've been through. It's not like I go around crying racism every day, but some days my kids are just out of control. They're brazen with it, almost proud. "Yeah, yeah, I hate white folks" or "I can't stand white people." That's racism, isn't it? So, I don't know your life, I, I, um, can't say whether or not you face racism, but I know what I go through, and it's very real.

BELL: This is actually a common theme in my interviews. Many teachers say they face racial discrimination in their schools.

MRS. DARLING: I believe them.

BELL: Really, just like that? Are you at all skeptical about the extent to which other white teachers face racial discrimination in urban schools?

MRS. DARLING: No, I don't think so, because I see it. I see it with my own eyes how sometimes a white teacher can be busting their ass, you know, and getting nowhere. Then a black teacher can just come in and snap their fingers and the kids automatically respond. I mean, I can't say for sure, but I think that's probably a race thing. Plus, it's not like we never talk about it. Maybe not like this, but we know what's going on in the school. I, it wouldn't surprise me to learn that other teachers, you know, teachers at other schools, go through some of the same stuff I go through.

In her answer, Mrs. Darling displayed a high degree of acceptance and a lesser degree of skepticism. Due to her personal experiences, she was perfectly comfortable accepting broader claims of white racial victimization. Also, during this brief exchange Mrs. Darling intimated that she and her white coworkers periodically discussed their respective experiences with racial discrimination, and those discussions had given her the impression that antiwhite bigotry was widespread within Brick City schools. Conversely, using me as a representative for people of color, or at the very least African Americans, Mrs. Darling was open to the idea of nonwhite racial victimization, but she would not fully commit to it ("I, I, um, can't say whether or not you face racism"). The ease and comfort with which white teachers accepted other white teachers' claims of racial victimization—in large part due to their own racialized experiences—was consistent and, with few exceptions, was not a consideration afforded to racial minorities.

Skepticism was exclusively relegated to the domain of nonwhite racial victimization. Typically, teachers who were younger and self-identified as liberals were open to the idea of sporadic instances of racism yet generally skeptical about the existence of broader, more systematic racial discrimination. These teachers acknowledged the possibility of individual acts of racially discriminatory behavior, but they rejected the interrelated ideas of institutional racism and white privilege.[51] Ms. Jarvis, only twenty-four years old, explained her discursive contradictions this way:

BELL: What would you say is the difference between a white teacher who claims to be a victim of racism, and a black teenager who claims the same thing? It seems like you believe the former and not the latter.

MS. JARVIS: [*Pause*] Well, it's not that, um, hold on a second, let me get this right [*pause*]. So, um, I wouldn't say I would necessarily believe one and not the other, but I would have to know the specific details, like what actually happened. Um, I think the reason it's not the same, or the reason I don't look at them the same, is because sometimes I think the whole race thing is overblown. I think, um, that sometimes people don't want to admit they're not good enough or smart enough, or whatever, you know, so they might fall back on race and just blame whites. I'm not saying that it can never be true. Some of these videos, these police shootings, are devastating to look at, but, um, even still, when you think about how big we are, um, as a country, I don't think you can make any conclusions based on a few bad apples.

BELL: Does that type of "wait and see" approach apply to other white teachers that work in Brick City schools?

MS. JARVIS: Um [*pause*], that's a really good question [*pause*]. I would have to say that it doesn't. Um, I know that makes me sound like the biggest hypocrite, but I know what I see and I know what I go through. I know what other teachers go through. I, I can't really explain it. It's like, it's everywhere, it's almost like the school system is just overly hostile, you know. I know that sounds weird, but that's the best way I can think of. It's the schools, they just mess everybody up.

When asked to distinguish between two hypothetical claims of racial victimization, one white, one nonwhite, Ms. Jarvis accepted the former while remaining skeptical of the latter. Like several other teachers, she referenced the litany of audio and video clips of African American men, women, and children being brutalized, and sometimes killed, by police officers and used them as examples of authentic grievance. Beyond those "few bad apples," however, Ms. Jarvis still believed that too many people of color "fall back on race." Also, and quite informatively, despite not possessing the language or academic jargon to label it as such, Ms. Jarvis made an implicit reference to institutional racism. That is, in justifying her general acceptance of white racial victimization within Brick City schools, she alluded to the schools themselves. By arguing that "the school system is just overly hostile" and that schools "just mess everybody up," Ms. Jarvis was pointing to an institutional structure that, above and beyond individual people, was unreceptive and even discriminatory toward white teachers.

Although acceptance was primarily reserved for white racial victimization, and skepticism was exclusively reserved for nonwhite racial victimization, overall both concepts were relatively benign. Aggression, on the other hand, was antagonistic and angry. Teachers within this category became upset, sometimes visibly so, at nonwhite claims of racial victimization. Phrases such as "Screw that," "Get over it," and "I call bullshit" were just a few of the verbal responses to the idea of ongoing racial discrimination against African Americans and other people of color. The teachers who displayed aggression reacted viscerally, often taking zero time to consider my questions before responding.[52] However, despite aggressively rejecting nonwhite claims of racial victimization, the teachers in this category were highly receptive of white claims of racial victimization. Again, with zero hesitation, these teachers regarded racial discrimination against white people—within and outside Brick City schools—as a near certainty, even as they rhetorically maintained their fidelity to colorblindness and postracialism.

Isaac Thornhill, a veteran middle school teacher and a self-proclaimed "staunch conservative," spoke of nonwhite claims of racial victimization in racially stereotypical and at times personal terms. Repeatedly admonishing "race pimps" and "social justice warriors" for "fanning the flames of racism and division," Mr. Thornhill rejected all claims of nonwhite racial victimization. When it came to talking about his own racialized experiences, however, Mr. Thornhill consistently blamed his personal frustration and professional failures on "black racism." For example, Mr. Thornhill attributed his difficulty, and initial failure, in gaining tenure to his race, claiming that "it was nearly impossible for white people to succeed in that environment."[53] When I questioned Mr. Thornhill about these discrepancies, he immediately engaged in a more aggressive form of authentic grievance.

> BELL: Earlier in the interview, you said you had no sympathy or patience for people making excuses or playing the race card. Do you feel that you are making excuses or playing the race card when you describe racial discrimination against white teachers?

> MR. THORNHILL: No. No, no, no, no, no. I don't think talking about my own experiences is playing the race card. That's ridiculous.

> BELL: Do you think it's possible that people of color who talk about racism are doing so based on their own experiences?

MR. THORNHILL: I, no. How many bad experiences can there be? If that were the case, black people would have to experience racism every second of every day. No offense, but that's how much they complain about racism. You always hear about that institutional racism bullshit, but if you look around, what do you see? You sure as hell don't see slavery. You don't see black people hanging from trees. No, you see affirmative action, you see black-only scholarships, you see a black president. Oh, and I don't know if you've heard, but BET, Black Entertainment Television, I mean what the hell is that? Could you imagine what would happen if there was a TV channel called White Entertainment Television? All the race pimps and social justice warriors would flip out. They might even burn down their own neighborhood. Don't get me started on that crap.

BELL: Obviously you know your own experiences better than anyone else, but what about other white teachers who complain about racism? Do you believe they are playing the race card?

MR. THORNHILL: Come on. No. I almost don't believe that's a serious question [laughs]. They hate us. They hate white people. Not everybody, that wouldn't be accurate, but a whole lot of my students simply can't stand white people. And the parents are worse. They don't take responsibility for anything. They drop their kids off looking a mess, they're looking a mess, and then they don't want to be bothered, they want to be left alone all day, which is funny because it isn't like they're going to work, most of them are on some kind of welfare. If I or anyone else dare call home and disturb their precious slumber, then all hell breaks loose. Especially if you're white. If you want to know the truth, I'm actually surprised more of us aren't coming forward. There's definitely a hostility directed at whites. And it's not just in the schools, either, it comes from the top down. It comes from the so-called president.

From being lazy to not caring about their kids, Mr. Thornhill believed in, and was not shy about expressing, a multitude of racial stereotypes, particularly stereotypes about African Americans. He and other teachers within the aggression category were so wedded to black stereotypes that they refused to even consider the possibility of nonwhite racial victimization. When asked if blacks and other people of color were simply speaking to their own lived realities, Mr. Thornhill immediately dismissed my question, instead asking, "How many bad experiences can there be?" Conversely, Mr. Thornhill considered his own racialized experiences absolute. Despite his antipathy toward blacks and other people of color who allegedly played the race card, Mr. Thornhill considered the insinuation that he himself engaged in a similar process "ridiculous." Furthermore, due to the perceived antiwhite atmosphere of his school—and, apparently, the country writ large—Mr. Thornhill had no trouble accepting the truthfulness of other white Brick City teachers who claimed to be victims of racial discrimination.

Reserved for nonwhite claims of racial victimization, authentic grievance in the form of aggression stood out because of the vitriol it engendered in white Brick City teachers. Time and again, white teachers defended their discursive contradictions by wading deep into the well of racial stereotypes, accusing people of color of playing the race card and refusing to entertain their veracity. Teachers within this category were outwardly angered not only by what they regarded as false claims of racial victimization but also by the insinuation, or mere suggestion, that their own racialized experiences could be looked at within the same vein. As one teacher put it, "You can't compare my life with some bullshit artist looking to play the race card." Still, looking beyond personal experience, the anger and aggression directed at "race hustlers" and "race pimps" did not preclude white Brick City teachers from accepting the authenticity of white racial victimization as a whole.

A different and, in many ways, more hostile response than racial rationalization, authentic grievance was yet another defensive mechanism used by white Brick City teachers to repair the white habitus and restore the white racial equilibrium.[54] As self-proclaimed longtime believers in colorblindness and American postracialism, many teachers were shaken by the realization that, based on their own responses, they were neither colorblind nor postracial, at least not to the degree or with the consistency that they had previously believed. When faced with their own ideological and experiential contradictions, a number of interviewees responded with authentic grievance, subjectively assigning legitimacy or illegitimacy to white versus nonwhite claims of racial victimization. Using acceptance, skepticism, and aggression, white Brick City teachers painted white claims of racial victimization as authentic while remaining skeptical about, and at times aggressively lashing out against, nonwhite claims of racial victimization.

Maybe There's Something to This Whole Race Thing

It's something that's been bothering me, like I've done everything I could not to admit it to myself. Maybe there's something to this whole race thing, you know. Being in the minority at my school has kind of opened my eyes a little bit. Is this how, you know, blacks feel everywhere else? Do I make black people feel the way I sometimes feel at work? The more I think about it, the more I realize I probably won't like the answer to those questions.

—SOPHIA TAYLOR, 38

Racial rationalization and authentic grievance were by far the most common strategies used by white Brick City teachers when trying to account for their ideological and experiential contradictions. A third response, *reluctant recognition*, while not as frequent, was just as illuminating. Reluctant recognition is the deliberate and careful consideration of personal racialized experiences, specifically assessing how they may or may not translate to the broader social world. The teachers who engaged in reluctant recognition paid special attention to racial status and racial space, questioning whether or not their racialized experiences within Brick City schools were applicable to racial minorities throughout the United States. Also, teachers in this category openly questioned whether they, outside Brick City schools, acted in ways that were similar to black students and black families within Brick City schools. These teachers, when faced with their discursive contradictions, grappled with them in nuanced ways, ultimately giving far more consideration to the intersection of race, ideology, and personal experience.

Reluctant recognition entailed both majority and minority comparisons. Some teachers chose to analyze their role as the racialized other, while other teachers chose to analyze their role as the racialized norm. To put it differently, some teachers recognized the similarities between their experiences in Brick City schools and those of people of color throughout the broader United States (minority comparison), while other teachers recognized the similarities between their black students in Brick City schools and themselves throughout the broader United States (majority comparison). At least one teacher made majority and minority comparisons and came to the conclusion that "unless we get the chance to live in each other's shoes and see the world through each other's eyes, we're never going to get past race, you know. Maybe we don't deserve to." As this particular quote indicates, reluctant recognition, tellingly, and perhaps accurately, often led to a deep sense of pessimism, engendering a negative outlook on race relations moving forward.

Mrs. Bradley, thirty-one, has been teaching in a predominantly black Brick City school for close to ten years. She, like my other interviewees, expressed a strong belief in colorblindness. Although she claimed to be passionate about fighting poverty, she thought "the race thing" had largely been "dealt with." Therefore, Mrs. Bradley, in addition to colorblindness, also believed in American postracialism. Both colorblindness and postracialism disappeared in their entirety once the conversation shifted to her own racialized experiences within Brick City schools. I asked her about this contradiction, and her response is captured in the following exchange.

BELL: Earlier in the interview, you said that people who complain about race, or racism, are looking to make an excuse and that we should all focus on being colorblind.

MRS. BRADLEY: Yeah, well, yeah, I feel that way. I think it's true.

BELL: OK, but you yourself complained about racism when describing your experiences at Taft Middle School. So, given your previous position, would you include yourself in those who use race as an excuse?

MRS. BRADLEY: Well, no. I don't think it's the same. I, um [pause], I, I think I talk about my own life, you know. Like, when I told you about being called the dumb white lady, or when a parent asks to talk to a black teacher, I mean, that really happened. I don't know what else to call it. I mean, is there another word? I don't think any of that would happen to me if I were a black teacher; it's because I'm white. To me, that's racism. It's not an excuse or anything, it really happened. It's really racism.

BELL: Well, along those lines, when a person of color recites a specific experience and describes it as racism, does that make it OK? Does relying on personal experience make talking about racism legitimate?

MRS. BRADLEY: [Pause] I don't know, like, how do I know it really happened, you know?

BELL: And what if someone said the same thing to you? What if someone assumed your racial experiences were exaggerated or made up?

MRS. BRADLEY: [Long pause] You know, that's a really good question. I don't think I've ever thought of it that way. I've never, um, I haven't considered it from that perspective before. Like, I'm sure people would hear me talk about work and think, "Yeah, right, she's so full of shit," you know, but it's true, I swear it's true. . . . I bet there's some stuff I'm forgetting [*pause*]. Hmmm, that's, that's kind of awful to think about. Like, what if I've been wrong, you know? I mean if even half the stuff my students say is true, then I'd hate white people too [*laughs*]. And here I am dismissing them. Wow, this is kind of sad. I don't know what to think.

Initially, Mrs. Bradley used authentic grievance to explain away her discursive contradictions. Without much thought, she stressed the authenticity of her own experiences while questioning those of people of color ("How do I know it really happened?"). After several follow-up questions, specifically a question that hypothesized the second-guessing of her own racialized experiences, Mrs. Bradley, seemingly for the first time, considered the possibility that people of color were telling the truth about the significance of race and racism in their lives. Taken aback, Mrs. Bradley put herself in the shoes of her black students, imagining how she would feel about white people if some of them actively discriminated against her and others, for whatever reason, did not seem to care. On recognizing her potential error ("and here I am dismissing them"), she became sad, confused, and pessimistic, struggling to make sense of the intersecting complexities of racial status and racialized experience.

Mrs. Clark took a different route to reluctant recognition, although the process and outcome were nearly identical. Instead of focusing on being a racial minority, Mrs. Clark paid more attention to majoritarian similarities. After a back-and-forth about the merits of nonwhite racial victimization in terms of both frequency and authenticity, Mrs. Clark remained skeptical about the extent to which nonwhites experience racism in the contemporary United States. As I prepared to move on in the interview, Mrs. Clark, unprompted, decided to reengage on the topic of racial victimization.

MRS. CLARK: It's just, I don't know, I've thought a lot about this, and it's weird. There's some students that hate white people no matter what. It doesn't matter who you are or what type of teacher you are, they're just not going to like you. I've been called a white bitch, a dumb white ho, a Becky (which I guess is code for white bimbo or whatever), but some students, I wonder whether or not they meant to be racist or insensitive or offensive at all. Like, I remember the first time a student told me that I was OK for a white lady, or white girl, I was cool for a white girl. At the time, all I could think was, Well, what the hell does that mean? What does that say about white people? Like, I got really upset. I even sent her to the office. Now, thinking back just now when we were talking, I think she was trying to be nice, you know? Maybe she was giving me a compliment. This whole idea about contradictions, was I being overly sensitive? Was I the one being politically correct? I think I took a compliment badly and punished Anaya for no reason [*long pause*].

BELL: Is everything OK?

MRS. CLARK: Yeah, I'm fine. I feel bad for Anaya. She never really liked me after that, and I think now I know why. Who can blame her, you know? But, um, I don't know, it just got me thinking, um, maybe sometimes I say or do things that black people find hurtful, even if I didn't mean it that way. Like, what's the word? Um, intent. Like, what if intent doesn't matter so much? What if it's more about how people feel, you know, how people are affected? So maybe we as white people might say something we think is harmless, but from, um, their perspective, um, for black people it isn't really harmless at all. Maybe it's extremely harmful, you know. I guess I can see why people still might want to talk about race.

After recalling a specific interaction with one of her black students, Mrs. Clark appeared to become visibly upset, prompting me to double-check that she was OK to continue. She assured me that she was, then proceeded to work through the racial meaning of this specific experience. Mrs. Clark openly grappled with the possibility that she misinterpreted the racial significance of a comment made by one of her students and, in her misunderstanding, punished the student "for no reason." Not content with relitigating this one experience, however, Mrs. Clark connected it to race and society more broadly, taking the time to differentiate between the *intent* and *outcome* of racialized interactions. That is, in her more common role as a member of the racial majority, Mrs. Clark wondered whether she had ever said or done anything, regardless of intent, that was received as offensive or "extremely harmful" by racial minorities. The mere possibility of such an occurrence caused her to take a more understanding tone toward color-consciousness ("I guess can see why people still might want to talk about race"). Still, much like Mrs. Bradley, Mrs. Clark only engaged reluctant recognition after specific follow-up questions from me, and she too was eventually left with a pessimistic view of race in the contemporary United States.

Reluctant recognition is the process by which white teachers came to appreciate racial status and racial experience in more meaningful and introspective ways. Although the teachers who engaged this process did so reluctantly, they at least tried to make a connection between their racialized experiences in Brick City schools and those of racial minorities throughout society as a whole. Some teachers focused on minority-based similarities, while others focused on majority-based similarities, yet they all saw the importance of racial status, particularly the way it shaped racial experience and racial understanding. All told, reluctant recognition sought clarity and perspective, not innocence or rationalization. It did not assign legitimacy or illegitimacy to racial grievance; rather, it pursued a greater understanding of racial grievance, seeking to discern why and how it came to be interpreted so differently. Although few in number, the teachers who displayed reluctant recognition challenged themselves in ways that other teachers did not, but in doing so, they came away more pessimistic about the future of race relations.

CONCLUSION

On April 4, 1968, Dr. Martin Luther King Jr. was shot and killed in Memphis, Tennessee. On November 4, 2008, Barack Obama was elected president of the United States, becoming the first person of color to ever hold that distinction. A mere forty years after the face of the civil rights movement was gunned down on a hotel balcony, American voters, in an Electoral College landslide, selected a black man to become the face of the nation. In just four decades' time, the United States transitioned from a nation of explicit race-consciousness, symbolized by an overt system of racial hierarchy and marred by extreme racial conflict, to one that is prized and characterized as culturally and institutionally postracial. Today this new racial orthodoxy praises colorblindness and bemoans color-consciousness. It constructs racism and antiracism as two sides of the same damaging, politically destructive coin. This ideological framing proved seductive for white Brick City teachers: even in the face of their own color-conscious experiences, they held tight to colorblindness as their normative racial ideology.

To varying degrees the general themes of colorblindness and postracialism could be found in almost all of my interviews, but as a general matter, white Brick City teachers believed that the best way to improve race relations, going forward, was to forgo any and all forms of racial recognition. Personal identity, politics and policy, and interpersonal communication all needed to dispense with race as an explanatory or intervening variable. Then and only then could America finally get past its "obsession" with race. Once the conversation shifted to Brick City schools, however, white teachers betrayed their own ideological stances. Within the context of nonwhite racialized spaces, interview respondents became extremely color-conscious and, to a teacher, displayed a hyperattentiveness to white racial identity and antiwhite discrimination. The same teachers who early in the interview claimed to be devoted to colorblindness then, later in the interview, offered a litany of thoughts, examples, and experiences detailing the salience of race. Perhaps most telling, and sociologically compelling, was the fact that without specific prompting from me, white Brick City teachers were completely oblivious to their ideological and experiential contradictions.

Once exposed to their own contradictory statements, white teachers became nervous, showing signs of racialized stress and being outside of their ideological comfort zones. This new—albeit temporary—reality led to a variety of defense mechanisms, all designed to protect the white habitus and restore the white racial equilibrium. Again struggling to speak in complete or coherent sentences (rhetorical incoherence), interview respondents used a combination of justification (racial rationalization) and adjudication (authentic grievance) to mitigate their own culpability in making race real and perpetuating the "mirage" of racial victimization. Though several teachers examined their contradictory stances introspectively (reluctant recognition), they were in the minority and, overall, not representative of my respondents as a whole. Taken together, these overlapping processes, with the lone exception of reluctant recognition, suggests that racial ideology is quite durable, so much so that not even personal experience is guaranteed to challenge it in a serious and sustained manner.

CONCLUSION: WHITE IDENTITY POLITICS
AND THE COMING CRISIS OF PLACE

America is run primarily by white, Christian men, and there is a segment
of our population who hates that, despises that power structure.
—former Fox News commentator BILL O'REILLY, May 29, 2007

It's a changing country, the demographics are changing. It's not a
traditional America anymore.—former Fox News commentator
BILL O'REILLY, November 6, 2012

It's impossible to fully understand modern American politics without
coming to terms with the fact that this country has been obsessed with
white people for 409 years.—STEVE PHILLIPS, *Brown Is the New White*

At the start of our interview, Mrs. Walker was visibly apprehensive. Sipping
from a cup of coffee in a thinly populated Starbucks, she jokingly mused
about swapping it out for wine or "something stronger." Although we had previously discussed my research project over the phone, Mrs. Walker showed
signs of hesitation when I began the face-to-face interview. In a muted and
somewhat nervous tone, she admitted that she "didn't really know what to
say." Compounding matters further was the fact that I myself was quite ner-

vous. Because this was one of my first interviews, I felt uneasy about my abilities as a researcher and uncertain about the empirical validity of interviewing white teachers. Shortly after the interview began, my uneasiness and uncertainty felt justified. Mrs. Walker gave one-word answers to each of my questions, and I, despite studious and detailed preparation, engaged in my own version of rhetorical incoherence. As we continued our conversation, however, I started to find my voice. I paid close attention to Mrs. Walker's responses, and I tailored my probes and follow-up questions in a way that facilitated a comprehensive and coequal construction of data. After our interview concluded, I sat quietly looking over my notes when, to my surprise, Mrs. Walker tapped me on the shoulder. I stood up and turned toward her. She smiled, gave me a hug, and remarked, "Thank you. I didn't realize I had so much to say."

Like Mrs. Walker, other white Brick City teachers also had much to say. As white teachers working in predominantly black schools, race was not something they could avoid, and white racial identity, specifically, was not something they could ignore. My interview respondents recounted a multitude of experiences—sometimes humorous, other times harrowing—that at once confirmed, contradicted, and complicated many of the now taken-for-granted constructions of whiteness and white racial identity in the United States. Yes, I found evidence that whiteness is generally invisible, often masquerading as the raceless norm, and had I stopped there, this study would neatly fit within the broader sociological literature. Thankfully, I did not stop there. I went past general constructions of whiteness, instead zeroing in on that which is situated within a specific racialized context. By doing so, I found that, in addition to general constructions as the invisible, raceless norm, whiteness—under certain spatial and experiential circumstances—could be made visible, constructed and lived as a meaningful racial identity.

In this conclusion I move beyond discussing white teachers from the Brick City School District and shift my focus to whiteness and white racial identity throughout the broader United States. More specifically, I elaborate on how my findings connect to, and what they mean for, broader social processes and race relations moving forward. How will whiteness be experienced and understood in a country that continues to undergo drastic demographic and cultural changes? How will white people respond to the new reality of a more diverse, more egalitarian, racially pluralistic society? What will a heightened sense of white racial identity mean for white people, and what will more forceful challenges to white racial hegemony mean for society? I place my findings within the context of these and other critical questions, and in doing so, I paint a somewhat unsettling picture about the months and years to come. Finally, I conclude the book with a brief discussion about the limitations of this study, and I make several suggestions for future research on white racial identity.

IS AMERICA BECOMING A NONWHITE RACIALIZED SPACE?

In many ways, public schools today act as a harbinger for things to come. Public education is now a majority-minority institution, meaning that there are collectively more nonwhite students than there are white students.[1] Though white students still constitute the single largest racial category, they are slightly outnumbered by the combined number of nonwhite students. Also, even though public schools—particularly urban public schools—are inundated with nonwhite students, their overall power structure remains predominantly white.[2] That is, teachers, staff members, security guards, counselors, nurses, principals, vice principals, and district administrators typically do not reflect the diversity of a rapidly changing student body.[3] Therefore, while students of color may be overrepresented in terms of physical bodies, whiteness remains atop the status hierarchy, as actual white people yield a disproportionately large share of the power, influence, and decision-making authority. Other institutions throughout the country—indeed, the country itself—operate in a similar fashion.[4]

As we move further into the twenty-first century, the United States will increasingly become blacker and browner.[5] Demographic realities are changing the racial complexity of physical space, and as a result, more and more of the country is becoming associated with people of color. As with public schools, however, demographics alone say very little about power dynamics, and currently there are no projections suggesting that racial minorities will overtake—or even reach parity with—white Americans in terms of political and economic power anytime soon.[6] Still, the perceived racial identity of physical space closely mirrors the racial composition of the people who occupy it.[7] Thus, the growing presence of nonwhite bodies can, and often does, facilitate the interruption of whiteness as the default form of American-ness, particularly in the minds of white people themselves.[8] This, I believe, will remain the case in the United States going forward, regardless of a power structure that is institutionally and operationally more receptive to whiteness.

Beyond sheer numbers, the culture of our country is changing as well. Rap music, once reviled as a deviant form of entertainment, is now one of the most popular genres in the country, even among white youth.[9] Public school curricula for K–12 are becoming more racially inclusive, and many colleges and universities are introducing courses that are critical of whiteness as a privileged racial category.[10] Harriet Tubman, abolitionist and pioneer of the Underground Railroad, was slated to replace, or at least join, Andrew Jackson on the twenty-dollar bill.[11] The Confederate flag has been removed from state capitols in the South, and, despite numerous protests, monuments of Confederate "heroes" are being removed from public spaces all across the country.[12] Also, in the wake of a number of officer-involved shootings, Black Lives Matter and other protest movements have engaged in a critical and sustained examination of how communities of color are policed in America. These killings, often recorded on smartphones by nearby civilians, have spawned marches, riots, protests during the national anthem, and a highly political, highly racialized public conversation about race and the criminal justice system.[13]

Another perceived cultural shift revolves around free speech, or the lack thereof. For a growing number of white and nonwhite Americans, the specter of political correctness has all but stifled public debate.[14] Any topic that is considered too sensitive or uncomfortable, especially for people of color, is to be avoided at all costs or, at the very least, spoken about only in dark places, far removed from the spotlight.[15] These ostensibly taboo topics include research findings about IQ differences between white people and people of color, the prevalence and pervasiveness of black intraracial violence (black-on-black crime), any criticism whatsoever of so-called black or brown cultural pathologies, and even the use of individual words, such as "illegal," "articulate," or "angry," in reference to specific minority groups.[16] Although the "problem" of political correctness is largely exaggerated, the culture of the country has changed, and white people today can be—and often are—held accountable for the stereotypical or racist things they say or do publicly.[17] All told, unlike the United States of decades and centuries past, the contemporary US is no longer a country where hegemonic whiteness can expect to go unchallenged, which for many white Americans is visibly and deeply unsettling.[18]

These demographic and cultural changes did not take place in a vacuum. The increasing visibility, cultural expression, and political power of racial minorities all took place within the physical space that is the United States. The country itself is becoming darker, a reality that looms large in the minds of many white Americans.[19] It is one thing for a white-dominated country to have individual pockets of nonwhite space, but it is something else altogether for the country as a whole to become spatially and institutionally multicultural.[20] Although the white majority still enjoys a disproportionate amount of political and economic power, their standing atop the racial hierarchy can no longer be taken for granted.[21] To be clear, I am not suggesting that the United States has reached racial parity in its cultural praxis and institutional functioning, but I do believe we are now in a position where white Americans can no longer claim ownership of the country, at least not without incurring a fierce and racially diverse backlash. Thus, much as with the arc of urban schools, millions of white Americans now believe that this once white and therefore "normal" country has become culturally, demographically, and spatially racialized.[22]

A NEW POLITICAL AWAKENING

On the evening of November 6, 2012—election night—before the presidential race between Democratic incumbent Barack Obama and Republican challenger Mitt Romney had officially been decided, conservative pundit and then Fox News political commentator Bill O'Reilly offered his assessment of what the incoming Obama-friendly results meant for the country. To his Fox News colleagues and presumably millions of viewers O'Reilly proclaimed, "It's a changing country, the demographics are changing. It's not a traditional America anymore, and there are 50 percent of the voting public who want *stuff*. They want things, and who is going to give them things? President Obama. He knows it, and he ran on it." In a defeated and somber tone, O'Reilly concluded that whereas "twenty years ago, President Obama would have been roundly defeated by an establishment candidate like Mitt Romney, the white establishment is now the minority."[23]

O'Reilly's words were far from a value-free description or politically neutral observation; he was lamenting the changing demographics of America, as well as the corresponding cultural shifts he believed to be a direct result. To O'Reilly, the demographic, cultural, and now political changes that gave rise to Barack Obama ran counter to so-called "traditional" American values. These new Americans, blacker and browner, were, according to O'Reilly, not sufficiently devoted to self-reliance and therefore constituted a voting electorate that was primarily concerned with government handouts or getting "stuff." Thus, in ridiculing the apparent nontraditional values of Obama voters, O'Reilly also displayed a wishful nostalgia for an America of a bygone era. That is, he showed his desire to return to a time when, after receiving 59 percent of the white vote, a presidential candidate—in this case, Romney—would have won in an electoral landslide, *roundly defeating* someone like Obama.[24]

O'Reilly wasn't alone in exhibiting what critical whiteness scholar John T. Warren terms the "rhetorical body of whiteness."[25] Other commentators and political pundits chimed in as well. The day after the 2012 election, on his popular talk radio show, polemical commentator Rush Limbaugh claimed that "we're outnumbered" and "we've lost the country." Comedian–turned–Fox News contributor Dennis Miller, reflecting on the same election, stated that he liked the country "the way it was" and bemoaned the possibility that "it's not going to be like that anymore." Miller went on to note, "Do I think it's the America that I saw from eighteen to fifty-eight, no, I don't. . . . It's not the America that I've grown comfortable with." Ann Coulter, another popular political commentator, explicitly tied President Obama's reelection to racial demographics when she asserted, without any evidence, that "Teddy Kennedy's 1965 Immigration Act was specifically designed to change the demographics of this nation. I think Mitt Romney would have won last night if he had the same demographics Ronald Reagan had."[26]

From Bill O'Reilly to Rush Limbaugh, from Dennis Miller to Ann Coulter, the various reactions to the 2012 presidential election all represented a growing trepidation over the newfound political power of nonwhite voters. Furthermore, in the world of zero-sum politics, these commentators interpreted the electoral increase in minority voting power as a concomitant decrease in white voting power.[27] Thus, from their perspective, the growing visibility and political efficacy of racial minorities not only increased their own sense of racial awareness but also precipitated feelings of loss, grievance, and, most germane to this study, victimization.[28] It would be easy to dismiss the comments of O'Reilly et al. as individual and emotional responses to a heartbreaking electoral defeat, but four years later—after explicitly engaging in a campaign of white identity politics—former reality television star and prominent birther Donald Trump was elected president of the United States.[29] Evidence suggests that this was no coincidence.[30]

WHITE IDENTITY POLITICS

Despite having no political experience, at any level, and running on a platform that included white nationalism,[31] Donald Trump won more than three hundred Electoral College votes, including victories in the traditional Democratic strongholds of Wisconsin, Michigan, and Pennsylvania. President Trump won white voters by a margin of 21 percentage points (58 percent to 37 percent), and subsequent analysis has shown that two of the biggest motivating factors among white Trump voters were "fear of diversity" and "cultural anxiety."[32] Even though the Trump administration was marred by conflict and controversy, white voters, particularly those without a college degree, remained loyal to him, as they were the only racial group among which a majority of voters approved of the president's job performance.[33] In just one term, the Trump administration, among other things, took a more punitive stance toward illegal immigration, moved toward curtailing *legal* immigration, successfully instituted a travel ban that disproportionately affected Muslim countries, and repeatedly promised to clamp down on so-called voter fraud in communities of color.[34] Coupled with multiple controversies surrounding race, such as referring to neo-Nazis as "very fine people" and African nations as "shithole countries," as well as a fiscal policy that saw billions of dollars in taxpayer funds go to rural, predominantly white states, the now former president's continued support from a majority of white Americans is emblematic of a modern and hyperpartisan strain of white identity politics.[35]

Ashley Jardina, a political scientist at Duke University, uses sweeping data to provide a window into the evolution and growth of white identity politics in the modern era.[36] By examining racial politics from the perspective of the white majority, Jardina shows, empirically, how in-group solidarity, as opposed to out-group hostility, has become a powerful political force, motivating millions of white voters. In response to a litany of cultural, economic, and, particularly, *demographic* changes (see earlier discussion), many white Americans, according to Jardina, have turned "inward," causing them to "circle the wagons, and to see their racial group as the one that is threatened." She continues, "The distinction between white prejudice and white identity also has implications for the types of political messages elites may use to persuade whites. Politicians need not appeal to racial animus to be politically successful. . . . Instead, they might campaign to preserve the status quo, or to protect whites' collective interests."[37] Jardina's framework of white identity politics, while paradigm-shifting as a work of scholarship, transcended academia altogether and was put to the test during the 2016 presidential election; it passed with flying colors.

In their detailed and wide-ranging book *Identity Crisis: The 2016 Presidential Campaign and the Battle for the Meaning of America*, political scientists John Sides, Michael Tesler, and Lynn Vavreck marshal a comprehensive array of data to demonstrate the extent to which racial politics have changed over the last few election cycles.[38] Starting with the election of Barack Obama, both major political parties began to undergo a fundamental realignment, one that saw white voters with conservative racial attitudes defect from the Democratic Party in great numbers.[39] Before the 2008 election, white Americans saw Republicans and Democrats as equally devoted to civil rights, and less than half of white voters without a college degree could accurately identify Democrats as the party most committed to protecting the rights of nonwhite citizens.[40] The election and reelection of Barack Obama, however, clarified the politics of race, and a growing number of white voters came to view Republicans as the party of white interests and Democrats as the party of nonwhite interests. This view of racial politics was exacerbated by the contentious, and explicitly racialized, presidential election of 2016.[41]

Race, racial identity, and racial attitudes all played major roles in the presidential contest between Donald Trump and Hillary Clinton. In large part through an explicit brand of white identity politics, Donald Trump activated white racial awareness and in-group solidarity in a way that had not been seen in modern presidential politics.[42] From the moment he announced his candidacy, Trump positioned himself as the defender of traditional America, vowing to stand up to rapid cultural change, fight political correctness, and "make America great again." At almost every step of the campaign, Trump found an outsider to denigrate or a foreign threat that endangered Americans. Examples include his pledge to build a wall along our southern border, his threat to shut down all Muslim immigration into the country, and his promise to defend the American heartland by getting tough on China. Ultimately, by othering and opposing various groups of color, criticizing demographic and cultural change, and vowing to restore America to an ostensibly glorified past, President Trump successfully appealed to white racial identity, fostering an "us versus them" mentality that eventually landed him in the White House.[43]

For her part, Hillary Clinton intensified this process by candidly talking about race throughout her campaign.[44] From the Democratic primary to the general election, the former first lady, US senator, and secretary of state spoke openly about politically controversial topics such as white privilege, unconscious bias, and institutional racism. At the height of the campaign Secretary Clinton gave a national speech about the growing threat of white nationalism in the form of the alt-right, and at the Democratic National Convention she offered a primetime slot to Mothers of the Movement, a group of African American mothers who have lost sons to gun violence, including at the hands of law enforcement.[45] Furthermore, Secretary Clinton was not shy about linking xenophobia and white nationalism to Trump's popularity, doing so on multiple occasions throughout the campaign.[46] Perhaps unbeknownst to Clinton, in an election broadly conceived as white political interests versus nonwhite political interests, she was perceived, by a significant portion of the white electorate, as supporting the latter.[47]

Sides, Tesler, and Vavreck show that the 2008, 2012, and 2016 presidential elections combined to have a profound effect on white identity politics.[48] As it stands now, a substantial percentage of the white voting public views politics as a zero-sum contest between leaders who would protect white rights and those who would challenge them.[49] For their part, both major political parties have taken notice. Many Democrats have cautioned party leaders against focusing too heavily on issues pertaining to racial minorities—ironically referred to as "identity politics"—and many Republicans have leaned hard into the Donald Trump playbook, waging culture wars and making overt appeals to white solidarity.[50] As a whole, the cultural and demographic racialization of the United States, specifically in the white imagination, has linked race and partisanship in ways that are without historical precedent.[51] Empirically, sociologists and other social scientists have only begun to grapple with these changes and what they mean for the country moving forward.[52]

TOWARD A FUTURE OF WHITENESS INTERRUPTED

Whiteness interrupted, the idea that white racelessness can be challenged in clear and patterned ways, was one of the very first themes that emerged from my interview data. Within the walls of Brick City schools, seemingly raceless teachers transitioned to white teachers as whiteness itself became a visible and visceral identity that could not be ignored. A second theme, white racial victimization, compounded this process. That is, as I conducted more interviews and analyzed more data, it became obvious that, for white Brick City teachers, their budding racial identities were not random; rather, they arose out of an iterative and interactional process that saw these teachers firmly positioned as the racialized other. This spatial—and explicitly racialized—dynamic led white teachers to react in multiple ways. While only some became reactionary and lashed out at black students and black families, they *all*, at one point or another, looked inward, acknowledging their own racial identity and turning to other white teachers for comfort and solidarity.

In assessing the documented demographic and cultural changes, as well as the emergence of a real and formidable white identity politics, I have somewhat begrudgingly come to the conclusion that whiteness interrupted is now taking place on a national scale. Within the collective recesses of the white racial frame,[53] the United States of America, long considered a white space, is becoming racialized, altering the culture and the very character of the country. Although white Americans are still a powerful and highly segregated group, they become a smaller share of the national population with each passing year. A number of them worry that unless this trend is confronted and eventually defeated, time itself will continue to weaken the strength of white hegemony and threaten the security of the white habitus. Thus, everything from neighborhoods to schools, from policing to the presidency, will be challenged—and sometimes changed—by the increasing presence and cultural influence of racial minorities. Consistent with my findings, this new reality has made white racial identity much more visible, and there are increasing signs that the interrelated processes of seeing white, feeling white, and being white are manifest beyond the urban classroom.

There is no realistic way for me to predict the future of race relations in the United States, but I do believe that the various processes outlined and discussed in this book will, to a certain degree, be replicated throughout the country as a whole. As our cultural and political history demonstrates, white racial identity can be activated, motivated, and mobilized to racially regressive ends.[54] That being said, however, especially owing to intraracial diversity and a growing multiracial population, it is impossible to know how *all* white Americans will respond to a rapidly changing society. Millions of white Americans welcome these changes, with some actively working toward a more diverse and egalitarian society. Others fall somewhere between rejection and acceptance, and still others are indifferent, rarely giving much thought to broader demographic and cultural changes. Complicating matters further is the variation among minority groups. Each nonwhite group has its own history, its own cultural practices, and its own internal politics. Also, due to intersectionality, intragroup membership is far from monolithic. All told, whether surveying white or nonwhite Americans, it is difficult to predict the long-term consequences of a nationally elevated white racial identity.

In the meantime, it seems prudent to pay attention to those spaces where nonwhite racialization has already taken place. These spaces include institutions, such as urban schools, certain residential areas, or, in some cases, even entire states. States like Arizona, Nevada, Florida, Colorado, and Georgia, for example, are racing toward majority-minority status, a milestone that four others, Hawaii, California, New Mexico, and Texas, have already reached. Although they each have their own internal culture and political structure, I believe that focusing on white racial identity—and race relations more broadly—within these states offers us a window into what has heretofore been a racially uncertain future. As it stands now, race scholars need to do a better job of incorporating physical space into their methodological considerations and overall research designs. Space, like people, can be racialized.

Therefore, any rigorous analysis of racial identity, racial experience, or racial ideology must also consider the racialization of the physical world.

LIMITATIONS AND SUGGESTIONS FOR FUTURE RESEARCH

When my findings are placed within the broader literature on white racial identity, several avenues for future research emerge, primarily stemming from the limitations of the study itself. First, as significant as my data are, they come from a small sample of teachers in one school district. Future research needs to consider a variety of school settings from different parts of the country. Next, even after racialized space is taken seriously, nonwhite racial variation needs to be given greater consideration. That is, any future work on white teachers must include those from predominantly Asian schools, predominantly Latino schools, and Native American reservations. With Asian Americans and Asian immigrants broadly constructed as model minorities, Latino Americans and Latino immigrants increasingly constructed as a racial threat, and Native Americans broadly forgotten, the possibility for empirical contributions and theoretical breakthroughs appear to be considerable. Finally, at least pertaining to schools, future work needs to take socioeconomic variation into account. Many nonwhite students from middle- and upper-class backgrounds also attend racially segregated schools with a predominantly white teaching staff. Therefore, in terms of white racial identity, the impact of *affluent* nonwhite racialized space remains unexplored and unknown.

Looking beyond urban education, other professions also need to be considered. While each may present its own set of challenges, particularly related to access, studying white correctional officers who work in prisons or jails, white police officers who work in inner-city communities, or white social workers who primarily serve people of color all seem to be worthwhile research endeavors. Even though none of these hypothetical studies would adequately account for socioeconomic variation, selection effects, or existing power differentials between white and nonwhite communities, each, in its own way, still has the potential to be substantively rich and theoretically significant. Also, professional spaces are not the only kinds of racialized spaces. In the future, researchers should pay attention to those white Americans who spend significant amounts of time in nonwhite spaces due to personal circumstances. Friendship networks, residential environments, and even intimate relationships all serve as potential opportunities to study the effects of nonwhite racialized space on white racial identity.

From a methodological standpoint, future studies must attend to the various limitations that currently exist within the research literature. To date, the vast majority of work on whiteness and white racial identity has been qualitative, historical, philosophical, or otherwise narratively constructed. Relatively few studies have utilized statistical or survey methods.[55] Going forward, more quantitative research is needed to complement, and empirically extend, the already robust historical, philosophical, and qualitative literatures. Also, within the pantheon of qualitative methods, few scholars have ventured outside the realm of in-depth interviews.[56] That includes this very study. In order to take the study of white racialization in new and empirically rich directions, more researchers need to utilize ethnography or participant observation in their work. Finally, considering the racial and material domination that contextualizes white racial identity, there remains a considerable need for public sociology and participatory action research.[57]

CONCLUSION

Today white people in America can no longer take whiteness for granted. The idea of whiteness as a raceless, meaningless identity, while by no means gone, has become harder to rationalize, particularly given its growing visibility to white people themselves. The demographics of the country are changing, deaths of despair are rising, and, just like their counterparts in the formal labor market, the wages of whiteness are flat.[58] In this study I have tried to analyze several of these processes on a much more localized scale. Instead of asking the general question *What does it mean to be white?*, I ask a similar yet more specific question: *What does it mean to be white in nonwhite racialized spaces?* The resegregation of public schools, in conjunction with the overwhelming whiteness of teaching, presented me with a unique opportunity to study white racial experience in different, and even opposing, racialized environments.

Ultimately, the data I collected for this project were comprehensive, theoretically illuminating, and empirically grounded. Owing to their race, white Brick City teachers felt under siege. In their own telling, they were stigmatized, sanctioned, and virtually powerless to alter the underlying conditions that led to their mistreatment. From a macro standpoint, similar to the way white teachers spoke about whiteness within Brick City schools, white racial identity throughout the broader United States is more aware of itself. It is more visible, more sensitive to (white) racial victimization, and more receptive to explicitly racial—or even racist—appeals. Unlike white Brick City teachers, however, a substantial number of white Americans nationwide are actively resisting underlying conditions, decrying demographic change, and embracing white identity politics. Thus, from the reemergence of white nationalism to the rise of Donald Trump, white racial identity is currently being mobilized on a national scale. Although this study is not without limitations, it does help to identify, analyze, and explain the broad, ongoing, and multifaceted process of *whiteness interrupted.*

APPENDIX: METHODOLOGY AND RESEARCH DESIGN

Science, in its traditional construction, aims for abstract knowledge—
timeless and universal—and the science-based professions draw their
legitimacy from an abstract and impersonal notion of expertise.
—MARJORIE DEVAULT, *Liberating Method*

Qualitative research thus refers to the meanings, concepts, definitions,
character, characteristics, metaphors, symbols, and descriptions of things.
In contrast, quantitative research refers to counts and measures of things.
—BRUCE BERG, *Qualitative Research Methods for the Social Sciences*

Interviewing gives us access to the observations of others.
—ROBERT WEISS, *Learning from Strangers*

QUALITATIVE METHODS

In describing the promise of qualitative methods, author and research methodologist John Creswell writes, "I think metaphorically of qualitative research as an intricate fabric composed of minute threads, many colors, different textures, and various blends of material." He continues, "The fabric is
not explained easily or simply."[1] As opposed to quantitative methods, which

are primarily concerned with *quantity*, at the root of qualitative methods is a question about *quality*.[2] Qualitative methods do not seek to provide broad generalizations or causal linkages—which, to be clear, are both vitally important to social scientific inquiry—but instead aim to provide an in-depth understanding of human interactions and various social processes.

Qualitative methods are especially adept at examining and understanding those social phenomena that do not lend themselves easily to counts and precise measurement.[3] While there are several drawbacks to such an orientation—namely, the lack of representativeness and generalizability—there are also certain benefits, including an intimate understanding of people, places, and events, a firsthand account of various social processes, and the ability to analyze human interaction from multiple vantage points.[4] Furthermore, qualitative research methods allow for inductive analysis, or the possibility of generating theory that emerges directly from the data itself.[5] As a result, research studies that employ qualitative methods often end up in very different places from where they began.

The complexity and diversity of qualitative methods enable scholars to investigate a wide range of social phenomena in the real world. Like any other methodological paradigm, qualitative research works best on certain kinds of questions. More specifically, qualitative methods are quite suitable for problems, questions, or issues that need to be explored.[6] At its core, this study was an exploratory project. My research design and selected methods were devised to explore the racialized experiences and meaning-making processes of white teachers who work in predominantly black schools. Principally, I wanted to examine the way white teachers themselves understood their lives as racial beings, and I also wanted to know whether or not this understanding varied in and between differently racialized environments. Given my theoretical and substantive focus, I ultimately decided that semi-structured, in-depth interviews afforded me the best opportunity to answer my questions successfully.[7]

THE RESPONSIVE INTERVIEW MODEL

The responsive interview model is a qualitative research technique designed to enable the interviewer and interviewee to construct data in a way that is mutually beneficial to both.[8] The interviewer gets rich and sophisticated data, while the interviewee gets the chance to play a meaningful role in the data construction process. Also, the responsive interview model builds on itself through different stages of data collection and analysis. That is, each new stage is, in large part, a product of those that came before it. New questions emerge from the answers given to old ones, and each additional interview purposefully incorporates the events, concepts, and themes of previous interviews. Finally, while the responsive interview model builds on itself, it maintains enough openness and flexibility to make space for new information as data collection continues. This process is repeated until saturation is reached.

The responsive interview model has four central features: richness of data, conversational partnerships, mutual construction of data, and analytical flexibility. Conversational partnerships differ from other interviewer-interviewee relationships because the researcher eschews any semblance of authority and treats all study participants as partners in the research process. Much like other critical epistemologies, conversational partnerships assume that real people know and can speak to their own reality better than any outside observer.[9] Although interviewees are not always attendant to historical and existing structures of power that contextualize their lives, their experiences—and the way they make sense of those experiences—*are real to them*. It is incumbent upon us as researchers to respect and value the way conversational partners experience and make sense of their own lives, even as we search for higher empirical truth.[10]

Building off the idea of conversational partnerships, the responsive interview model is a research method in which the interviewer and interviewee engage in the mutual construction of data. In this sense, scholars do not come into the interview with an expert/novice mindset, or with the intention of imposing their will on research participants. To the contrary, given that it is they who are recalling and interpreting their own experiences, conversational partners are integral to the type and quality of data that are constructed. Also, in the responsive interview model, researchers have to be able to respond in the moment. While it is useful, and highly salient, to build on events, concepts, and themes from previous interviews—as well as the broader research literature—ultimately each individual interview is its own entity, and all interviewees have their own "distinct experience, knowledge, and perspective."[11] With this in mind, researchers have to be able to respond to what is being said contemporaneously, whether or not it comports with data that have already been collected.

Taken together, conversational partnerships and the mutual construction of data often lead to a rich collection of stories, events, concepts, and themes that provide a window into whatever social process is under study. The rich data collected in the responsive interview go beyond the surface of individual experience and instead delve deeper into the interpretations and feelings that are engendered by experience. It is not enough for a conversational partner to merely recall a process or an event that took place sometime in their life. The goal is to get them to share how they experienced it in the moment, how they responded to it, and how they make sense of it now. It is the responsibility of the interviewer to create an environment in which this type of data gathering is possible. With the assistance of conversational partners, the ultimate goal of the responsive interview model is to construct nuanced, rich, and complex data that vividly, and sometimes intimately, illustrate how interview respondents make sense of and talk about their own social worlds.

Finally, taking its cue from grounded theory, the responsive interview model employs a flexible, yet systematic, mode of data analysis.[12] First conceptualized by Barney Glaser and Anselm Strauss in 1967, grounded theory, with its inductive approach, seeks to counterbalance the methodological hegemony of deductive analysis in the social sciences.[13] That is, rather than using quantitative techniques to test existing theories, grounded theory posits that data itself should supply the building blocks of theory construction. Tenets of grounded theory include the constant comparative method, memo writing, and the strict belief that everything, from initial research questions to the final theoretical model, should emanate from actual data.[14] These tenets and several others are all central to data collection and data analysis in the responsive interview model.[15]

PURPOSEFUL/THEORETICAL SAMPLING

One of the benefits of the responsive interview model is the possibility of theoretical and purposeful sampling. Although the two techniques are similar in application, there are substantive differences between them.[16] Purposeful sampling is similar to theoretical sampling in that they both identify a specific subset of the population for study. The primary difference is that while purposeful sampling seeks to gain a deeper understanding about the lives, experiences, and worldviews of certain individuals, theoretical sampling is more concerned with building a general theory about a specific process or phenomena.[17] Ideally, though, both purposeful and theoretical sampling identify and recruit a specific group of people who all have the unique ability to speak to a particular process or experience. Thus, the data collected from these individuals are considered reliable, rich, and relevant to the topic at hand.

This study had a very explicit focus: to empirically examine how nonwhite racialized space affects the social construction of whiteness and white racial identity. More specifically, I wanted to explore the way white teachers experience, make meaning of, and discuss their own racial identities within predominantly black schools. Initially, when I first sought to incorporate nonwhite racialized space into the study of white racial identity, I did not have a clear idea about how best to proceed. I spent a considerable amount of time brainstorming and trying to come up with a suitable sampling frame that could substantively speak to the questions I had about racialized space and the social construction of whiteness. At one point, I stared making lists of different scenarios, occupations, and other physical spaces that, even if temporarily, made white people the numerical minority. The initial conceptualization of this project, specifically in terms of sampling frame, research site, and access, was somewhat difficult.

In thinking through different research possibilities, I recalled Mrs. Wilkes and how she talked about race and white racial identity at Capitol Heights. If you recall, Mrs. Wilkes believed that being white was a disadvantage and that it unfairly limited her overall chances of successfully teaching black students. Rather than referring to whiteness in a general sense, Mrs. Wilkes made a specific claim about a specific space: a predominantly black school. In her telling, white teachers at Capitol Heights were subjected to a localized form of racial stigmatism and racialized mistreatment, and it was something that they thought about often and openly discussed. From then on, my thoughts about this project became increasingly clear. As I learned just how extensive the demographic gap between white teachers and nonwhite students was in many inner-city schools, I committed to focusing on white teachers in urban education. Having settled on a sampling frame, I then turned my attention to access.

RECRUITMENT/SNOWBALL SAMPLING

To recruit research participants for this project, I employed a snowball sample. Snowball sampling, although often done out of convenience, is not necessarily a convenience sampling technique.[18] According to the late qualitative methodologist Bruce Berg, convenience samples rely on "available subjects" or "those who are close at hand or easily accessible," while snowball samples are a reliable way to "locate subjects with certain attributes or characteristics necessary in the study."[19] At its core, snowball sampling entails the intentional enlistment of research participants in locating and recruiting additional research participants.[20] For me, this process took on a specific form. At the conclusion of each interview, I asked my respective interviewees if they knew of other white teachers who worked in schools with predominantly black student bodies and might be willing to talk about their racialized experiences. Starting with several personal acquaintances who met the specific parameters of my target population, I conducted several rounds of snowball sampling, recruiting and ultimately interviewing thirty-two white teachers from the Brick City School District: twenty-five women and seven men.[21]

The teachers who participated in this study were carefully screened on the basis that they all grew up in predominantly white neighborhoods, all currently live in predominantly white neighborhoods, and all have predominantly white social networks. This screening process was designed to ensure that the racialized environments of their respective workplaces—"black schools"—were experiential departures from those spaces that shaped the bulk of their past and present life experiences. I conducted preliminary phone interviews with potential respondents, asking them a series of questions about their exposure to, and experiences with, people from different racial backgrounds. To varying degrees, the teachers who composed my final sample acknowledged having little contact and sparse experiences with racial minorities outside of Brick City schools. What's more, with few exceptions, teachers also admitted that the majority of the contact they did have with racial minorities was, at best, superficial in nature. Thus, the racial context of Brick City schools provided white teachers with a real and meaningful departure from what they experienced in almost every other aspect of their lives.

ENTERING THE FIELD

"But why does it have to be white teachers?" Mr. Davidson, a high school math teacher, questioned why I wanted to interview white teachers from the BCSD. At the start of our interview, Mr. Davidson displayed a healthy skepticism, and even suspicion, about the ultimate purpose of my study. Although my interviews ended up going well, Mr. Davidson was not the only teacher who showed up to our face-to-face meeting with lingering uncertainty. Despite my best efforts, numerous teachers came into the interview with questions about why I wanted to speak with them personally. This reality led me to reevaluate my recruitment process, especially the content of my initial emails and phone conversations. I realized that I needed to be absolutely clear about why I was conducting this research and why I specifically wanted to interview white teachers from predominantly black schools. I also realized that interrogating whiteness, particularly by interviewing white people themselves, would take an incredible amount of reflection, reassessment, and reflexivity.

Although there is a considerable literature on the importance of "insider/outsider" status when conducting qualitative research, there is still no consensus on how best to handle demographic differences between researcher and research participant.[22] As a black man, the process of interviewing white teachers—the vast majority of whom were women—about their racial identities, was methodologically and experientially challenging.[23] What's more, previous studies have shown that many white people are reluctant or hesitant to openly discuss issues of race and racism.[24] Thus, navigating my outsider status, as well as the sensitive topic of white racial identity, proved to be a difficult, though not insurmountable, hurdle to clear. In the end, perhaps what I learned most from this experience is that when it comes to in-depth interviews—and qualitative fieldwork more broadly—repetition is key.

As I reached out to potential interviewees, particularly after several teachers showed up to our interview with lingering questions and concerns, I took great care to ensure that both my reason for inquiry and my overall research design were presented in a clear and transparent manner. For some, this required multiple phone calls, and on two occasions I was specifically asked to provide relevant literature on the overall concept of whiteness.[25] In any instance where I felt the potential interviewee was troubled or triggered by the possibility of opening up and speaking about their racialized experiences, I did not pursue a formal interview. Also, when presented with concerns during phone conversations, I addressed each of them openly and honestly, and if any teacher seemed reluctant to talk during the interview itself, I reminded them that they could halt the interview at any moment for any reason, no questions asked. Ultimately, this process led to a relatively smooth transition from identification to recruitment to interview to analysis.

DATA ANALYSIS IN THE RESPONSIVE INTERVIEW MODEL

There are seven steps to data analysis in the responsive interview model. First, each interview is transcribed and summarized. Researchers need to make sure that each summary includes "the main points expressed, along with the name (or the pseudonym) of the interviewee, the time and location of the interview," and "the reasons the interviewee was included in the study."[26] Also, memos with interesting passages and notable quotes should be kept throughout each interview. Second, each interview should be coded for "relevant concepts, themes, events, examples, names, places, or dates."[27] Coding in the responsive interview model should be rigorous, thoughtful, and deliberate. Third, relevant codes should be identified and sorted from across a number of interviews, culminating in a single data file and file summary of each code. These individual files, while not mutually exclusive, will each hold data pertaining to specific concepts, themes, quotes, events, and so on.

Fourth, the data within each file need to be sorted, resorted, and summarized. During this step, excerpts between different subgroups should be compared to one another, and any similarities or differences should be noted. Fifth, after analyzing the original and resorted data files, a picture should begin to emerge, sometimes more than one. At this point, different pictures should be compared to one another, and it is up to the researchers to weigh each of them and determine which one best represents the process or processes under study. Sixth, each composite should be used to generate new questions for subsequent interviews, and any additional data should be contrasted, and possibly merged, with the already existing data files. Finally, researchers, particularly those seeking to generate theory, should determine how well their results generalize to other empirical processes. This iterative process should be repeated until theoretical saturation is reached.

As I looked over my raw interview data, countless concepts and themes leaped from the pages, forcing me to decide which ones to code and which ones to bypass. At first, I decided that I would take my time and code every single concept and theme, thereby exploring every possible picture that could be painted by the data. I soon realized that such an approach was untenable and that even though the data presented numerous options, I, as the researcher, would have to make hard choices and decide how best to proceed. In fact, as the architects of the responsive interview model themselves note, when it comes to the overabundance of concepts and themes in your raw interview data, "you cannot code them all, but you want to make sure you examine everything in your data that is relevant to your research problem."[28] Following this advice, I focused my coding on those concepts and themes that specifically addressed racialized space, white racial identity, and white racial discourse.

My data analysis was a deliberate yet straightforward process. Once I completed an interview, I would immediately transcribe and summarize it, making sure to include things like age, gender, teaching experience, the tone and tenor of the interview, my rapport with the interviewee, and where the interview took place. Next I coded each interview, looking for relevant concepts, themes, events, examples, and notable quotations. With each additional interview, I compared and contrasted codes, looking for any similarities, contradictions, and emergent patterns within the data. Each code, spanning multiple interviews, was then given its own data file. I studied the content within each file, constantly comparing it to data from old and new interview transcriptions. By doing so, I was able to update and improve my analysis, incorporating new codes and augmenting old ones based on the data. After several rounds of comparing and contrasting codes, I reviewed and resorted each individual data file, using the new files to improve my protocol for subsequent interviews. I continued this iterative process throughout the remainder of my time in the field.

THEORETICAL SATURATION

Glenn Bowen describes theoretical saturation—also referred to as data saturation—as the point "when the researcher gathers data to the point of diminishing returns, when nothing new is being added." He continues, "Theoretical saturation, in effect, is the point at which no new insights are obtained, no new themes are identified, and no issues arise regarding a category of data."[29] Theoretical saturation is a trademark of grounded theory, which, again, serves as one of the foundational pillars of the responsive interview model.[30] Therefore, when working toward saturation, this research followed many of the steps, and in some ways took on the appearance, of a grounded theory study. Data collection and data analysis took place simultaneously, which allowed for a cyclical process of fieldwork informing analysis and analysis informing fieldwork. With this methodological and analytical framework in mind, my ultimate goal was to get to the point where each additional interview provided no new insight about the impact of racialized space on white racial identity.

Aside from the introductory questions that were designed to build rapport, the only standardized aspect of my interview protocol was the section that pertained to white racial awareness. Beyond that, each version of my protocol, and thus each interview, was predicated on a combination of prior data analysis and the contemporaneous interview itself. While all but my first interviews were influenced by those that came before, I made sure that each individual interview retained a certain amount of sovereignty, owing both to the general structure and corresponding flexibility of the responsive interview model.[31] This methodological design led to a superfluity of unstructured data. These data were similar enough that, after just a handful of interviews, a composite picture began to emerge, yet distinct enough that each additional interview provided new concepts and themes to incorporate into my overall analysis. After several dozen interviews, this latter point became less and less pronounced. Thus, I tempered the pace at which I sought new interviewees from the Brick City School District.

I spent close to two years sifting through over a thousand pages, including interview transcriptions, interview notes, file summaries, file resummaries, and summary memos. I analyzed various codes, excerpts, concepts, themes, and notable quotations—both within and across interviews—and during this time several composites began to emerge. I recognized early on that the concept of white racelessness did not hold within Brick City Schools and that neither age nor gender, years of experience nor political ideology did much to alter the development and expression of localized racial identities. Also, as my fieldwork progressed, the themes of white racial victimization, colorblind discourse, and postracial politics permeated my interview data, leading to a more complete and thematically sound picture. As this particular composite continued to evolve, I integrated its core elements into my interview proto-col and tested it against new data. Initially, this iterative process yielded new insights and took my analysis in new directions, but as my interview total increased, each additional teacher yielded little to no new information. After interviewing thirty-two teachers, I reached theoretical saturation and for-mally exited the field.

REFLECTION AND REFLEXIVITY

In social scientific inquiry, there necessarily exists a critical interplay be-tween various research methodologies, structures of power, and the demo-graphic identities of researchers and research participants.[32] Historically and today, sociologists and other social scientists have routinely influenced—and have been influenced by—the cultural, political, and economic contexts in which they carried out their work.[33] Although time and maturity have, to a certain degree, mitigated these processes, it remains true that the "social" in social science cannot be neatly separated from the "social" in social context or the "social" in social interaction.[34] Therefore, demographic variation be-tween researcher and respondent, particularly within a stratified society, can be just as integral to the research process as the collection, analysis, and dis-semination of data.[35] This reality did not escape me as I repeatedly sat down to conduct interviews with people who (1) looked nothing like me, and (2) had substantially different backgrounds, life experiences, and, in many cases, worldviews.

Interracial discussions of race and racial identity are fraught with possibilities of consternation and confrontation.[36] A racial and cultural mismatch will sometimes, though not inevitably, lead to a genuine miscommunication about sensitive subject matter.[37] The same is true for gender.[38] With these and other adverse possibilities casting a shadow over the entire interview process, I was pleasantly surprised by the fruitfulness of my initial set of interviews. On meeting up with interviewees, I never dove right into the interview; instead I took some time to just talk and relieve any lingering tension. Thus, between preinterview phone conversations and rapport-building dialogue, I spent a considerable amount of time working to assuage the doubts and concerns of every teacher who participated in this study. From both a methodological and a substantive standpoint, this strategy paid off, as the vast majority of conversational partners—even after an initial bit of reluctance—opened up about their thoughts, feelings, and experiences in illuminating, and at times emotional, ways.

For my part, I stayed true to the responsive interview model, never straying too far from its core methods and procedures. My questions not only were designed to invoke thinking but also were delivered in a welcoming, nonthreatening, and nonconfrontational manner. Furthermore, moving beyond the responsive interview model and thinking about qualitative methods more broadly, self-reflection and reflexivity are of the utmost importance. Both self-reflection and reflexivity were instrumental throughout my time in the field, as the sensitive subject matter of race, whiteness, and white racial identity yielded numerous answers that, for an African American man, had the potential to be very upsetting. Wittingly or unwittingly, teachers routinely expressed their belief in racial stereotypes, and on multiple occasions, they made statements about racial inequality that were simply not true. Through it all, I remained calm, kept my composure, and monitored my reactions accordingly. At no time did I break from my cordial and respectful demeanor, not even when made to listen to dehumanizing and hurtful stereotypes about African Americans and other people of color.[39]

Although initially it was somewhat difficult to fully digest the litany of racialized statements, racial stereotypes, and, on several occasions, outright racism expressed by white Brick City teachers, I did find that it became easier over time. Because data collection and data analysis in the responsive interview model occur simultaneously, I was constantly engaging with interview data in real time, a process that allowed me to become more accustomed to, and better prepared for, the possibility of racially inflammatory discourse. Also, I constantly reminded myself that *I chose this project*. Nobody forced me to study race, nor did anyone demand that I investigate whiteness. These were choices that I made of my own volition, and if the subject matter was too much for me to handle, then I had no business taking on such an endeavor. Finally, throughout the entire process of identification and recruitment, I repeatedly stressed to my conversational partners that I wanted them to open up and be honest with me. Therefore, it would have been unethical—and quite frankly unfair—for me to then turn around and chastise or otherwise judge them upon their doing so. Thus, self-reflection and reflexivity kept me grounded while navigating the fraught, stressful, and potentially tumultuous terrain of mixed-race, mixed-gender fieldwork.

NOTES

PREFACE AND ACKNOWLEDGMENTS

Epigraphs: Martin Luther King Jr., *Why We Can't Wait* (New York: Signet Classics, 2000), 69–70; Alison Bailey, "Strategic Ignorance," in *Race and Epistemologies of Ignorance*, ed. Shannon Sullivan and Nancy Tuana (Albany: SUNY Press, 2007), 80; George Floyd was murdered by police officers on May 25, 2020, in Minneapolis, Minnesota, and "I can't breathe" were a few of his very last words.

1. Floyd has not been the only African American man to speak these words while being killed by police officers. In the summer of 2014, Eric Garner, accused of selling loose cigarettes, was choked to death by a police officer, Daniel Pantaleo, in Staten Island, New York. Garner's death was also captured on film, and in the video he can be heard saying, "I can't breathe" a total of eleven times before eventually succumbing to his injuries.

2. This list is by no means exhaustive. Also, it should be noted that several other high-profile cases, such as Trayvon Martin, Jordan David, and Ahmaud Arbery, also involved the murder of unarmed African Americans. In these three cases, however, the accused assailants were not working as police officers.

3. Similar to King's assassination, Floyd's murder has set off a wave of both peaceful protests and violent riots. Also, unlike protests and riots of years and decades past—the 1992 Los Angeles riot, for example—the reaction to Floyd's death, similar to the reaction to King's, has been far-reaching and widespread, accruing in a number of states as opposed to one isolated locality.

4. Alex Woodward, "Hundreds of Thousands of Protestors Take to America's Streets to Call for Racial Justice," *Independent*, June 7, 2020, https://www.independent.co.uk/news/world/americas/george-floyd-protest-black-lives-matter-memorial-a9552806.html.

5. For domestic protests, see Lara Putnam, Erica Chenoweth, and Jeremy Pressman, "The Floyd Protests Are the Broadest in U.S. History—and Are Spreading to White,

Small-Town America," *Washington Post*, June 6, 2020, https://www.washingtonpost.com/politics/2020/06/06/floyd-protests-are-broadest-us-history-are-spreading-white-small-town-america/. For international protests, see Rachel Pannett, James Marson, and Gabriele Steinhauser, "George Floyd's Death in U.S. Sparks Outcry Abroad," *Wall Street Journal*, June 3, 2020, https://www.wsj.com/articles/george-floyds-death-in-u-s-sparks-outcry-abroad-11591123234.

6. Nate Cohn and Kevin Quealy, "How Public Opinion Has Moved on Black Lives Matter," *New York Times*, June 10, 2020, https://www.nytimes.com/interactive/2020/06/10/upshot/black-lives-matter-attitudes.html.

7. For Democrats, see Ed Kilgore, "Congressional Democrats Unveil Police Reform Bill," *New York Magazine*, June 8, 2020, https://nymag.com/intelligencer/2020/06/congressional-democrats-unveil-police-reform-bill.html. For Republicans, see Lisa Hagan, "Republicans Consider Police Reform Bill," *US News and World Report*, June 8, 2020, https://www.usnews.com/news/national-news/articles/2020-06-12/republicans-in-congress-consider-police-reform-bills.

8. For the NBA, see "Adam Silver, NBA Teams Express Outrage after George Floyd's Death," NBA.com, June 11, 2020, https://www.nba.com/article/2020/05/31/nba-teams-respond-tragic-death-george-floyd. For the NFL, see "Rodger Goodell Issues Statement on Death of George Floyd, Nationwide Protests," NFL.com, May 30, 2020, https://www.nfl.com/news/roger-goodell-issues-statement-on-killing-of-george-floyd-nationwide-protests.

9. For just one example of athletes, see Cindy Boren, "Michael Jordan Pledges 100 Million to Improve Social Justice Because 'This Is a Tipping Point,'" *Washington Post*, June 7, 2020, https://www.washingtonpost.com/sports/2020/06/07/michael-jordan-pledged-100-million-improve-social-justice-because-this-is-tipping-point/. For celebrities, see Christi Carras, "White Celebrities Partner with NAACP to 'Take Responsibility' for Racism," *Los Angeles Times*, June 11, 2020, https://www.latimes.com/entertainment-arts/story/2020-06-11/i-take-responsibility-video-white-celebrities-naacp.

10. For Netflix and Amazon Prime, see Todd Spangler, "Netflix Launches 'Black Lives Matter' Collection of Movies, TV Shows, and Documentaries," *Variety*, June 10, 2020, https://variety.com/2020/digital/news/netflix-black-lives-matter-collection-1234630160/; Thomas Umstead, "Streaming Services, Cable Nets Show Support for Black Community amid George Floyd Protests," Multichannel.com, May 31, 2020, https://www.multichannel.com/news/netflix-amazon-prime-show-support-black-lives-matter-amid-george-floyd-protests. For *New York Times* Bestsellers List, see Marguerite Ward, "The *New York Times* Bestsellers List This Week Is Almost Entirely Comprised of Books about Race and White Privilege in America," *Business Insider*, June 11, 2020, https://www.businessinsider.com/new-york-times-bestseller-list-books-about-race-in-america-2020-6.

11. For NASCAR, see Steve Almasy, "NASCAR Bans Confederate Flags at All Races, Events," CNN.com, June 10, 2020, https://www.cnn.com/2020/06/10/us/nascar-bans-confederate-flag-spt-trnd/index.html. For military bases, see Rebecca Kheel, "Pentagon Leaders Open to Renaming Army Bases Named after Confederate Leaders,"

The Hill, June 8, 2020, https://thehill.com/policy/defense/501736-army-head-open-to
-renaming-bases-named-after-confederate-leaders.

12. Patrick Hipes, "How to Watch George Floyd's Funeral Online and on TV,"
Deadline.com, June 9, 2020, https://deadline.com/2020/06/george-floyd-funeral
-livestream-houston-how-to-watch-online-tv-1202953901/.

13. See Reñee Graham, "Support for Black Lives Matter Is Dropping—among
White Americans," *Boston Globe*, September 1, 2020, https://www.bostonglobe.com
/2020/09/01/opinion/support-black-lives-matter-is-dropping-among-white
-americans/.

INTRODUCTION

Epigraphs: Ruth Frankenberg, *White Women, Race Matters: The Social Construction
of Whiteness* (Minneapolis: University of Minnesota Press, 1993), 228–229; Karyn D.
McKinney, *Being White: Stories of Race and Racism* (New York: Routledge, 2005), 3;
Monica McDermott and Frank L. Samson, "White Racial and Ethnic Identity in the
United States," *Annual Review of Sociology* 31 (2005): 256.

1. In order to maintain confidentiality, I use pseudonyms for all teacher, student,
and school names throughout the book.

2. John Hartigan, *Racial Situations: Class Predicaments of Whiteness in Detroit*
(Princeton, NJ: Princeton University Press, 1999); McDermott and Samson, "White
Racial and Ethnic Identity"; Pamela Perry, *Shades of White: White Kids and Racial
Identities in High School* (Durham, NC: Duke University Press, 2002).

3. For a nonexhaustive overview, see Richard D. Alba, *Ethnic Identity: The Transformation of White America* (New Haven, CT: Yale University Press, 1990); Robin J. Di-
Angelo and David Allen, "'My Feelings Are Not about You': Personal Experience as a
Move of Whiteness," *InterActions: UCLA Journal of Education and Information Studies*
2, no. 2 (2006), https://escholarship.org/uc/item/6dk67960; Richard Delgado and Jean
Stefancic, eds., *Critical White Studies: Looking behind the Mirror* (Philadelphia: Tem-
ple University Press, 1997); Ashley W. Doane and Eduardo Bonilla-Silva, eds., *White
Out: The Continuing Significance of Racism* (New York: Routledge, 2003); Frankenberg,
White Women, Race Matters; Grace Elizabeth Hale, *Making Whiteness: The Culture of
Segregation in the South, 1890–1940* (New York: Vintage Books, 2010); Janet E. Helms,
Black and White Racial Identity: Theory, Research, and Practice (Westport, CT: Green-
wood, 1990); Mike Hill, *Whiteness: A Critical Reader* (New York: NYU Press, 1997);
Cheryl Hyde, "The Meanings of Whiteness," *Qualitative Sociology* 18, no. 1 (1995):
87–95; Matthew F. Jacobson, *Whiteness of a Different Color: European Immigrants and
the Alchemy of Race* (Cambridge, MA: Harvard University Press, 1999); Zeus Leonardo,
"The Color of Supremacy: Beyond the Discourse of 'White Privilege,'" *Educational Philosophy and Theory* 36, no. 2 (2004): 137–152; Amanda E. Lewis, "There Is No 'Race' in
the Schoolyard: Color-Blind Ideology in an (Almost) All-White School," *American Educational Research Journal* 38, no. 4 (2001): 781–811; Amanda E. Lewis, "What Group?
Studying Whites and Whiteness in the Era of Colorblindness," *Sociological Theory* 22,
no. 4 (2004); George Lipsitz, *The Possessive Investment in Whiteness: How White People
Profit from Identity Politics* (Philadelphia: Temple University Press, 2006); Ian Haney

López, *White by Law: The Legal Construction of Race* (New York: NYU Press, 1997); McDermott and Samson, "White Racial and Ethnic Identity"; Peggy McIntosh, "White Privilege: Unpacking the Invisible Knapsack," *Peace and Freedom Magazine*, July/August 1989, 10–12; Alice McIntyre, *Making Meaning of Whiteness: Exploring Racial Identity with White Teachers* (Albany: SUNY Press, 1997); McKinney, *Being White*; Charles W. Mills, *The Racial Contract* (Ithaca, NY: Cornell University Press, 1997); Nell I. Painter, *The History of White People* (New York: Norton, 2010); Beverly D. Tatum, *Why Are All the Black Kids Sitting Together in the Cafeteria? And Other Conversations about Race*, 20th anniv. ed. (New York: Basic Books, 2017); George Yancy, *Look, a White! Philosophical Essays on Whiteness* (Philadelphia: Temple University Press, 2012).

4. On whiteness as the raceless norm, see Harlon Dalton, "Failing to See," in *White Privilege: Essential Readings on the Other Side of Racism*, 5th ed., ed. Paula S. Rothenberg (New York: Worth, 2016), 15–18; Ashley W. Doane, "Rethinking Whiteness Studies," in Doane and Bonilla-Silva, *White Out*, 3–20; Richard Dyer, "The Matter of Whiteness," in Rothenberg, *White Privilege*, 9–14; Toni Morrison, *Playing in the Dark: Whiteness and the Literary Imagination* (New York: Vintage Books, 1993); Yancy, *Look, a White!* On whiteness as a form of structural privilege, see Cynthia Kaufman, "A User's Guide to White Privilege," *Radical Philosophy Review* 4, nos. 1–2 (2001): 30–38; McIntosh, "White Privilege"; Rothenberg, *White Privilege*. On whiteness as emanating from a particular standpoint, see Robin J. DiAngelo, "'Why Can't We All Just Be Individuals?': Countering the Discourse of Individualism in Anti-racist Education," *Inter-Actions: UCLA Journal of Education and Information Studies* 6, no. 1 (2010), https://escholarship.org/uc/item/5fm4h8wm; DiAngelo and Allen, "'My Feelings Are Not about You'"; Frankenberg, *White Women, Race Matters*; Tukufu Zuberi and Eduardo Bonilla-Silva, eds., *White Logic, White Methods: Racism and Methodology* (Lanham, MD: Rowman and Littlefield, 2008).

5. Alba, *Ethnic Identity*; Cheryl I. Harris, "Whiteness as Property," *Harvard Law Review* 106, no. 8 (1993): 1707–1791; Jacobson, *Whiteness of a Different Color*; Haney López, *White by Law*; David R. Roediger, *Working toward Whiteness: How America's Immigrants Became White; The Strange Journey from Ellis Island to the Suburbs* (New York: Basic Books, 2006); Mary C. Waters, *Ethnic Options: Choosing Identities in America* (Berkeley: University of California Press, 1990).

6. Mary Bucholtz, "The Whiteness of Nerds: Superstandard English and Racial Markedness," *Journal of Linguistic Anthropology* 11, no. 1 (2001): 84–100; Doane and Bonilla-Silva, *White Out*; Evelyn N. Glenn, "Yearning for Lightness: Transnational Circuits in the Marketing and Consumption of Skin Lighteners," *Gender and Society* 22, no. 3 (2008): 281–302; Harris, "Whiteness as Property"; Margaret L. Hunter, "Buying Racial Capital: Skin-Bleaching and Cosmetic Surgery in a Globalized World," *Journal of Pan African Studies* 4, no. 4 (2011): 142–164.

7. For detailed critiques, see Eric Arnesen, "Whiteness and the Historians' Imagination," *International Labor and Working-Class History* 60, no. 3 (2001): 3–32; Douglas Hartmann, Joseph Gerteis, and Paul R. Croll, "An Empirical Assessment of Whiteness Theory: Hidden from How Many?," *Social Problems* 56, no. 3 (2009): 403–424; McDermott and Samson, "White Racial and Ethnic Identity."

8. Dalton, "Failing to See"; Doane, "Rethinking Whiteness Studies"; Dyer, "The Matter of Whiteness"; Lipsitz, *The Possessive Investment in Whiteness*.

9. Michelle Fine, Lois Weis, Judi Addelston, and Julia Marusza, "Secure Times: Constructing White Working-Class Masculinities in the Late 20th Century," *Gender and Society* 11, no. 1 (1997): 52–68; Hartigan, *Racial Situations*; Lorraine Delia Kenny, *Daughters of Suburbia: Growing Up White, Middle Class, and Female* (New Brunswick, NJ: Rutgers University Press, 2000); Monica McDermott, *Working-Class White: The Making and Unmaking of Race Relations* (Berkeley: University of California Press, 2006); Lynn Weber, "A Conceptual Framework for Understanding Race, Class, Gender, and Sexuality," *Psychology of Women Quarterly* 22, no. 1 (1998): 13–32.

10. For several notable exceptions, see Hartigan, *Racial Situations*; Charles A. Gallagher, "White Racial Formation: Into the 21st Century," in *Critical White Studies: Looking behind the Mirror*, ed. Richard Delgado and Jean Stefancic (Philadelphia: Temple University Press, 1997), 6–11; Lauri Johnson, "'My Eyes Have Been Opened': White Teachers and Racial Awareness," *Journal of Teacher Education* 53, no. 2 (2002): 153–167; McKinney, *Being White*; Edward W. Morris, *An Unexpected Minority: White Kids in an Urban School* (New Brunswick, NJ: Rutgers University Press, 2006); Perry, *Shades of White*.

11. Critical whiteness studies is an interdisciplinary field of research that explicitly focuses on the history, attitudes, and lived experiences of whites in America and abroad. Several relevant anthologies include Delgado and Stefancic, *Critical White Studies*; Mike Hill, *Whiteness*; Birgit B. Rasmussen, Eric Klinenberg, Irene J. Nexica, and Matt Wray, *The Making and Unmaking of Whiteness* (Durham, NC: Duke University Press, 2001).

12. Hartigan, *Racial Situations*, 13; Gallagher, "White Racial Formation," 7.

13. William J. Hussar and Tabitha M. Bailey, *Projections of Education Statistics to 2022*, 41st ed. (Washington, DC: US Department of Education, 2014), http://nces.ed .gov/pubs2014/2014051.pdf.

14. According to the National Center for Education Statistics, in 2014, 50.2 percent of all public school students were either Hispanic, African American, Asian American, American Indian/Alaska Native, or two or more races. In the same year, 49.8 percent of public school students were white.

15. Ulrich Boser, "Teacher Diversity Revisited: A New State by State Analysis," Center for American Progress, May 2014, https://cdn.americanprogress.org/wp-content /uploads/2014/05/TeacherDiversity.pdf.

16. National Center for Education Statistics, "Spotlight A: Characteristics of Public School Teachers by Race/Ethnicity," last updated February 2019, https://nces.ed.gov /programs/raceindicators/spotlight_a.asp.

17. US Department of Education, "The State of Racial Diversity in the Education Workforce," July 2016, https://www2.ed.gov/rschstat/eval/highered/racial-diversity /state-racial-diversity-workforce.pdf.

18. Charles T. Clotfelter, *After Brown: The Rise and Retreat of School Desegregation* (Princeton, NJ: Princeton University Press, 2011); Jonathan Kozol, *The Shame of the Nation: The Restoration of Apartheid Schooling in America* (New York: Broadway

Books, 2005); Gary Orfield, Erica D. Frankenberg, and Chungmei Lee, "The Resurgence of School Segregation," *Educational Leadership* 60, no. 4 (2003): 16–20.

19. Ann Ferguson, *Bad Boys: Public Schools in the Making of Black Masculinity* (Ann Arbor: University of Michigan Press, 2000); Anne Gregory and Pharmicia M. Mosley, "The Discipline Gap: Teachers' Views on the Over-representation of African American Students in the Discipline System," *Equity and Excellence in Education* 37, no. 1 (2004): 18–30; Anne Gregory, Russell J. Skiba, and Pedro A. Noguera, "The Achievement Gap and the Discipline Gap: Two Sides of the Same Coin?," *Educational Researcher* 39, no. 1 (2010): 59–68; Pedro A. Noguera, "The Trouble with Black Boys: The Role and Influence of Environmental and Cultural Factors on the Academic Performance of African American Males," *Urban Education* 38, no. 4 (2003): 431–459.

20. Émile Durkheim, *The Rules of Sociological Method* (New York: Free Press, 1938).

21. To be clear, and as I will detail throughout the book, even though white teachers did not view them as such, predominantly or exclusively white spaces are also racialized environments.

22. Cameron McCarthy, Warren Crichlow, Greg Dimitriadis, and Nadine Dolby, *Race, Identity, and Representation in Education* (New York: Routledge, 2013); Bree Picower, "The Unexamined Whiteness of Teaching: How White Teachers Maintain and Enact Dominant Racial Ideologies," *Race, Ethnicity and Education* 12, no. 2 (2009): 197–215; R. Patrick Solomona, John P. Portelli, Beverly J. Daniel, and Arlene Campbell, "The Discourse of Denial: How White Teacher Candidates Construct Race, Racism and 'White Privilege,'" *Race, Ethnicity and Education* 8, no. 2 (2005): 147–169.

23. Ulrich Boser, "Teacher Diversity Revisited"; Constance A. Lindsay, Erica Blom, and Alexandra Tilsley, "Diversifying the Classroom: Examining the Teacher Pipeline," Urban Institute, October 5, 2017, https://www.urban.org/features /diversifying-classroom-examining-teacher-pipeline.

24. I provide a detailed breakdown of my research methodology in the appendix.

25. Hartigan, *Racial Situations*; Lipsitz, *The Possessive Investment in Whiteness*; Shannon Sullivan and Nancy Tuana, eds., *Race and Epistemologies of Ignorance* (Albany: SUNY Press, 2007); George Yancy, *Black Bodies, White Gazes: The Continuing Significance of Race in America*, 2nd ed. (Lanham, MD: Rowman and Littlefield, 2016).

26. Frankenberg, *White Women, Race Matters*; Kaufman, "A User's Guide to White Privilege"; Lipsitz, *The Possessive Investment in Whiteness*; McKinney, *Being White*; McIntosh, "White Privilege"; Rothenberg, *White Privilege*.

27. Doane and Bonilla-Silva, *White Out*; Eduardo Bonilla-Silva, "Rethinking Racism: Toward a Structural Interpretation," *American Sociological Review* 62, no. 3 (1997): 465–480; Matthew Desmond and Mustafa Emirbayer, "What Is Racial Domination?," *Du Bois Review* 6, no. 2 (2009): 335–355; Joe R. Feagin, *Systemic Racism: A Theory of Oppression* (New York: Routledge, 2013); Harris, "Whiteness as Property"; Lipsitz, *The Possessive Investment in Whiteness*.

28. Matthew Desmond and Mustafa Emirbayer, *Racial Domination, Racial Progress: The Sociology of Race in America* (New York: McGraw-Hill, 2010), 37.

29. Desmond and Emirbayer, *Racial Domination, Racial Progress*; Joe R. Feagin, *The White Racial Frame: Centuries of Racial Framing and Counter-framing* (New

York: Routledge, 2010); Feagin, *Systemic Racism*; Lipsitz, *The Possessive Investment in Whiteness*.

30. Eduardo Bonilla-Silva and David Dietrich, "The Sweet Enchantment of Color-Blind Racism in Obamerica," *Annals of the American Academy of Political and Social Science* 634, no. 1 (2011): 190–206; Martin Gilens, *Why Americans Hate Welfare: Race, Media, and the Politics of Antipoverty Policy* (Chicago: University of Chicago Press, 2009); Donald R. Kinder and Lynn M. Sanders, *Divided by Color: Racial Politics and Democratic Ideals* (Chicago: University of Chicago Press, 1996); Howard Schuman, Charlotte Steeh, Lawrence Bobo, and Maria Krysan, *Racial Attitudes in America: Trends and Interpretations* (Cambridge, MA: Harvard University Press, 1997); Donald R. Kinder and David O. Sears, "Prejudice and Politics: Symbolic Racism versus Racial Threats to the Good Life," *Journal of Personality and Social Psychology* 40, no. 3 (1981): 414; Paul M. Sniderman and Thomas L. Piazza, *The Scar of Race* (Cambridge, MA: Harvard University Press, 1993).

31. Dalton, "Failing to See"; Dyer, "The Matter of Whiteness"; Neil Gotanda, "A Critique of 'Our Constitution Is Color-Blind,'" *Stanford Law Review* 44, no. 1 (1991): 1.

32. Harris, "Whiteness as Property"; Haney López, *White by Law*.

33. Jacobson, *Whiteness of a Different Color*; Roediger, *Working toward Whiteness*.

34. Bonilla-Silva, "Rethinking Racism"; Eduardo Bonilla-Silva, *Racism without Racists: Color-Blind Racism and the Persistence of Racial Inequality in the United States* (Lanham, MD: Rowman and Littlefield, 2006); Feagin, *The White Racial Frame*; Leonardo, "The Color of Supremacy"; Lipsitz, *The Possessive Investment in Whiteness*; McIntosh, "White Privilege"; Michael Omi and Howard Winant, *Racial Formation in the United States: From the 1960s to the 1990s* (New York: Routledge, 1994).

35. Christine E. Sleeter, "How White Teachers Construct Race," in *Race, Identity, and Representation in Education*, ed. Cameron McCarthy, Warren Crichlow, Greg Dimitriadis, and Nadine Dolby (New York: Routledge, 1993): 157–171; Amanda E. Lewis, "Everyday Race-Making: Navigating Racial Boundaries in Schools," *American Behavioral Scientist* 47, no. 3 (2003): 283–305; Dyan Watson, "'Urban, but Not Too Urban': Unpacking Teachers' Desires to Teach Urban Students," *Journal of Teacher Education* 62, no. 1 (2011): 23–34.

36. For a detailed overview of privatization and neoliberal education policy, see David Hursh, "Assessing No Child Left Behind and the Rise of Neoliberal Education Policies," *American Educational Research Journal* 44, no. 3 (2007): 493–518; Michael Fabricant and Michelle Fine, *Charter Schools and the Corporate Makeover of Public Education: What's at Stake?* (New York: Teachers College Press, 2015); Diane Ravitch, *Reign of Error: The Hoax of the Privatization Movement and the Danger to America's Public Schools* (New York: Vintage Books, 2013).

37. Ann Berlak and Sekani Moyenda, *Taking It Personally: Racism in the Classroom from Kindergarten to College* (Philadelphia: Temple University Press, 2001); Jennifer L. Hochschild and Nathan Scovronick, *The American Dream and the Public Schools* (Oxford: Oxford University Press, 2003); Jonathan Kozol, *Savage Inequalities: Children in America's Schools* (1991; repr., New York: Broadway Books, 2012); Gary Orfield and Chungmei Lee, "Why Segregation Matters: Poverty and Educational Inequality," Civil

Rights Project at Harvard University, January 2005, https://eric.ed.gov/?q=Why
+Segregation+Matters%3a+Poverty+and+Educational+Inequality&id=ED489186.

38. Dennis J. Condron and Vincent J. Roscigno, "Disparities Within: Unequal
Spending and Achievement in an Urban School District," *Sociology of Education* 76,
no. 1 (2003): 18–36; Hochschild and Scovronick, *The American Dream and Public
Schools*; Jaekyung Lee, "Racial and Ethnic Achievement Gap Trends: Reversing the
Progress toward Equity?," *Educational Researcher* 31, no. 1 (2002): 3–12; Zeus
Leonardo and W. Norton Grubb, *Education and Racism: A Primer on Issues and
Dilemmas* (New York: Routledge, 2018); Monique Morris, *Pushout: The Criminaliza-
tion of Black Girls in Schools* (New York: New Press, 2016); Jeannie Oakes, *Keeping
Track: How Schools Structure Inequality* (New Haven, CT: Yale University Press, 2005);
Sean F. Reardon, "The Widening Academic Achievement Gap between the Rich and
the Poor: New Evidence and Possible Explanations," *Whither Opportunity* 1, no. 1
(2011): 91–116.

39. Robin J. DiAngelo, *What Does It Mean to Be White? Developing White Racial
Literacy* (New York: Peter Lang, 2016); Frankenberg, *White Women, Race Matters*;
Helms, *Black and White Racial Identity*; McDermott and Samson, "White Racial and
Ethnic Identity"; McKinney, *Being White*.

40. Hartigan, *Racial Situations*; Cynthia Levine-Rasky, "Framing Whiteness: Working through the Tensions in Introducing Whiteness to Educators," *Race, Ethnicity and
Education* 3, no. 3 (2000): 271–292; Amanda E. Lewis, *Race in the Schoolyard: Negotiating the Color Line in Classrooms and Communities* (New Brunswick, NJ: Rutgers University Press, 2003); Perry, *Shades of White*.

41. Dalton, "Failing to See"; Dyer, "The Matter of Whiteness"; Debby Irving, *Waking Up White and Finding Myself in the Story of Race* (Cambridge, MA: Elephant
Room, 2016); L. Johnson, "'My Eyes Have Been Opened'"; Lipsitz, *The Possessive Investment in Whiteness*; McKinney, *Being White*; Perry, *Shades of White*.

42. Elijah Anderson, "The Iconic Ghetto," *Annals of the American Academy of Political and Social Science* 642, no. 1 (2012): 8–24; Elijah Anderson, "The White Space," *Sociology of Race and Ethnicity* 1, no. 1 (2015): 10–21; George Lipsitz, "The Racialization
of Space and the Spatialization of Race: Theorizing the Hidden Architecture of
Landscape," *Landscape Journal* 26, no. 1 (2007): 10–23.

43. Elijah Anderson, *Code of the Streets: Decency, Violence, and the Moral Life of
the Inner City* (New York: Norton, 2000); Patricia H. Collins, *Black Feminist Thought:
Knowledge, Consciousness, and the Politics of Empowerment* (New York: Routledge,
2002); Sonja M. Brown Givens and Jennifer L. Monahan, "Priming Mammies, Jezebels, and Other Controlling Images: An Examination of the Influence of Mediated Stereotypes on Perceptions of an African American Woman," *Media Psychology*
7, no. 1 (2005): 87–106; Simone Ispa-Landa and Jordan Conwell, "'Once You Go to a
White School, You Kind of Adapt': Black Adolescents and the Racial Classification of
Schools," *Sociology of Education* 88, no. 1 (2015): 1–19; A. E. Lewis, "Everyday Race-
Making"; Omi and Winant, *Racial Formation*; Allison Roda and Amy Stuart Wells,
"School Choice Policies and Racial Segregation: Where White Parents' Good Inten-
tions, Anxiety, and Privilege Collide," *American Journal of Education* 119, no. 2 (2013):

261–293; Dyan Watson, "What Do You Mean When You Say 'Urban'? Speaking Honestly about Race and Students," *Rethinking Schools* 26, no. 1 (2011): 48–50.

44. Lawrence D. Bobo, "Somewhere between Jim Crow and Post-racialism: Reflections on the Racial Divide in America Today," *Daedalus* 140, no. 2 (2011): 11–36; Bonilla-Silva and Dietrich, "The Sweet Enchantment of Color-Blind Racism in Obamerica"; Eduardo Bonilla-Silva and Tyrone A. Forman, "'I Am Not a Racist But . . .': Mapping White College Students' Racial Ideology in the USA," *Discourse and Society* 11, no. 1 (2000): 50–85; Eduardo Bonilla-Silva, Tyrone A. Forman, Amanda E. Lewis, and David G. Embrick, "'It Wasn't Me!': How Will Race and Racism Work in 21st Century America," *Research in Political Sociology* 12, no. 1 (2003): 111–134; Charles A. Gallagher, "Color-Blind Privilege: The Social and Political Functions of Erasing the Color Line in Post-race America," *Race, Gender and Class* 10, no. 4 (2003): 22–37; Jennifer C. Mueller, "Producing Colorblindness: Everyday Mechanisms of White Ignorance," *Social Problems* 64, no. 2 (2017): 219–238; Michael Tesler and David O. Sears, *Obama's Race: The 2008 Election and the Dream of a Post-racial America* (Chicago: University of Chicago Press, 2010).

45. Gallagher, "White Racial Formation"; Hartigan, *Racial Situations*; A. E. Lewis, "There Is No 'Race' in the Schoolyard"; McKinney, *Being White*; E. W. Morris, *An Unexpected Minority*; Perry, *Shades of White*.

46. Dora Apel, *Imagery of Lynching: Black Men, White Women, and the Mob* (New Brunswick, NJ: Rutgers University Press, 2004); Martha Hodes, "The Sexualization of Reconstruction Politics: White Women and Black Men in the South after the Civil War," *Journal of the History of Sexuality* 3, no. 3 (1993): 402–417; Martha Hodes, *White Women, Black Men: Illicit Sex in the Nineteenth-Century South* (New Haven, CT: Yale University Press, 2014).

47. Collins, *Black Feminist Thought*; Marjorie L. DeVault, "Talking and Listening from Women's Standpoint: Feminist Strategies for Interviewing and Analysis," *Social Problems* 37, no. 1 (1990): 96–116; Linda T. Smith, *Decolonizing Methodologies: Research and Indigenous Peoples*, 2nd ed. (London: Zed Books, 2013); France W. Twine and Jonathan W. Warren, eds., *Racing Research, Researching Race: Methodological Dilemmas in Critical Race Studies* (New York: NYU Press, 2000); Zuberi and Bonilla-Silva, *White Logic, White Methods*.

48. Pierre Bourdieu and Loïc Wacquant, *An Invitation to Reflexive Sociology* (Chicago: University of Chicago Press, 1992).

49. Margaret A. Hagerman, *White Kids: Growing Up with Privilege in a Racially Divided America* (New York: NYU Press, 2018), 14.

ONE. WHITE RACELESSNESS

Epigraphs: Hale, *Making Whiteness*, xi; Kaufman, "A User's Guide to White Privilege," 30; Linda Martin Alcoff, *The Future of Whiteness* (Cambridge, MA: Polity, 2015), 22.

1. Desmond and Emirbayer, *Racial Domination, Racial Progress*; Omi and Winant, *Racial Formation*.

2. Craig Calhoun, ed., *Sociology in America: A History* (Chicago: University of Chicago Press, 2007).

3. For biological theories, see Angela Saini, *Superior: The Return of Race Science* (Boston: Beacon, 2019); Audrey Smedley and Brian D. Smedley, "Race as Biology Is Fiction, Racism as a Social Problem Is Real: Anthropological and Historical Perspectives on the Social Construction of Race," *American Psychologist* 60, no. 1 (2005): 16. For cultural theories, see Oscar Lewis, "The Culture of Poverty," *Scientific American* 215, no. 4 (1966): 19–25; Mario L. Small and Katherine Newman, "Urban Poverty after the Truly Disadvantaged: The Rediscovery of the Family, the Neighborhood, and Culture," *Annual Review of Sociology* 27, no. 1 (2001): 23–45. For social structural theories, see Bonilla-Silva, "Rethinking Racism"; Desmond and Emirbayer, *Racial Domination, Racial Progress*; Feagin, *Systemic Racism*.

4. Linda Martin Alcoff, "Epistemologies of Ignorance: Three Types," in Sullivan and Tuana, *Race and Epistemologies of Ignorance*; Doane, "Rethinking Whiteness Studies"; Charles W. Mills, "White Ignorance," in Sullivan and Tuana, *Race and Epistemologies of Ignorance*, 26–31; Aldon D. Morris, "Sociology of Race and W. E. B. DuBois: The Path Not Taken," in *Sociology in America: A History*, ed. C. Calhoun (Chicago: University of Chicago Press, 2007), 503–534; Howard Winant, "The Dark Side of the Force: One Hundred Years of the Sociology of Race," in Calhoun, *Sociology in America: A History*, 535–571.

5. A. D. Morris, "Sociology of Race and W. E. B. Du Bois."

6. Winant, "The Dark Side of the Force."

7. David R. Roediger, *Black on White: Black Writers on What It Means to Be White* (New York: Random House, 2010).

8. W. E. B. Du Bois, *Darkwater: Voices from within the Veil* (Mineola, NY: Dover, 1999); Joyce A. Ladner, *The Death of White Sociology: Essays on Race and Culture* (Baltimore: Black Classic Press, 1998); Ida B. Wells, *Southern Horrors: Lynch Law in All Its Phases* (1892; repr., Auckland: Floating Press, 2014).

9. A. D. Morris, "Sociology of Race and W. E. B. Du Bois"; Winant, "The Dark Side of the Force."

10. Frankenberg, *White Women, Race Matters*, 1.

11. Frankenberg, *White Women, Race Matters*; Morrison, *Playing in the Dark*.

12. Doane, "Rethinking Whiteness Studies," 4.

13. While not an exhaustive list, such studies include Karen Brodkin, *How Jews Became White Folks and What That Says about Race in America* (New Brunswick, NJ: Rutgers University Press, 1998); Delgado and Stefancic, *Critical White Studies*; Feagin, *The White Racial Frame*; Frankenberg, *White Women, Race Matters*; Matthew W. Hughey, *White Bound: Nationalists, Antiracists, and the Shared Meanings of Race* (Palo Alto, CA: Stanford University Press, 2012); Mike Hill, *Whiteness*; Noel Ignatiev, *How the Irish Became White*, new ed. (New York: Routledge, 1996); Jacobson, *Whiteness of a Different Color*; Kaufman, "A User's Guide to White Privilege"; Leonardo, "The Color of Supremacy"; Lipsitz, *The Possessive Investment in Whiteness*; Haney López, *White by Law*; Morrison, *Playing in the Dark*; Rasmussen et al., *The Making and Unmaking of Whiteness*; David R. Roediger, *The Wages of Whiteness: Race and the Making of the American Working Class* (New York: Verso, 1992); Matt Wray, *Not Quite White: White Trash and the Boundaries of Whiteness* (Durham, NC: Duke University Press, 2006); Yancy, *Look, a White!*

14. Delgado and Stefancic, *Critical White Studies*; Irving, *Waking Up White*.

15. Lipsitz, *The Possessive Investment in Whiteness*, 1.

16. Dalton, "Failing to See"; Dyer, "The Matter of Whiteness"; Jean Halley, Amy Eshleman, and Ramya M. Vijaya, *Seeing White: An Introduction to White Privilege and Race* (Lanham, MD: Rowman and Littlefield, 2011); Kaufman, "A User's Guide to White Privilege"; McIntosh, "White Privilege"; Rasmussen et al., *The Making and Unmaking of Whiteness*; Stephanie M. Wildman and Adrienne D. Davis, "Making Systems of Privilege Visible," in *Critical White Studies: Looking behind the Mirror*, ed. R. Delgado and J. Stefancic (Philadelphia: Temple University Press, 1997), 314–319; Yancy, *Look, a White!*

17. DiAngelo, *What Does It Mean to Be White?*

18. Frankenberg, *White Women, Race Matters*; DiAngelo, *What Does It Mean to Be White?*; Irving, *Waking Up White*; L. Johnson, "'My Eyes Have Been Opened.'"

19. Robert P. Amico, *Exploring White Privilege* (New York: Routledge, 2017); Dalton, "Failing to See"; DiAngelo, *What Does It Mean to Be White?*; Dyer, "The Matter of Whiteness"; Frankenberg, *White Women, Race Matters*; Kaufman, "A User's Guide to White Privilege"; A. E. Lewis, "There Is No 'Race' in the Schoolyard"; Lipsitz, *The Possessive Investment in Whiteness*; McIntosh, "White Privilege"; McKinney, *Being White*; Perry, *Shades of White*.

20. Feagin, *The White Racial Frame*.

21. Just to be absolutely clear, I never got the sense that Ms. Hall was mocking or trying to belittle the question or the study. If anything, it appeared to be more of a nervous laughter, possibly even discomfort.

22. Bonilla-Silva, *Racism without Racists*; Robin DiAngelo and Özlem Sensoy, "Getting Slammed: White Depictions of Race Discussions as Arenas of Violence," *Race, Ethnicity and Education* 17, no. 1 (2014): 103–128.

23. Kimberlé Crenshaw, "Mapping the Margins: Identity Politics, Intersectionality, and Violence against Women of Color," *Stanford Law Review* 43, no. 6 (1991): 1241–1299; Leslie McCall, "The Complexity of Intersectionality," *Signs: Journal of Women in Culture and Society* 30, no. 3 (2005): 1771–1800; Weber, "A Conceptual Framework for Understanding Race, Class, Gender, and Sexuality."

24. Amy Best, *Representing Youth: Methodological Issues in Critical Youth Studies* (New York: NYU Press, 2007); William A. Corsaro, *The Sociology of Childhood* (Los Angeles: Sage, 2017); Erin N. Winkler, *Learning Race, Learning Place: Shaping Racial Identities and Ideas in African American Childhoods* (New Brunswick, NJ: Rutgers University Press, 2012).

25. Hagerman, *White Kids*.

26. Lawrence Bobo, James R. Kluegel, and Ryan A. Smith, "Laissez-Faire Racism: The Crystallization of a Kinder, Gentler, Antiblack Ideology," in *Racial Attitudes in the 1990s: Continuity and Change*, ed. Steven A. Tuch and Jack K. Martin (Westport, CT: Praeger, 1997), 23–25; Eduardo Bonilla-Silva, "The Linguistics of Color Blind Racism: How to Talk Nasty about Blacks without Sounding 'Racist,'" *Critical Sociology* 28, nos. 1–2 (2002): 41–64.

27. Robin DiAngelo, *White Fragility: Why It's So Hard for White People to Talk about Racism* (Boston: Beacon, 2018).

28. Tristan Bridges and Cheri J. Pascoe, "Hybrid Masculinities: New Directions in the Sociology of Men and Masculinities," *Sociology Compass* 8, no. 3 (2014): 246–258; Kim A. Case and Annette Hemmings, "Distancing Strategies: White Women Preservice Teachers and Antiracist Curriculum," *Urban Education* 40, no. 6 (2005): 606–626.

29. Hae Yeon Choo and Myra Marx Ferree, "Practicing Intersectionality in Sociological Research: A Critical Analysis of Inclusions, Interactions, and Institutions in the Study of Inequalities," *Sociological Theory* 28, no. 2 (2010): 131.

30. Frankenberg, *White Women, Race Matters*; Joyce A. Ladner, "Tomorrow's Tomorrow: The Black Woman," in *Imagine a World: Pioneering Black Women Sociologists*, ed. Delores P. Aldridge (Lanham, MD: University Press of America, 2009), 91–100; Morrison, *Playing in the Dark*; Benita Roth, *Separate Roads to Feminism: Black, Chicana, and White Feminist Movements in America's Second Wave* (Cambridge: Cambridge University Press, 2004); Weber, "A Conceptual Framework for Understanding Race, Class, Gender, and Sexuality."

31. Rose M. Brewer, "Theorizing Race, Class and Gender: The New Scholarship of Black Feminist Intellectuals and Black Women's Labor," in *Theorizing Black Feminisms: The Visionary Pragmatism of Black Women*, ed. Stanlie M. James and Abena P. A. Busia (New York: Routledge, 1993), 13–30; Choo and Ferree, "Practicing Intersectionality"; Collins, *Black Feminist Thought*; Crenshaw, "Mapping the Margins"; bell hooks, *Ain't I a Woman: Black Women and Feminism* (Boston: South End, 1981); Deborah K. King, "Multiple Jeopardy, Multiple Consciousness: The Context of a Black Feminist Ideology," *Signs: Journal of Women in Culture and Society* 14, no. 1 (1988): 42–72; McCall, "The Complexity of Intersectionality."

32. Collins, *Black Feminist Thought*; Crenshaw, "Mapping the Margins"; hooks, *Ain't I a Woman*; Roth, *Separate Roads to Feminism*.

33. Brewer, "Theorizing Race, Class and Gender"; Choo and Ferree, "Practicing Intersectionality"; McCall, "The Complexity of Intersectionality."

34. Choo and Ferree, "Practicing Intersectionality."

35. Choo and Ferree, "Practicing Intersectionality," 134.

36. Kenny, *Daughters of Suburbia*; McKinney, *Being White*; Perry, *Shades of White*.

37. Brodkin, *How Jews Became White Folks*; Thomas A. Gugliemo, *White on Arrival: Italians, Race, Color, and Power in Chicago, 1890–1945* (New York: Oxford University Press, 2003); John Higham, *Strangers in the Land: Patterns of American Nativism, 1860–1925* (New Brunswick, NJ: Rutgers University Press, 2002); Ignatiev, *How the Irish Became White*; Jacobson, *Whiteness of a Different Color*.

38. Charles A. Gallagher, "Playing the White Ethnic Card: Using Ethnic Identity to Deny Contemporary Racism," in *White Out: The Continuing Significance of Racism*, ed. Ashley W. Doane and Eduardo Bonilla-Silva (New York: Routledge, 2003), 146.

39. Roediger, *Working toward Whiteness*.

40. Brodkin, *How Jews Became White Folks*; Ignatiev, *How the Irish Became White*; Jacobson, *Whiteness of a Different Color*; Haney López, *White by Law*; Roediger, *Working toward Whiteness*.

41. Roediger, *Working toward Whiteness*.

42. Bridges and Pascoe, "Hybrid Masculinities."

43. DeVault, "Talking and Listening from Women's Standpoint"; Herbert J. Rubin and Irene S. Rubin, *Qualitative Interviewing: The Art of Hearing Data* (Thousand Oaks, CA: Sage, 2011).

44. Sandra G. Harding, ed., *The Feminist Standpoint Theory Reader: Intellectual and Political Controversies* (New York: Routledge, 2004).

45. Choo and Ferree, "Practicing Intersectionality"; Joe R. Feagin and Melvin P. Sikes, *Living with Racism: The Black Middle-Class Experience* (Boston: Beacon, 1994); hooks, *Ain't I a Woman*; Mills, "White Ignorance"; Mueller, "Producing Colorblindness"; Tim Wise, *White like Me: Reflections on Race from a Privileged Son* (New York: Soft Skull, 2011).

TWO. THE COLOR LINE AND THE CLASSROOM

Epigraphs: W. E. B. Du Bois, *The Souls of Black Folk* (New York: Barnes and Noble Classics, 2003), 3; William H. Watkins, *The White Architects of Black Education: Ideology and Power in America, 1865–1954* (New York: Teachers College Press, 2001), 10; E. Anderson, "The White Space," 11.

1. Once again, I just want to be clear that, despite their general lack of awareness, the teachers in this study were, indeed, products of racialized space. That said, however, most of them did not see their racially segregated, predominantly white neighborhoods, homes, and schools as racialized, and I am trying to convey whiteness and white racial identity from their perspective.

2. E. Anderson, "The Iconic Ghetto"; E. Anderson, "The White Space"; Paul A. Jargowsky, *Poverty and Place: Ghettos, Barrios, and the American City* (New York: Russell Sage Foundation, 1997); Lipsitz, "The Racialization of Space"; Charles W. Mills, *The Racial Contract* (Ithaca, NY: Cornell University Press, 1997).

3. E. Anderson, "The White Space"; Jargowsky, *Poverty and Place*; George Lipsitz, *How Racism Takes Place* (Philadelphia: Temple University Press, 2011).

4. Desmond and Emirbayer, *Racial Domination, Racial Progress*; Kevin M. Kruse, *White Flight: Atlanta and the Making of Modern Conservatism* (Princeton, NJ: Princeton University Press, 2005).

5. William J. Wilson, *The Truly Disadvantaged: The Inner City, the Underclass, and Public Policy* (Chicago: University of Chicago Press, 1987).

6. Camille Z. Charles, "The Dynamics of Racial Residential Segregation," *Annual Review of Sociology* 29, no. 1 (2003): 167–207; Desmond and Emirbayer, *Racial Domination, Racial Progress*; David M. Freund, *Colored Property: State Policy and White Racial Politics in Suburban America* (Chicago: University of Chicago Press, 2010); Hale, *Making Whiteness*; Lipsitz, "The Racialization of Space"; Douglas S. Massey and Nancy A. Denton, *American Apartheid: Segregation and the Making of the Underclass* (Cambridge, MA: Harvard University Press, 1993); Stephen G. Meyer, *As Long as They Don't Move Next Door: Segregation and Racial Conflict in American Neighborhoods* (Lanham, MD: Rowman and Littlefield, 2000).

7. Lipsitz, *How Racism Takes Place*.

8. Elliot Jaspin, *Buried in the Bitter Waters: The Hidden History of Racial Cleansing in America* (New York: Basic Books, 2008); James W. Loewen, *Sundown Towns: A*

Hidden Dimension of American Racism (New York: New Press, 2018); Richard Rothstein, *The Color of Law: A Forgotten History of How Our Government Segregated America* (New York: Norton, 2017); Isabel Wilkerson, *The Warmth of Other Suns: The Epic Story of America's Great Migration* (New York: Vintage Books, 2011).

9. Jaspin, *Buried in the Bitter Waters*; Loewen, *Sundown Towns*; Jessica Trounstine, *Segregation by Design: Local Politics and Inequality in American Cities* (Cambridge: Cambridge University Press, 2018).

10. E. Anderson, "The White Space"; Philip Dray, *At the Hands of Persons Unknown: The Lynching of Black America* (New York: Random House, 2003); Harris, "Whiteness as Property"; Haney López, *White by Law.*

11. Lipsitz, "The Racialization of Space," 12.

12. Lipsitz, *How Racism Takes Place*; Charles W. Mills, *The Sociological Imagination: 40th Anniversary Edition* (New York: Oxford University Press, 2000).

13. E. Anderson, "Iconic Ghetto"; E. Anderson, "White Space"; Lipsitz, "The Racialization of Space"; Mills, *The Racial Contract.*

14. E. Anderson, "The Iconic Ghetto"; E. Anderson, "The White Space," 12 (quote).

15. E. Anderson, "The White Space," 13.

16. Mills, *The Racial Contract*, 41–42.

17. E. Anderson, "Iconic Ghetto"; Lipsitz, "The Racialization of Space"; Jargowsky, *Poverty and Place*; Mills, *The Racial Contract.*

18. Desmond and Emirbayer, *Racial Domination, Racial Progress*, 202.

19. Kaufman, "A User's Guide to White Privilege"; Lipsitz, *The Possessive Investment in Whiteness*; Rothenberg, *White Privilege*; Wise, *White like Me.*

20. E. Anderson, "White Space"; Desmond and Emirbayer, *Racial Domination, Racial Progress*; Lipsitz, *How Racism Takes Place*; Mills, *The Racial Contract.*

21. Jane H. Hill, *The Everyday Language of White Racism* (Hoboken, NJ: Wiley and Sons, 2009).

22. Hartigan, *Racial Situations*; A. E. Lewis, *Race in the Schoolyard*; McKinney, *Being White*; Perry, *Shades of White.*

23. E. Anderson, "White Space"; Charles, "The Dynamics of Racial Residential Segregation"; Desmond and Emirbayer, *Racial Domination, Racial Progress*; Freund, *Colored Property*; Kruse, *White Flight*; Maria Krysan, "Whites Who Say They'd Flee: Who Are They, and Why Would They Leave?," *Demography* 39, no. 4 (2002): 675–696; Massey and Denton, *American Apartheid*; Meyer, *As Long as They Don't Move Next Door*; John Yinger, *Closed Doors, Opportunities Lost: The Continuing Costs of Housing Discrimination* (New York: Russell Sage Foundation, 1995).

24. David W. Adams, *Education for Extinction: American Indians and the Boarding School Experience, 1875–1928* (Lawrence: University Press of Kansas, 1995); James D. Anderson, *The Education of Blacks in the South, 1860–1935* (Chapel Hill: University of North Carolina Press, 1988); Desmond and Emirbayer, *Racial Domination, Racial Progress*; Watkins, *The White Architects of Black Education.*

25. E. Anderson, "White Space"; Zeus Leonardo, *Race, Whiteness, and Education* (New York: Routledge, 2009).

26. Leonardo and Grubb, *Education and Racism.*

27. Adams, *Education for Extinction*; J. D. Anderson, *Education of Blacks in the South*; Karen Anderson, *Little Rock: Race and Resistance at Central High School* (Princeton, NJ: Princeton University Press, 2010); Matthew F. Delmont, *Why Busing Failed: Race, Media, and the National Resistance to School Desegregation* (Berkeley: University of California Press, 2016); Desmond and Emirbayer, *Racial Domination, Racial Progress*; Kozol, *The Shame of the Nation*; Dana Goldstein, *The Teacher Wars: A History of America's Most Embattled Profession* (New York: Anchor Books, 2015); Amanda E. Lewis and John B. Diamond, *Despite the Best Intentions: How Racial Inequality Thrives in Good Schools* (New York: Oxford University Press, 2015); Charles J. Ogletree, *All Deliberate Speed: Reflections on the First Half Century of* Brown v. Board of Education (New York: Norton, 2004); Carla Shedd, *Unequal City: Race, Schools, and Perceptions of Injustice* (New York: Russell Sage, 2015).

28. Jennifer L. Hochschild and Nathan Scovronick, *The American Dream and the Public Schools* (New York: Oxford University Press, 2003); Heather B. Johnson, *The American Dream and the Power of Wealth: Choosing Schools and Inheriting Inequality in the Land of Opportunity* (New York: Routledge, 2014); Linn Posey-Maddox, *When Middle-Class Parents Choose Urban Schools: Class, Race, and the Challenge of Equity in Public Education* (Chicago: University of Chicago Press, 2014); Roda and Wells, "School Choice Policies and Racial Segregation"; Dyan Watson, "Norming Suburban: How Teachers Talk about Race without Using Race Words," *Urban Education* 47, no. 5 (2012): 983–1004.

29. Erwin Chemerinsky, "The Segregation and Resegregation of American Public Education: The Court's Role," NCL *Review* 81 (2002): 1597; Beverly D. Tatum, *Can We Talk about Race? And Other Conversations in an Era of School Resegregation* (Boston: Beacon, 2007); Watson, "'Urban, but Not Too Urban.'"

30. Robert W. Fairlie and Alexandra M. Resch, "Is There 'White Flight' into Private Schools? Evidence from the National Educational Longitudinal Survey," *Review of Economics and Statistics* 84, no. 1 (2002): 21–33; Matthew D. Lassiter and Andrew B. Lewis, eds., *The Moderates' Dilemma: Massive Resistance to School Desegregation in Virginia* (Charlottesville: University of Virginia Press, 1998); Christine H. Rossell, "School Desegregation and White Flight," *Political Science Quarterly* 90, no. 4 (1975): 675–695.

31. Delmont, *Why Busing Failed*; Lassiter and Lewis, *The Moderates' Dilemma*; George Lewis, *Massive Resistance: The White Response to the Civil Rights Movement* (London: Hoddor Arnold, 2006); Clive Webb, ed., *Massive Resistance: Southern Opposition to the Second Reconstruction* (New York: Oxford University Press, 2005).

32. Reynolds Farley, Howard Schuman, Suzanne Bianchi, Diane Colasanto, and Shirley Hatchett, "'Chocolate City, Vanilla Suburbs': Will the Trend toward Racially Separate Communities Continue?," *Social Science Research* 7, no. 4 (1978): 319–344.

33. Clotfelter, *After* Brown; Hochschild and Scovronick, *The American Dream and Public Schools*.

34. Hochschild and Scovronick, *The American Dream and Public Schools*, 36.

35. Clotfelter, *After* Brown; Glenn Firebaugh and Kenneth E. Davis, "Trends in Antiblack Prejudice, 1972–1984: Region and Cohort Effects," *American Journal of Sociol-*

ogy 94, no. 2 (1988): 251–272; Hochschild and Scovronick, *The American Dream and Public Schools*.

36. Clotfelter, *After Brown*; Kozol, *The Shame of the Nation*; Ogletree, *All Deliberate Speed*; Gary Orfield and Susan E. Eaton, *Dismantling Desegregation: The Quiet Reversal of Brown v. Board of Education* (New York: New Press, 1996); Orfield, Frankenberg, and Lee, "The Resurgence of School Segregation"; Tatum, *Can We Talk about Race?*

37. Delmont, *Why Busing Failed*; Desmond and Emirbayer, *Racial Domination, Racial Progress*; Hochschild and Scovronick, *The American Dream and Public Schools*; Kozol, *The Shame of the Nation*; Lassiter and Lewis, *The Moderates' Dilemma*; Sean F. Reardon and Ann Owens, "60 Years after *Brown*: Trends and Consequences of School Segregation," *Annual Review of Sociology* 40 (2014): 199–218; Webb, *Massive Resistance*.

38. Carol Anderson, *White Rage: The Unspoken Truth of Our Racial Divide* (New York: Bloomsbury, 2016); Delmont, *Why Busing Failed*; Desmond and Emirbayer, *Racial Domination, Racial Progress*; Ogletree, *All Deliberate Speed*; Webb, *Massive Resistance*.

39. Charles T. Clotfelter, "School Desegregation, 'Tipping,' and Private School Enrollment," *Journal of Human Resources* 11, no. 1 (1976): 28–50; Fairlie and Resch, "Is There 'White Flight' into Private Schools?"; Hochschild and Scovronick, *The American Dream and Public Schools*; Orfield and Eaton, *Dismantling Desegregation*; Sean F. Reardon and John T. Yun, "Private School Racial Enrollments and Segregation," Civil Rights Project at Harvard University, June 26, 2002, https://eric.ed.gov/?q=Private+School+Racial+Enrollments+and+Segregation&id=ED467108.

40. Lawrence Bobo, "Whites' Opposition to Busing: Symbolic Racism or Realistic Group Conflict?," *Journal of Personality and Social Psychology* 45, no. 6 (1983): 1196; Delmont, *Why Busing Failed*; Desmond and Emirbayer, *Racial Domination, Racial Progress*; Hochschild and Scovronick, *The American Dream and Public Schools*; Kruse, *White Flight*; J. Dennis Lord, "School Busing and White Abandonment of Public Schools," *Southeastern Geographer* 15, no. 2 (1975): 81–92; David O. Sears, Carl P. Hensler and Leslie K. Speer, "Whites' Opposition to 'Busing': Self-Interest or Symbolic Politics?," *American Political Science Review* 73, no. 2 (1979): 369–384; Karl E. Taeuber and David R. James, "Racial Segregation among Public and Private Schools," *Sociology of Education* 55, no. 2 (1982): 133–143; Tatum, *Can We Talk about Race?*

41. Dan T. Carter, *The Politics of Rage: George Wallace, the Origins of the New Conservatism, and the Transformation of American Politics* (Baton Rouge: LSU Press, 2000); Joseph Crespino, *In Search of Another Country: Mississippi and the Conservative Counterrevolution* (Princeton, NJ: Princeton University Press, 2009); Kevin M. Kruse and Julian E. Zelizer, *Fault Lines: A History of the United States since 1974* (New York: Norton, 2019); Ian Haney López, *Dog Whistle Politics: How Coded Racial Appeals Have Reinvented Racism and Wrecked the Middle Class* (New York: Oxford University Press, 2015); Lisa McGirr, *Suburban Warriors: The Origins of the New American Right* (Princeton, NJ: Princeton University Press, 2015).

42. Ansley T. Erickson, *Making the Unequal Metropolis: School Desegregation and Its Limits* (Chicago: University of Chicago Press, 2016); Joe R. Feagin, *White Party, White Government: Race, Class, and US Politics* (New York: Routledge, 2012); Haney López,

Dog Whistle Politics; Stephen Steinberg, *Turning Back: The Retreat from Racial Justice in American Thought and Policy* (Boston: Beacon, 1995).

43. Joyce A. Baugh, *The Detroit School Busing Case:* Milliken v. Bradley *and the Controversy over Desegregation* (Lawrence: University Press of Kansas, 2011); Desmond and Emirbayer, *Racial Domination, Racial Progress*; Tatum, *Can We Talk about Race?*

44. Milliken v. Bradley, 418 U.S. 717 (1974).

45. Baugh, *Detroit School Busing Case*; John R. Logan, Elisabeta Minca, and Sinem Adar, "The Geography of Inequality: Why Separate Means Unequal in American Public Schools," *Sociology of Education* 85, no. 3 (2012): 287–301; Thomas F. Pettigrew, "Justice Deferred a Half Century after *Brown v. Board of Education*," *American Psychologist* 59, no. 6 (2004): 521; Thomas J. Sugrue, *The Origins of the Urban Crisis: Race and Inequality in Postwar Detroit* (Princeton, NJ: Princeton University Press, 2014).

46. Parents Involved in Community Schools v. Seattle School District No. 1, 551 U.S. 701 (2007).

47. Clotfelter, *After* Brown; Desmond and Emirbayer, *Racial Domination, Racial Progress*; Jonathan Fischbach, Will Rhee, and Robert Cacace, "Race at the Pivot Point: The Future of Race-Based Policies to Remedy De Jure Segregation after Parents Involved in Community Schools," *Harvard Law Review* 43 (2008): 491.

48. Two additional cases, in particular, were instrumental to school desegregation following the *Brown* decision. The first, *Green v. County School Board of New Kent County* (1968), mandated that school boards must formulate actual school desegregation plans in lieu of the often farcical "freedom of choice" plans that were ways to get around or avoid compliance with the *Brown*. The second case, *Swann v. Charlotte-Mecklenburg* (1971), held that school busing could be used to achieve racial integration in public schools, even when schools were segregated because of neighborhood proximity as opposed to racial classification. Collectively, the *Green* and *Swann* decisions made no distinction between de facto and de jure segregation.

49. Clotfelter, *After* Brown; Desmond and Emirbayer, *Racial Domination, Racial Progress*; Kozol, *The Shame of the Nation*; Pettigrew, "Justice Deferred"; Reardon and Owens, "60 Years after *Brown*."

50. Gloria J. Browne-Marshall, *Race, Law, and American Society: 1607–Present*, 2nd ed. (New York: Routledge, 2013).

51. William J. Wilson, *The Declining Significance of Race: Blacks and Changing American Institutions* (Chicago: University of Chicago Press, 1978).

52. Jargowsky, *Poverty and Place*; William J. Wilson, *When Work Disappears: The World of the New Urban Poor* (New York: Vintage Books, 2011).

53. Charles, "The Dynamics of Racial Residential Segregation"; Massey and Denton, *American Apartheid*; Patrick Sharkey, *Stuck in Place: Urban Neighborhoods and the End of Progress toward Racial Equality* (Chicago: University of Chicago Press, 2013); Sugrue, *The Origins of the Urban Crisis*; Wilson, *The Truly Disadvantaged*.

54. Massey and Denton, *American Apartheid*; Wilson, *The Truly Disadvantaged*.

55. Douglas B. Downey, "Black/White Differences in School Performance: The Oppositional Culture Explanation," *Annual Review of Sociology* 34 (2008): 107–126; Douglas B. Downey and James W. Ainsworth-Darnell, "The Search for Oppositional

Culture among Black Students," *American Sociological Review* 67, no. 1 (2002): 156–164; Signithia Fordham and Jonathan U. Ogbu, "Black Students' School Success: Coping with the 'Burden of "Acting White,"'" *Urban Review* 18, no. 3 (1986): 176–206; Ronald G. Fryer, "'Acting White': The Social Price Paid by the Best and Brightest Minority Students," *Education Next* 6, no. 1 (2006): 52–59; Angel L. Harris, "I (Don't) Hate School: Revisiting Oppositional Culture Theory of Blacks' Resistance to Schooling," *Social Forces* 85, no. 2 (2006): 797–834; Richard Majors and Janet M. Billson, *Cool Pose: The Dilemma of Black Manhood in America* (New York: Simon and Schuster, 1993); Noguera, "The Trouble with Black Boys"; Jonathan U. Ogbu, ed., *Minority Status, Oppositional Culture, and Schooling* (New York: Routledge, 2008); Shedd, *Unequal City*.

56. Hochschild and Scovronick, *The American Dream and Public Schools*; Gloria Ladson-Billings, "It's Not the Culture of Poverty, It's the Poverty of Culture: The Problem with Teacher Education," *Anthropology and Education Quarterly* 37, no. 2 (2006): 104–109; Jeanne Theoharis, Gaston Alonso, Noel S. Anderson, and Celina Su, *Our Schools Suck: Students Talk Back to a Segregated Nation on the Failures of Urban Education* (New York: NYU Press, 2009).

57. H. B. Johnson, *The American Dream and the Power of Wealth*; Heather B. Johnson and Thomas M. Shapiro, "Good Neighborhoods, Good Schools: Race and the Good Choices," in *White Out: The Continuing Significance of Racism*, ed. Ashley W. Doane and Eduardo Bonilla-Silva (New York: Routledge, 2003), 173–187.

58. Freeden Blume Oeur, *Black Boys Apart: Racial Uplift and Respectability in All-Male Public Schools* (Minneapolis: University of Minnesota Press, 2018); Ravitch, *Reign of Error*.

59. David Hursh, "Assessing No Child Left Behind and the Rise of Neoliberal Education Policies," *American Educational Research Journal* 44, no. 3 (2007): 493–518; US National Commission on Excellence in Education, *A Nation at Risk: The Imperative for Education Reform* (Washington, DC: National Commission on Excellence and Education, 1983).

60. Christopher Lubienski, "Innovation in Education Markets: Theory and Evidence on the Impact of Competition and Choice in Charter Schools," *American Educational Research Journal* 40, no. 2 (2003): 395–443.

61. While campaigning for the Republican nomination during the 2000 presidential campaign, then candidate and eventual president George W. Bush coined the phrase "the soft bigotry of low expectations." The crux of Bush's position was that not holding disadvantaged students of color to the same academic standards as their more affluent, white peers was itself a form of racism. This thinking served as the ideological basis for the No Child Left Behind policy he would sign into law as president.

62. David Hursh, "The Growth of High-Stakes Testing in the USA: Accountability, Markets and the Decline in Educational Equality," *British Educational Research Journal* 31, no. 5 (2005): 605–622; Oeur, *Black Boys Apart*; Ravitch, *Reign of Error*.

63. Johnson and Shapiro, "Good Neighborhoods, Good Schools."

64. Pauline Lipman, *The New Political Economy of Urban Education: Neoliberalism, Race, and the Right to the City* (Abingdon, UK: Taylor and Francis, 2013); Oeur, *Black Boys Apart*.

65. To take but two examples, both Hurricane Katrina and the Great Recession played massive roles in the reconfiguration of space and the restructuring of schools. After Hurricane Katrina, corporate lobbyists flooded the Louisiana state legislature, pushing elected officials to replace public housing with private condos and public schools with private charters; see Naomi Klein, *The Shock Doctrine: The Rise of Disaster Capitalism* (New York: Picador, 2007). Similarly, the Great Recession devastated black homeowners, leading to a massive loss of wealth, as well as the financial looting and gentrification of black neighborhoods. In both cases, national disasters were used as an opportunity to further neoliberal hegemony and remake the physical world.

66. Jordan T. Camp, *Incarcerating the Crisis: Freedom Struggles and the Rise of the Neoliberal State* (Berkeley: University of California Press, 2016); David Harvey, *A Brief History of Neoliberalism* (New York: Oxford University Press, 2007).

67. In the decades after the civil rights movement, neoliberalism rose to prominence alongside colorblindness as two dominant ideologies in the United States. Central to both are frames including the overlapping frames of individualism and meritocracy. Another commonality of these ideologies is the belief that government intervention, or social engineering, not only is unneeded but actually does harm and may even be its own form of bigotry. Both neoliberalism and colorblindness have become normative throughout the broader United States.

68. The language of neoliberalism utilizes various discursive frames to rationalize and explain away contradictions, oversights, and contravening evidence to its legitimacy as a political program. For example, white Brick City teachers clung to popular discursive tropes such as "the race card," "personal responsibility," and "reverse discrimination" to justify existing social arrangements and minimize the stories and lived experiences of their black students and parents. I detail this process further in chapters 4 and 5.

69. Camp, *Incarcerating the Crisis*; Harvey, *A Brief History of Neoliberalism*; Lipman, *The New Political Economy of Urban Education*; Oeur, *Black Boys Apart*.

70. Since the Great Recession, Brick City has consistently ranked in the top ten for cities with the highest percentage of residents living below the poverty line.

71. Robert J. Sampson, *Great American City: Chicago and the Enduring Neighborhood Effect* (Chicago: University of Chicago Press, 2012); Robert J. Sampson, Jeffrey D. Morenoff, and Thomas Gannon-Rowley, "Assessing 'Neighborhood Effects': Social Processes and New Directions in Research," *Annual Review of Sociology* 28, no. 1 (2002): 443–478; Sharkey, *Stuck in Place*; Wilson, *The Truly Disadvantaged*.

72. Delbert S. Elliot, William J. Wilson, David Huizinga, Robert J. Sampson, Amanda Elliott, and Bruce Rankin, "The Effects of Neighborhood Disadvantage on Adolescent Development," *Journal of Research in Crime and Delinquency* 33, no. 4 (1996): 389–426; Gary W. Evans, "The Environment of Childhood Poverty," *American Psychologist* 59, no. 2 (2004): 77–92; Sampson, *Great American City*; Sharkey, *Stuck in Place*; Wilson, *The Truly Disadvantaged*.

73. Camp, *Incarcerating the Crisis*; Matthew Desmond, *Evicted: Poverty and Profit in the American City* (New York: Broadway Books, 2016); Oeur, *Black Boys Apart*; Victor M. Rios, *Punished: Policing the Lives of Black and Latino Boys* (New York: NYU Press,

2011); Loïc Wacquant, *Punishing the Poor: The Neoliberal Government of Social Insecurity* (Durham, NC: Duke University Press, 2009); Wilson, *When Work Disappears*.

74. E. Anderson, "The Iconic Ghetto"; E. Anderson, "The White Space"; Jargowsky, *Poverty and Place*; A. E. Lewis, *Race in the Schoolyard*; Lipsitz, *How Racism Takes Place*; Massey and Denton, *American Apartheid*; Wilson, *The Truly Disadvantaged*.

75. In recent years—and spanning the tenure of multiple school superintendents—the Brick City School District has begun a "renewed emphasis" on student achievement. The district has adopted what they term an "all hands on deck" approach to closing the racial *and* economic achievement gaps. This "new" approach includes more money for technology, teachers, and staff, corporate and nonprofit partnerships, and an ambiguous "commitment to innovation." Comparatively, there have been few district-wide efforts to combat, or even mitigate, the effects that concentrated poverty has on its student body.

76. I should note here that one dynamic that complicates my methodology and overall analysis is the socioeconomic incongruity between white teachers (who primarily came from middle-class and affluent backgrounds) and black students (who primarily came from working-class and impoverished backgrounds). Because schools were both racially and economically segregated, it is not completely clear whether or not my interview respondents were associating poverty with blackness. That is, there is a decent chance that, from the standpoint of teachers, the culture, attitudes, and behaviors discussed throughout my fieldwork were references to their students' class standing, not their race. This is a methodological and analytical question that I cannot fully account for. I say more about this particular limitation in the concluding chapter.

77. Nancy A. Denton, "The Persistence of Segregation: Links between Residential Segregation and School Segregation," *Minnesota Law Review* 80 (1995): 795; Downey and Ainsworth-Darnell, "The Search for Oppositional Culture among Black Students"; Vivian L. Gadsden and Ezekiel J. Dixon-Roman, "'Urban' Schooling and 'Urban' Families: The Role of Context and Place," *Urban Education* 52, no. 4 (2017): 431–459; Hochschild and Scovronick, *The American Dream and Public Schools*; John R. Logan, Deirdre Oakley, and Jacob Stowell, "School Segregation in Metropolitan Regions, 1970–2000: The Impacts of Policy Choices on Public Education," *American Journal of Sociology* 113, no. 6 (2008): 1611–1644; Noguera, "The Trouble with Black Boys"; Reardon and Owens, "60 Years after *Brown*"; Tatum, *Can We Talk about Race?*; Watson, "Norming Suburban."

78. John H. McWhorter, *Losing the Race: Self-Sabotage in Black America* (New York: Simon and Schuster, 2000).

79. Randall Kennedy, *Nigger: The Strange Career of a Troublesome Word* (New York: Vintage Books, 2008).

80. On three separate occasions, interview respondents described the death of Trayvon Martin as an unfortunate situation or otherwise tragic event.

81. Bonilla-Silva, "Rethinking Racism," 469.

82. Four teachers, all under the age of thirty-five, did not take exception to being racially identified as white. These teachers also politically identified as progressive Democrats.

83. Just to be clear, Grand Ledge is a pseudonym for a predominantly white, middle-class, suburban school district just on the outside of Brick City.

84. Whenever I felt that interviews were becoming too painful for my interviewees, I would offer to take a break or stop the interview. Each time I did so, however, interview respondents would insist that we continue.

85. I provide a more detailed analysis of this process in chapter 4.

THREE. BECOMING WHITE TEACHERS

Epigraph: A. E. Lewis, Race in the Schoolyard, 6–7.

1. DiAngelo, What Does It Mean to Be White?; Frankenberg, White Women, Race Matters; Hale, Making Whiteness; McIntosh, "White Privilege."

2. Herbert Blumer, Symbolic Interactionism: Perspective and Method (Berkeley: University of California Press, 1986).

3. Blumer, Symbolic Interactionism; Norman K. Denzin, Symbolic Interactionism and Cultural Studies: The Politics of Interpretation (Cambridge, MA: Blackwell, 1992); Manford H. Kuhn, "Major Trends in Symbolic Interaction Theory in the Past Twenty-Five Years," Sociological Quarterly 5, no. 1 (1964): 61–84; George H. Mead, "Social Consciousness and the Consciousness of Meaning," Psychological Bulletin 7, no. 12 (1910): 397; David A. Snow, "Extending and Broadening Blumer's Conceptualization of Symbolic Interactionism," Symbolic Interaction 24, no. 3 (2001): 367–377; Sheldon Stryker, Symbolic Interactionism: A Social Structural Version (San Francisco: Benjamin-Cummings, 1980).

4. Blumer, Symbolic Interactionism.

5. Charles H. Cooley, Human Nature and the Social Order (New York: Charles Scribner's Sons, 1902); John Dewey, "The Reflex Arc Concept in Psychology," Psychological Review 3, no. 4 (1896): 357; Erving Goffman, The Presentation of Self in Everyday Life (1956; repr., New York: Random House, 2008); John P. Hewitt, Self and Society: A Symbolic Interactionist Social Psychology (London: Pearson, 1976); William James, The Principles of Psychology (1890; repr., New York: Cosimo Classics, 2007); Mead, "Social Consciousness and the Consciousness of Meaning"; Stryker, Symbolic Interactionism.

6. Kathy Charmaz, Scott R. Harris, and Leslie Irvine, The Social Self and Everyday Life: Understanding the World through Symbolic Interactionism (Hoboken, NJ: Wiley-Blackwell, 2019); Stryker, Symbolic Interactionism.

7. Denzin, Symbolic Interactionism and Cultural Studies, 3.

8. Blumer, Symbolic Interactionism; Charmaz, Harris, and Irvine, The Social Self and Everyday Life; Denzin, Symbolic Interactionism and Cultural Studies; Stryker, Symbolic Interactionism.

9. Blumer, Symbolic Interactionism; Charmaz, Harris, and Irvine, The Social Self and Everyday Life.

10. Denzin, Symbolic Interactionism and Cultural Studies; Charmaz, Harris, and Irvine, The Social Self and Everyday Life; Kuhn, "Major Trends in Symbolic Interaction Theory."

11. Blumer, Symbolic Interactionism; Joel M. Charon, Symbolic Interactionism: An Introduction, an Interpretation, an Integration (New York: Pearson, 2010); Denzin, Sym-

bolic Interactionism and Cultural Studies; Dewey, "The Reflex Arc Concept in Psychology"; Hewitt, *Self and Society*; Robert E. Park, "Reflections on Communication and Culture," *American Journal of Sociology* 44, no. 2 (1938): 187–205.

12. Blumer, *Symbolic Interactionism*, 5.

13. Blumer, *Symbolic Interactionism*; Denzin, *Symbolic Interactionism and Cultural Studies*; Hartigan, *Racial Situations*; Gallagher, "White Racial Formation"; McDermott, *Working-Class White*; McKinney, *Being White*; E. W. Morris, *An Unexpected Minority*; Perry, *Shades of White*.

14. Blumer, *Symbolic Interactionism*; Charmaz, Harris, and Irvine, *The Social Self and Everyday Life*; Denzin, *Symbolic Interactionism and Cultural Studies*.

15. Gallagher, "White Racial Formation"; Hartigan, *Racial Situations*; bell hooks, *Representing Whiteness in the Black Imagination* (New York: Routledge, 1992); Hughey, *White Bound*; Julie Landsman, *A White Teacher Talks about Race* (Lanham, MD: Rowman and Littlefield, 2009); A. E. Lewis, *Race in the Schoolyard*; McDermott, *Working-Class White*; McKinney, *Being White*; E. W. Morris, *An Unexpected Minority*; Perry, *Shades of White*; Tatum, *Why Are All the Black Kids Sitting Together in the Cafeteria?*

16. Matthew W. Hughey, "The (Dis)Similarities of White Racial Identities: The Conceptual Framework of 'Hegemonic Whiteness,'" *Ethnic and Racial Studies* 33, no. 8 (2010): 1289–1309; Amanda E. Lewis, "What Group? Studying Whites and Whiteness in the Era of Colorblindness," *Sociological Theory* 22, no. 4 (2004); McDermott and Samson, "White Racial and Ethnic Identity."

17. Gallagher, "White Racial Formation."

18. Gallagher, "White Racial Formation"; Hartigan, *Racial Situations*; A. E. Lewis, *Race in the Schoolyard*; McKinney, *Being White*; E. W. Morris, *An Unexpected Minority*; Perry, *Shades of White*.

19. McKinney, *Being White*.

20. Mueller, "Producing Colorblindness"; H. R. Outten, Michael T. Schmitt, Daniel A. Miller, and Amber L. Garcia, "Feeling Threatened about the Future: Whites' Emotional Reactions to Anticipated Ethnic Demographic Changes," *Personality and Social Psychology Bulletin* 38, no. 1 (2012): 14–25; Victoria C. Plaut, Flannery G. Garnett, Laura E. Buffardi, and Jeffrey Sanchez-Burks, "'What about Me?': Perceptions of Exclusion and Whites' Reactions to Multiculturalism," *Journal of Personality and Social Psychology* 101, no. 2 (2011): 337.

21. Gallagher, "White Racial Formation," 7.

22. Hughey, "The (Dis)Similarities of White Racial Identities"; A. E. Lewis, *Race in the Schoolyard*; McDermott, *Working-Class White*; Pamela Perry, "White Means Never Having to Say You're Ethnic: White Youth and the Construction of 'Cultureless' Identities," *Journal of Contemporary Ethnography* 30, no. 1 (2001): 56–91.

23. Perry, *Shades of White*.

24. Valley Grove and Clavey are pseudonyms. Perry, *Shades of White*.

25. Perry, *Shades of White*, 78.

26. Gallagher, "White Racial Formation"; Hartigan, *Racial Situations*; McKinney, *Being White*; E. W. Morris, *An Unexpected Minority*.

27. Robin DiAngelo and Özlem Sensoy, "Getting Slammed: White Depictions of

Race Discussions as Arenas of Violence," *Race, Ethnicity and Education* 17, no. 1 (2014): 103–128; E. W. Morris, *An Unexpected Minority*.

28. Arlie R. Hochschild, *Strangers in Their Own Land: Anger and Mourning on the American Right* (New York: New Press, 2018); McKinney, *Being White*; Mueller, "Producing Colorblindness."

29. Hartigan, *Racial Situations*; E. W. Morris, *An Unexpected Minority*; Perry, *Shades of White*.

30. Anne Case and Angus Deaton, *Deaths of Despair and the Future of Capitalism* (Princeton, NJ: Princeton University Press, 2020); Hartigan, *Racial Situations*; Hochschild, *Strangers in Their Own Land*; E. W. Morris, *An Unexpected Minority*; Perry, *Shades of White*.

31. McKinney, *Being White*, 2.

32. DiAngelo and Sensoy, "Getting Slammed"; Gallagher, "White Racial Formation"; McDermott and Samson, "White Racial and Ethnic Identity"; McKinney, *Being White*; E. W. Morris, *An Unexpected Minority*; Perry, *Shades of White*.

33. Hartigan, *Racial Situations*; Hochschild, *Strangers in Their Own Land*; McKinney, *Being White*; E. W. Morris, *An Unexpected Minority*; Perry, *Shades of White*.

34. Hochschild, *Strangers in Their Own Land*; Gallagher, "White Racial Formation"; E. W. Morris, *An Unexpected Minority*; Outten et al., "Feeling Threatened"; Perry, *Shades of White*; Plaut et al., "'What about Me?'"

35. Mrs. McCormick was one of my very first interviews, which is why I found her answers about teaching in predominantly black schools somewhat surprising. As I continued my fieldwork, however, a clear pattern emerged, and the disparate answers given by the same interview respondents, all based on context, was something that I came to expect.

36. Lisa Delpit, *Other People's Children: Cultural Conflict in the Classroom* (New York: New Press, 2006).

37. Despite their disproportionate amount of power within the school, the teachers I interviewed still constructed white racial identity as a disadvantage. To them, they occupied a precarious position. I talk more about this process in chapter 4.

38. Sara Ahmed, "A Phenomenology of Whiteness," *Feminist Theory* 8, no. 2 (2007): 149–168; John T. Warren, "Doing Whiteness: On the Performative Dimensions of Race in the Classroom," *Communication Education* 50, no. 2 (2001): 91–108.

39. Warren, "Doing Whiteness," 92.

40. Delpit, *Other People's Children*.

41. While some teachers genuinely believed in the necessity and importance of Black Lives Matter, other teachers, despite promoting the organization within their classrooms and schools, believed them to be "silly," "unnecessary," and a symbol of "everything that's wrong with society."

42. Gilens, *Why Americans Hate Welfare*; Linda Gordon, *Pitied but Not Entitled: Single Mothers and the History of Welfare* (Cambridge, MA: Harvard University Press, 1994); Kenneth J. Neubeck and Noel A. Cazenave, *Welfare Racism: Playing the Race Card against America's Poor* (New York: Routledge, 2002); Mark Peffley, Jon Hurwitz, and Paul M. Sniderman, "Racial Stereotypes and Whites' Political Views of Blacks

in the Context of Welfare and Crime," *American Journal of Political Science* 41, no. 1 (1997): 30–60; Jill S. Quadagno, *The Color of Welfare: How Racism Undermined the War on Poverty* (New York: Oxford University Press, 1994).

43. Both Florence and Nelly Fisher are pseudonyms. Also, Nelly Fisher was a former full-time teacher who continued to substitute following her retirement.

44. It should be noted that, while performing whiteness was seen as a way to take control of white racial identity, the teachers I interviewed believed that doing so had limits. That is, being a specific, more racially amenable kind of white teacher only went so far. A big part of their racial identity came from without. Meaning, whether they liked it or not, their racial identity was often assigned to them by black students and black families.

45. Although I speak more about political correctness in chapter 4, I feel it is important to point out here that performing whiteness to appease black students, black families, and black coworkers was seen by many white teachers as its own form of political correctness.

46. This new form of white racial socialization was localized to Brick City schools. The racial awareness they exhibited did not follow them outside of their respective classrooms and schools, which, in part, accounts for the white racelessness demonstrated in chapter 1.

FOUR. THE WHITE RACE CARD

Epigraph: Perry, *Shades of White*, 3.

1. Richard T. Ford, *The Race Card: How Bluffing about Bias Makes Race Relations Worse* (London: Macmillan, 2008).

2. Larry Elder, *Stupid Black Men: How to Play the Race Card—and Lose* (New York: Macmillan, 2008).

3. Tim Wise, *Colorblind: The Rise of Post-racial Politics and the Retreat from Racial Equity* (San Francisco: City Lights Books, 2010).

4. Ford, *The Race Card*.

5. Desmond and Emirbayer, *Racial Domination, Racial Progress*; Ford, *The Race Card*; Wise, *Colorblind*; George Yancy, *Backlash: What Happens When We Talk Honestly about Racism in America* (Lanham, MD: Rowman and Littlefield, 2018).

6. Each of these publications, to name but a few, has included multiple pieces admonishing liberals, particularly liberals of color, for allegedly playing the race card. At the heart of this critique is typically one of three themes: (1) the race card is used when liberals and people of color cannot win a political debate on the merits, (2) white liberals deploy the race card in order to pander to people of color for votes, and (3) people of color use the race card to make excuses for their collective moral and cultural failings. In recent years, the discourse surrounding the race card has overlapped with that surrounding so-called identity politics.

7. Jon Hurwitz and Mark Peffley, "Playing the Race Card in the Post–Willie Horton Era: The Impact of Racialized Code Words on Support for Punitive Crime Policy," *Public Opinion Quarterly* 69, no. 1 (2005): 99–112; Tali Mendelberg, *The Race Card: Campaign Strategy, Implicit Messages, and the Norm of Equality* (Princeton, NJ: Prince-

ton University Press, 2017); Neubeck and Cazenave, *Welfare Racism*; Linda Williams, *Playing the Race Card: Melodramas of Black and White from Uncle Tom to O. J. Simpson* (Princeton, NJ: Princeton University Press, 2002).

8. Kinder and Sanders, *Divided by Color*; Maria Krysan, "Prejudice, Politics, and Public Opinion: Understanding the Sources of Racial Policy Attitudes," *Annual Review of Sociology* 26, no. 1 (2000): 135–168; Felicia Pratto, Jim Sidanius, Lisa M. Stallworth, and Bertram F. Malle, "Social Dominance Orientation: A Personality Variable Predicting Social and Political Attitudes," *Journal of Personality and Social Psychology* 67, no. 4 (1994): 741; Schuman et al., *Racial Attitudes in America*; Sniderman and Piazza, *Scar of Race*.

9. For detailed review of these studies, see Lawrence D. Bobo, Camille Z. Charles, Maria Krysan, and Alicia D. Simmons, "The Real Record on Racial Attitudes," *Social Trends in American Life: Findings from the General Social Survey since 1972*, edited by Peter V. Marsden (Princeton, NJ: Princeton University Press, 2012), 38–83; and Krysan, "Prejudice, Politics, and Public Opinion."

10. DiAngelo, *What Does It Mean to Be White?*

11. Elder, *Stupid Black Men*; McWhorter, *Losing the Race*.

12. DiAngelo, *What Does It Mean to Be White?*

13. Bonilla-Silva, *Racism without Racists*; Meghan Burke, *Colorblind Racism* (Cambridge: Polity, 2018); Leslie G. Carr, *"Color-Blind" Racism* (Thousand Oaks, CA: Sage, 1997).

14. Irving, *Waking Up White*; Tatum, *Why Are All the Black Kids Sitting Together in the Cafeteria?*

15. To be clear, most teachers were willing to admit that racism against nonwhites still exists, but they rejected the idea that it was systematic. Yes, we still have individual bigots, but no, that was not seen as "an excuse for failure."

16. Aarti Iyer, Colin Wayne Leach, and Faye J. Crosby, "White Guilt and Racial Compensation: The Benefits and Limits of Self-Focus," *Personality and Social Psychology Bulletin* 29, no. 1 (2003): 117–129; Shelby Steele, *White Guilt: How Blacks and Whites Together Destroyed the Promise of the Civil Rights Era* (New York: HarperCollins, 2009).

17. Interview respondents were especially protective of urban education. To the extent that urban schools were dysfunctional, which they readily admitted to, it was because of education policy, school administrators, and most of all, the culture, behavior, and work ethic of the students who attended them.

18. Joe R. Feagin and Vera Hernan, *White Racism: The Basics* (New York: Routledge, 2000); David T. Wellman, *Portraits of White Racism* (Cambridge: Cambridge University Press, 1993).

19. Defending themselves against charges of racism was a common theme running throughout my interview data. This particular theme can be found in chapters 3, 4, and 5.

20. Lawrence Bobo and James R. Kluegel, "Opposition to Race-Targeting: Self-Interest, Stratification Ideology, or Racial Attitudes?," *American Sociological Review* 58 (1993): 443–464; DiAngelo and Sensoy, "Getting Slammed"; Joe R. Feagin and Eileen

O'Brian, *White Men on Race: Power, Privilege, and the Shaping of Cultural Consciousness* (Boston: Beacon, 2003); Michael Kimmel, *Angry White Men: American Masculinity at the End of an Era*, rev. ed. (New York: Nation Books, 2017); David O. Sears, Colette Van Laar, Mary Carrillo, and Rick Kosterman, "Is It Really Racism? The Origins of White Americans' Opposition to Race-Targeted Policies," *Public Opinion Quarterly* 61, no. 1 (1997): 16–53; Solomona et al., "The Discourse of Denial"; Sabina E. Vaught and Angelina E. Castagno, "'I Don't Think I'm a Racist': Critical Race Theory, Teacher Attitudes, and Structural Racism," *Race, Ethnicity and Education* 11, no. 2 (2008): 95–113.

21. Barbara Trepagnier, *Silent Racism: How Well-Meaning White People Perpetuate the Racial Divide*, 2nd ed. (London: Routledge, 2017).

22. A number of teachers talked about how they wished they could do more for their students economically. They brought up things like food insecurity, housing insecurity, disconnected phones, dirty clothes, and poor hygiene. Again, though, with only a few exceptions, teachers failed to connect any of these conditions to race or racism.

23. For a more detailed discussion of race and ideology, see chapter 5.

24. For a more detailed discussion of *doing whiteness*, see chapter 3.

25. DiAngelo, *What Does It Mean to Be White?*

26. DiAngelo, *What Does It Mean to Be White?*, 151, emphasis in original.

27. DiAngelo, *What Does It Mean to Be White?*; Frankenberg, *White Women, Race Matters*; Kaufman, "A User's Guide to White Privilege"; L. Johnson, "'My Eyes Have Been Opened'"; McIntosh, "White Privilege"; McKinney, *Being White*.

28. hooks, *Representing Whiteness*.

29. DiAngelo, *What Does It Mean to Be White?*

30. Mr. Ball is a pseudonym.

31. DiAngelo, *What Does It Mean to Be White?*; Joe R. Feagin and Debra Van Ausdale, *The First R: How Children Learn Race and Racism* (Lanham, MD: Rowman and Littlefield, 2001); McKinney, *Being White*.

32. Stuart Hall and Paul du Gay, eds., *Questions of Cultural Identity* (London: Sage, 1996).

33. Several teachers remarked about their black colleagues being "from the culture." When I pressed them, they could not exactly define what they meant by this construction. As far as I can tell, being black, demographically, was enough to be considered a product of black culture.

34. As this reasoning implies, white teachers all but took an essentialist approach to black teachers and black students. On the whole, they made little room for intraracial variation among the black bodies that populated their respective schools.

35. For a more detailed account of how white teachers attempted to leverage "black culture," please see my discussion on "becoming white teachers" in chapter 3.

36. During this part of the interview, Mrs. Edwards repeatedly used the word "merit" when explaining her version of a high-quality teacher, and her thoughts about career advancement. From schools to society, she made it clear that she was a firm believer in American meritocracy.

37. I say "typically" here because there are some exceptions. That is, there are plenty of whites in America who do believe in the existence of institutional racism, and there are plenty of nonwhite people who accuse people of color and their white allies of playing the race card. To this day, it is not a simple black/white binary in terms of who does and who does not chastise others for making claims of nonwhite racial victimization.

38. While white Brick City teachers were in the minority, numerically, white people still comprised a disproportionate number of principals, vice principals, and other positions of power. Therefore, their comparison to racial minorities throughout America writ large is empirically and experientially limited.

FIVE. COLORBLIND

Epigraph: Gallagher, "Color-Blind Privilege," 24–25.

1. Plessy v. Ferguson, 163 U.S. 537 (1896).

2. Justice Harlan quoted in Ralph Hofstader, *Great Issues in American History* (New York: Vintage Books, 1982), 58. It should be noted that even though colorblindness as an ideology traverses several centuries of American history, it has not always been used in the same way. See the progressive vision of Martin Luther King Jr., for example, contrasted with the often neoliberal, reactionary way it is used in the contemporary United States.

3. Carr, *"Color-Blind" Racism*; Lawrence Goldstone, *Inherently Unequal: The Betrayal of Equal Rights by the Supreme Court, 1865–1903* (New York: Walker, 2011).

4. Bonilla-Silva, *Racism without Racists*; Bonilla-Silva and Dietrich, "The Sweet Enchantment of Color-Blind Racism in Obamerica"; Burke, *Colorblind Racism*; Carr, *"Color-Blind" Racism*; Douglas Hartmann, Paul R. Croll, Ryan Larson, Joseph Gerteis, and Alex Manning, "Colorblindness as Identity: Key Determinants, Relations to Ideology, and Implications for Attitudes about Race and Policy," *Sociological Perspectives* 60, no. 5 (2017): 866–888; Ian Haney López, "'A Nation of Minorities': Race, Ethnicity, and Reactionary Colorblindness," *Stanford Law Review* 59 (2007): 985–1063.

5. Bonilla-Silva and Dietrich, "The Sweet Enchantment of Color-Blind Racism in Obamerica"; Wise, *Colorblind*.

6. Bobo, Kluegel, and Smith, "Laissez-Faire Racism"; Bobo and Kluegel, "Opposition to Race-Targeting"; Bonilla-Silva, *Racism without Racists*; Gallagher, "Color-Blind Privilege"; Sniderman and Piazza, *Scar of Race*; Laurie Cooper Stoll, *Should Schools Be Colorblind?* (Cambridge: Polity, 2019); Wise, *Colorblind*.

7. Bobo, "Somewhere between Jim Crow and Post-racialism"; Feagin and Vera, *White Racism*.

8. For a small sampling of this work, see Bettina L. Love and Brandelyn Tosolt, "Reality or Rhetoric? Barack Obama and Post-racial America," *Race, Gender and Class* 17, nos. 3–4 (2010): 19–37; McWhorter, *Losing the Race*; Sniderman and Piazza, *Scar of Race*; Shelby Steele, *The Content of Our Character: A New Vision of Race in America* (New York: St. Martin's, 1990); Stephan Thernstrom and Abigail Thernstrom, *America in Black and White: One Nation, Indivisible* (New York: Simon and Schuster, 1999).

9. Bonilla-Silva and Dietrich, "The Sweet Enchantment of Color-Blind Racism in Obamerica"; Gallagher, "Color-Blind Privilege"; Wise, *Colorblind*.

10. See chapter 4.

11. Gregory S. Parks and Matthew W. Hughey, eds., *The Obamas and a (Post)Racial America?* (Oxford: Oxford University Press, 2011); Lydia Lum, "The Obama Era: A Post-racial Society?," *Diverse: Issues in Higher Education* 25, no. 26 (2009): 14–16; Michael Tesler, *Post-Racial or Most-Racial? Race and Politics in the Obama Era* (Chicago: University of Chicago Press, 2016); Michael Tesler and David O. Sears, *Obama's Race: The 2008 Election and the Dream of a Post-racial America* (Chicago: University of Chicago Press, 2010).

12. Feagin, *The White Racial Frame.*

13. Bobo, Kluegel, and Smith, "Laissez-Faire Racism"; Bonilla-Silva, *Racism without Racists*; Feagin, *The White Racial Frame.*

14. Bobo, "Somewhere between Jim Crow and Post-racialism"; Bobo, Kluegel, and Smith, "Laissez-Faire Racism"; Feagin, *The White Racial Frame*; Parks and Hughey, *The Obamas and a (Post)Racial America?*; Tesler, *Post-Racial or Most-Racial?*; Wise, *Colorblind.*

15. It should be noted that, because I focus on ideological and discursive contradictions, this chapter revisits much of the data that structured chapters 3 and 4. Similarly, I touch on a number of concepts and themes that were discussed in previous chapters, albeit in new and illuminating ways.

16. Feagin, *The White Racial Frame*, ix.

17. Feagin, *The White Racial Frame*, ix, emphasis in original.

18. For example, several teachers specifically denounced the Ku Klux Klan, white supremacists, and "those neo-Nazi types." Overt racism was uniformly denounced across all interviews.

19. Bobo, Kluegel, and Smith, "Laissez-Faire Racism"; Bonilla-Silva, *Racism without Racists*; Carr, *"Color-Blind" Racism*; Feagin, *The White Racial Frame*; Charles A. Gallagher, "Color-Blind Privilege."

20. Bonilla-Silva, *Racism without Racists.*

21. Bonilla-Silva, *Racism without Racists*, 211.

22. Bonilla-Silva, *Racism without Racists*; Bonilla-Silva and Dietrich, "The Sweet Enchantment of Color-Blind Racism in Obamerica"; Carr, *"Color-Blind" Racism*; Tyrone A. Forman and Amanda E. Lewis, "Racial Apathy and Hurricane Katrina: The Social Anatomy of Prejudice in the Post–Civil Rights Era," *Du Bois Review* 3, no. 1 (2006): 175–202; Wise, *Colorblind.*

23. Bonilla-Silva, *Racism without Racists.*

24. Bonilla-Silva, *Racism without Racists*, 23.

25. E. Anderson, *Code of the Street*; Bonilla-Silva, *Racism without Racists*; Bonilla-Silva and Dietrich, "The Sweet Enchantment of Color-Blind Racism in Obamerica"; Richard J. Herrnstein and Charles Murray, *The Bell Curve: Intelligence and Class Structure in American Life* (New York: Simon and Schuster, 1994); McWhorter, *Losing the Race*; Saini, *Superior*; Small and Newman, "Urban Poverty after the Truly Disadvantaged."

26. Jessica S. Cobb, "Inequality Frames: How Teachers Inhabit Color-Blind Ideology," *Sociology of Education* 90, no. 4 (2017): 315–332; Gallagher, "Color-Blind Privi-

lege"; Hartmann et al., "Colorblindness as Identity"; Uma M. Jayakumar and Annie S. Adamian, "The Fifth Frame of Colorblind Ideology: Maintaining the Comforts of Colorblindness in the Context of White Fragility," *Sociological Perspectives* 60, no. 5 (2017): 912–936; Monica McDermott, "Color-Blind and Color-Visible Identity among American Whites," *American Behavioral Scientist* 59, no. 11 (2015): 1452–1473; Marianne Modica, "Unpacking the 'Colorblind Approach': Accusations of Racism at a Friendly, Mixed-Race School," *Race, Ethnicity and Education* 18, no. 3 (2015): 396–418; Laurie C. Stoll, "Constructing the Color-Blind Classroom: Teachers' Perspectives on Race and Schooling," *Race, Ethnicity and Education* 17, no. 5 (2014): 688–705; Stoll, *Should Schools Be Colorblind?*

27. Bonilla-Silva, *Racism without Racists*; Cobb, "Inequality Frames"; Jayakumar and Adamian, "The Fifth Frame of Colorblind Ideology"; Mueller, "Producing Colorblindness."

28. Bonilla-Silva, *Racism without Racists*.

29. Bobo, "Somewhere between Jim Crow and Post-racialism"; Carr, *"Color-Blind" Racism*; Gallagher, "Color-Blind Privilege"; Hartmann et al., "Colorblindness as Identity."

30. Bonilla-Silva and Dietrich, "The Sweet Enchantment of Color-Blind Racism in Obamerica"; Hartmann et al., "Colorblindness as Identity"; McDermott, "Color-Blind and Color-Visible Identity among American Whites."

31. Bonilla-Silva et al., "'It Wasn't Me!'"; Cobb, "Inequality Frames"; Gallagher, "Color-Blind Privilege"; Hartmann et al., "Colorblindness as Identity"; Modica, "Unpacking the 'Colorblind Approach.'"

32. This particular line was an homage to Martin Luther King Jr.'s famous 1963 "I Have a Dream" speech.

33. Desmond and Emirbayer, *Racial Domination, Racial Progress*.

34. In 2014, Michael Brown, an unarmed African American male, was shot and killed by Darren Wilson, a white police officer. Mostly peaceful protests, and some rioting, ensued after Wilson was not charged with a crime.

35. Bonilla-Silva, *Racism without Racists*, 2.

36. While most teachers dismissed racism, some of the more politically progressive teachers did talk seriously about the debilitating and constraining effects of poverty.

37. When the interviewee described the activist's trademark blue vest, I was able to determine that the guy in question was DeRay McKesson, a prominent Black Lives Matter advocate.

38. Jean Yonemura Wing, "Beyond Black and White: The Model Minority Myth and the Invisibility of Asian American Students," *Urban Review* 39, no. 4 (2007): 455–487; Tianlong Yu, "Challenging the Politics of the 'Model Minority' Stereotype: A Case for Educational Equality," *Equity and Excellence in Education* 39, no. 4 (2006): 325–333; Qin Zhang, "Asian Americans beyond the Model Minority Stereotype: The Nerdy and the Left Out," *Journal of International and Intercultural Communication* 3, no. 1 (2010): 20–37.

39. For a good breakdown of voting patterns by race, see Haney López, *Dog Whistle Politics*.

40. At one point when talking about President Obama, Mrs. Edwards referred to him as a Muslim and even indicated that she did not believe he was an American citizen. She also expressed her belief that President Obama was racially biased against white people.

41. Wing, "Beyond Black and White"; Zhang, "Asian Americans beyond the Model Minority Stereotype."

42. The few teachers who mentioned Japanese internment or Chinese exclusion (four in total) were all either history or social studies teachers.

43. Desmond and Emirbayer, *Racial Domination, Racial Progress*, 36.

44. Like many people, white and nonwhite alike, Mrs. Peterson did not differentiate between race and ethnicity. She assumed all Asian and Asian American groups are highly educated and economically successful, which is factually inaccurate.

45. *Merriam-Webster*, s.v. "post- (prefix)," accessed November 25, 2020, https://www.merriam-webster.com/dictionary/post.

46. Louise Seamster and Victor Ray, "Against Teleology in the Study of Race: Toward the Abolition of the Progress Paradigm," *Sociological Theory* 36, no. 4 (2018): 315–342; Andreas Wimmer, "Race-Centrism: A Critique and a Research Agenda," *Ethnic and Racial Studies* 38, no. 13 (2015): 2186–2205.

47. Seamster and Ray, "Against Teleology in the Study of Race," 316.

48. Bobo, "Somewhere between Jim Crow and Post-racialism"; Bobo, Kluegel, and Smith, "Laissez-Faire Racism"; Bonilla-Silva, *Racism without Racists*; Desmond and Emirbayer, *Racial Domination, Racial Progress*; Kasey Henricks, "When Questions Do Not Yield Answers: Foreclosures of Racial Knowledge Production," *Sociology Compass* 10, no. 11 (2016): 1028–1037; Rahsaan Mahadeo, "Why Is the Time Always Right for White and Wrong for Us? How Racialized Youth Make Sense of Whiteness and Temporal Inequality," *Sociology of Race and Ethnicity* 5, no. 2 (2019): 186–199.

49. Eduardo Bonilla-Silva, Carla Goar, and David G. Embrick, "When Whites Flock Together: The Social Psychology of White Habitus," *Critical Sociology* 32, nos. 2–3 (2006): 229–253.

50. By "nonpersonal," I mean racial victimization that is not experienced by them personally.

51. Feagin, *Systemic Racism*; Gallagher, "Color-Blind Privilege"; Rothenberg, *White Privilege*; Wise, *Colorblind*.

52. To be clear, at no point were any of my interviewees aggressive toward me.

53. He moved to a new school and has since been granted tenure. Both schools have predominantly black student bodies.

54. Bonilla-Silva, *Racism without Racists*; Bonilla-Silva, Goar, and Embrick, "When Whites Flock Together."

CONCLUSION

Epigraphs: Bill O'Reilly made the 2007 comments on his radio show in response to President George W. Bush's push for comprehensive immigration reform; O'Reilly made the 2012 comments live on Fox News in reaction to what appeared to be—and eventually was—the reelection of President Barack Obama; Steve Phillips, *Brown Is the*

New White: How the Demographic Revolution Has Created a New American Majority (New York: New Press, 2016), 45.

1. William J. Hussar and Tabitha M. Bailey, *Projections of Education Statistics to 2022*, 41st ed. (Washington, DC: US Department of Education, 2014), http://nces.ed .gov/pubs2014/2014051.pdf.

2. US Department of Education, "The State of Racial Diversity in the Education Workforce," July 2016, https://www2.ed.gov/rschstat/eval/highered/racial-diversity /state-racial-diversity-workforce.pdf.

3. For a discussion about the demographic gap—and its attendant consequences— between white teachers and nonwhite students in public schools, see the introduction to this book, as well as chapters 2 and 3.

4. D. Cohn and A. Caumont, "10 Demographic Trends That Are Shaping the U.S. and the World," Pew Research, March 31, 2016, https://www.pewresearch.org/fact -tank/2016/03/31/10-demographic-trends-that-are-shaping-the-u-s-and-the-world/.

5. For a detailed breakdown of projected demographic changes, see Jonathan Vespa, Lauren Medina, and David M. Armstrong, "Demographic Turning Points for the United States: Population Projections for 2020 to 2060," March 2018; rev. February 2020, https://www.census.gov/content/dam/Census/library/publications/2020/demo /p25-1144.pdf.

6. Nathan Robinson, "Rich White Men Rule America: How Long Will We Tolerate That?," *Guardian*, May 20, 2019, https://www.theguardian.com/commentisfree/2019 /may/20/rich-white-men-rule-america-minority-rule.

7. E. Anderson, "The White Space"; Lipsitz, *How Racism Takes Place*.

8. For several empirical examples, see Maureen A. Craig and Jennifer A. Richeson, "More Diverse Yet Less Tolerant? How the Increasingly Diverse Racial Landscape Affects White Americans' Racial Attitudes," *Personality and Social Psychology Bulletin* 40, no. 6 (2014): 750–761; Maureen A. Craig and Jennifer A. Richeson, "On the Precipice of a 'Majority-Minority' America: Perceived Status Threat from the Racial Demographic Shift Affects White Americans' Political Ideology," *Psychological Science* 25, no. 6 (2014): 1189–1197; Felix Danbold and Yuen J. Huo, "No Longer 'All-American'? Whites' Defensive Reactions to Their Numerical Decline," *Social Psychological and Personality Science* 6, no. 2 (2015): 210–218; Outten et al., "Feeling Threatened."

9. Bakari Kitwana, *Why White Kids Love Hip-Hop: Wankstas, Wiggers, Wannabes, and the New Reality of Race in America* (New York: Civitas Books, 2005).

10. College courses on whiteness, white privilege, and white racism can be found in a growing number of colleges and universities across America, including in many prestigious institutions such as Syracuse University, the University of Wisconsin–Madison, and Yale University.

11. For Harriet Tubman, see Jackie Calmes, "Harriet Tubman Ousts Andrew Jackson in Change for a $20," *New York Times*, April 21, 2016, https://www.nytimes.com /2016/04/21/us/women-currency-treasury-harriet-tubman.html.

12. For Confederate flags, see "After 54 Years, Confederate Flag Comes Down in S.C.," CBS News, last updated July 10, 2015, http://www.cbsnews.com/news/confederate -flag-south-carolina-statehouse-grounds-comes-down/. For Confederate monuments,

see Associated Press, "New Orleans Removes Another Confederate Monument; Jefferson Davis Statue Comes Down amid Cheers and Jeers," *Los Angeles Times*, May 11, 2017, http://www.latimes.com/nation/nationnow/la-na-jefferson-davis-statue-20170511-story.html.

13. The prevalence of public police shootings has prompted a combination of political leaders, law enforcement officials, community activists, business leaders, professional athletes, and even celebrities to openly discuss the intersection of race, crime, and punishment. For a brief overview of police violence, see "Black Lives Upended by Policing: The Raw Videos Sparking Outrage," *New York Times*, updated April 19, 2018, https://www.nytimes.com/interactive/2017/08/19/us/police-videos-race.html.

14. See Jonathan Chait, "Not a Very P.C. Thing to Say: How the Language Police Are Perverting Liberalism," *New York Magazine*, January 27, 2015, http://nymag.com/daily/intelligencer/2015/01/not-a-very-pc-thing-to-say.html.

15. See B. Weiss, "Meet the Renegades of the Intellectual Dark Web," *New York Times*, May 8, 2018, https://www.nytimes.com/2018/05/08/opinion/intellectual-dark-web.html.

16. For a detailed overview of the main grievances of the "Intellectual Dark Web," see Henry Farrell, "The 'Intellectual Dark Web' Explained: What Jordan Peterson Has in Common with the Alt-Right," *Vox*, May 10, 2018, https://www.vox.com/the-big-idea/2018/5/10/17338290/intellectual-dark-web-rogan-peterson-harris-times-weiss.

17. In one high-profile example, Roseanne Barr was fired from her highly rated television show after sending a racist tweet about Valerie Jarrett, longtime adviser to former president Barack Obama. For a summary, see John Koblin, "After Racist Tweet, Roseanne Barr's Show Cancelled by ABC," *New York Times*, May 29, 2018, https://www.nytimes.com/2018/05/29/business/media/roseanne-barr-offensive-tweets.html.

18. For a detailed review, see Justin Gest, *The New Minority: White Working Class Politics in an Age of Immigration and Inequality* (New York: Oxford University Press, 2016); M. Norris, "As America Changes, Some Anxious Whites Feel Left Behind," *National Geographic*, April 2018, https://www.nationalgeographic.com/magazine/2018/04/race-rising-anxiety-white-america/.

19. Gest, *The New Minority*; Norris, "As America Changes."

20. For example, cultural displacement was a major motivating factor for white voters in the 2016 presidential election. The more anxious that working-class whites felt about demographic and cultural changes, the more likely they were to vote for Donald Trump. For analysis, see Daniel Cox, Rachel Lienesch, and Robert P. Jones, "Beyond Economics: Fears of Cultural Displacement Pushed the White Working Class to Trump," PRRI/*Atlantic*, May 9, 2017, https://www.prri.org/research/white-working-class-attitudes-economy-trade-immigration-election-donald-trump/.

21. For an example of growing white anxiety, see Gest, *The New Minority*; T. Kludt and B. Stelter, "White Anxiety Finds a Home at Fox News," CNN, August 9, 2018, https://www.cnn.com/2018/09/28/media/fox-news-laura-ingraham-tucker-carlson-white-nationalism/index.html.

22. Craig and Richeson, "More Diverse Yet Less Tolerant?"; Gest, *The New Mi-*

nority; Robert P. Jones, *The End of White Christian America* (New York: Simon and Schuster, 2016).

23. You can see O'Reilly's comments here: "Fox's O'Reilly: 50% of Voters Will Support Obama Because They 'Feel That They Are Entitled to Things,'" Media Matters, November 6, 2012, https://www.mediamatters.org/video/2012/11/06/foxs -oreilly-50-of-voters-will-support-obama-be/191188.

24. For example, in the 1988 presidential election, Republican George H. W. Bush, after getting 60 percent of the white vote, won in an electoral college landslide, 426–111, over his Democratic opponent, Michael Dukakis. See "How Groups Voted in 1988," Roper Center, accessed November 15, 2020, http://ropercenter.cornell.edu/how -groups-voted-1988. By comparison, in the 2012 presidential election, despite getting 59 percent of the white votes, Republican challenger Mitt Romney lost in an electoral college landslide, 332–206, to Democratic incumbent Barack Obama. See "How Groups Voted in 2012," Roper Center, accessed November 15, 2020, https://ropercenter .cornell.edu/how-groups-voted-2012.

25. John T. Warren, *Performing Purity: Whiteness, Pedagogy, and the Reconstruction of Power* (New York: Peter Lang, 2003). Warren describes the rhetorical body of whiteness as the "communicative systems of whiteness that influence our understandings or race," and as a "rhetoric as a way of knowing, in which whiteness is an epistemological construct" (19).

26. For Limbaugh, see "Limbaugh: 'We're Outnumbered. . . . We've Lost the Country,'" Media Matters, November 7, 2012, https://www.mediamatters.org/video /2012/11/07/limbaugh-were-outnumbered-weve-lost-the-country/191210. For Miller, see "Dennis Miller Reacts to Romney Losing Election, America under Obama," Real Clear Politics, November 7, 2012, http://www.realclearpolitics.com/video/2012/11/07 /dennis_miller_reacts_to_romney_losing_election_america_under_obama.html. Finally, Ann Coulter made these comments to Sean Hannity on *Hannity* (Fox News), November 7, 2012.

27. Ashley Jardina, *White Identity Politics* (Cambridge: Cambridge University Press, 2019); Michael I. Norton and Samuel R. Sommers, "Whites See Racism as a Zero-Sum Game That They Are Now Losing," *Perspectives on Psychological Science* 6, no. 3 (2011): 215–218.

28. See chapter 4.

29. The birther movement was a collection of right-wing conservatives who questioned President Obama's citizenship. That is, the birther movement rejected President Obama's eligibility to be president.

30. Craig and Richeson, "More Diverse Yet Less Tolerant?"; Craig and Richeson, "On the Precipice of a 'Majority-Minority' America"; Danbold and Huo, "No Longer 'All-American'?"; Jardina, *White Identity Politics*; Brenda Major, Alison Blodorn, and Gregory Major Blascovich, "The Threat of Increasing Diversity: Why Many White Americans Support Trump in the 2016 Presidential Election," *Group Processes and Intergroup Relations* 21, no. 6 (2016): 931–940; Outten et al., "Feeling Threatened."

31. Candidate Trump famously accused Mexico of sending rapists and murderers into the United States, questioned the impartiality of a federal judge based solely on his

Mexican heritage, proposed banning all Muslims from entering the United States, and was endorsed by numerous white supremacists, including David Duke, the alt-right, and the Ku Klux Klan.

32. It should be noted, here, that while Trump's naked appeals to white nationalism won over some white voters, it also cost him with others. Many lifelong conservatives and operatives of the Republican Party, refusing to vote for Trump because of his racism and xenophobia, either stayed home, voted third-party, or even supported the Democratic candidate, Hillary Clinton. This accounts for Trump's only receiving 58 percent of the white vote despite bringing in a number of white nonvoters and many from the Democratic Party. For fear of diversity, see Sean McElwee and Jason McDaniel, "Fear of Diversity Made People More Likely to Vote for Trump," *The Nation*, March 14, 2017, https://www.thenation.com/article/fear-of-diversity-made -people-more-likely-to-vote-trump/. For cultural anxiety, see Cox, Lienesch, and Jones, "Beyond Economics."

33. For a detailed analysis of Trump's approval rating among white voters, see Thomas B. Edsall, "We Aren't Seeing White Support for Trump for What It Is," *New York Times*, August 28, 2019, https://www.nytimes.com/2019/08/28/opinion/trump -white-voters.html.

34. For a detailed look at President Trump's immigration crackdown, see S. Pierce, J. Bolter, and A. Selee, "U.S. Immigration Policy under Trump: Deep Changes and Lasting Impacts," Migration Policy Institute, July 2018, https://www.migrationpolicy .org/research/us-immigration-policy-trump-deep-changes-impacts. For analyses of President Trump's legal immigration policies, see S. Anderson, "Trump Is Fighting to Dramatically Restrict Legal Immigration," *Reason*, March 21, 2019, https://reason.com /archives/2019/03/21/trump-is-fighting-to-dramatically-restri. For a timeline of the president's travel ban, see American Civil Liberties Union, "Timeline of the Muslim Ban" (January 27, 2017–February 10, 2020), accessed November 15, 2020, https:// www.aclu-wa.org/pages/timeline-muslim-ban. Finally, for an analysis of President Trump's voter fraud claims, see L. King, "Trump's Claims of Massive Voter Fraud are Baseless, Election Integrity Panel Member Says," *USA Today*, August 4, 2018, https:// www.usatoday.com/story/news/politics/2018/08/04/donald-trumps-widespread-voter -fraud-claim-untrue-election-official/905262002/.

35. For President Trump's comments on white nationalists, see R. Gray, "Trump Defends White-Nationalist Protestors: 'Some Very Fine People on Both Sides,'" *Atlantic*, August 15, 2017, https://www.theatlantic.com/politics/archive/2017/08/trump-defends -white-nationalist-protesters-some-very-fine-people-on-both-sides/537012/. For President Trump's comments on African countries, see A. Vitali, K. Hunt, and F. Thorp, "Trump Referred to Haiti and African Nations as 'Shithole' Countries," NBC News, January 11, 2018, https://www.nbcnews.com/politics/white-house/trump-referred -haiti-african-countries-shithole-nations-n836946. For taxpayer funds going to rural, predominantly white states, see Don Lee, "Trump Dispenses Billions of Dollars in Aid to Farmers, Hoping to Shore Up Rural Base," *Los Angeles Times*, November 27, 2019, https://www.latimes.com/politics/story/2019-11-27/trump-dispenses-billions-aid-to

-farmers-shore-up-rural-base. For a detailed and empirical analysis of white identity politics, see Jardina, *White Identity Politics*. Also, while it is too soon to deconstruct the 2020 presidential election, early exit polls indicate Trump lost white support, particularly among college-educated white voters, and he gained nonwhite support, particularly among Hispanic and African American males.

36. Jardina, *White Identity Politics*.

37. Jardina, *White Identity Politics*, 16.

38. John Sides, Michael Tesler, and Lynn Vavreck, *Identity Crisis: The 2016 Presidential Campaign and the Battle for the Meaning of America* (Princeton, NJ: Princeton University Press, 2018).

39. In *Identity Crisis*, Sides, Tesler, and Vavreck describe conservative racial attitudes as those that see ongoing racial inequality, particularly between white and black people, as the fault of black people themselves, as opposed to ongoing discrimination. Whether pathological culture, poor work ethic, an inability to delay gratification, opposition to schools, single parent homes, or even genetic inferiority, people who hold conservative racial attitudes see black people, and not racism, as the most prominent reason for contemporary racial inequality.

40. Sides, Tesler, and Vavreck, *Identity Crisis*.

41. Brian F. Schaffner, Matthew MacWilliams, and Tatishe Nteta, "Understanding White Polarization in the 2016 Vote for President: The Sobering Role of Racism and Sexism," *Political Science Quarterly* 133, no. 1 (2018): 9–34; Tyler T. Reny, Loren Collingwood, and Ali A. Valenzuela, "Vote Switching in the 2016 Election: How Racial and Immigration Attitudes, Not Economics, Explain Shifts in White Voting," *Public Opinion Quarterly* 83, no. 1 (2019): 91–113; Sides, Tesler, and Vavreck, *Identity Crisis*.

42. Jardina, *White Identity Politics*; Sides, Tesler, and Vavreck, *Identity Crisis*.

43. Jardina, *White Identity Politics*; Major, Blodorn, and Major Blascovich, "The Threat of Increasing Diversity"; Cox, Lienesch, and Jones, "Beyond Economics"; Sides, Tesler, and Vavreck, *Identity Crisis*.

44. Sides, Tesler, and Vavreck, *Identity Crisis*.

45. For more about Hillary's speech on Trump and the alt-right, see Maria L. La Ganga, "Clinton Slams Trump's 'Racist Ideology' That Ushers Hate Groups into Mainstream," *Guardian*, August 25, 2016, https://www.theguardian.com/us-news/2016/aug/25/hillary-clinton-alt-right-racism-speech-donald-trump-nevada. For more about the Mothers of the Movement speaking at the DNC, see W. Drabold, "Meet the Mothers of the Movement: Speaking at the Democratic National Convention," *Time*, July 26, 2016, https://time.com/4423920/dnc-mothers-movement-speakers/.

46. In one high-profile example, at a campaign fundraiser, Hillary infamously referred to half of Trump's supporters as a "basket of deplorables." For more on these comments, see Z. Miller, "Hillary Clinton Says Half of Donald Trump's Supporters Are in 'Basket of Deplorables,'" *Time*, September 10, 2016, https://time.com/4486437/hillary-clinton-donald-trump-basket-of-deplorables/.

47. Jardina, *White Identity Politics*; Schaffner, MacWilliams, and Nteta, "Under-

standing White Polarization in the 2016 Vote for President"; Sides, Tesler, and Vavreck, *Identity Crisis*.

48. Sides, Tesler, and Vavreck, *Identity Crisis*.

49. Reny, Collingwood, and Valenzuela, "Vote Switching in the 2016 Election"; Schaffner, MacWilliams, and Nteta, "Understanding White Polarization in the 2016 Vote for President"; Sides, Tesler, and Vavreck, *Identity Crisis*.

50. For a detailed summary of white vs. nonwhite identity politics, see G. Lopez, "The Battle over Identity Politics, Explained," Vox, August 17, 2017, https://www.vox .com/identities/2016/12/2/13718770/identity-politics. For a summary of explicit racial appeals, see M. Rhor, "In 2018 Midterms, Campaign Ads Engaged in Racist Rhetoric," *USA Today*, November 7, 2018, https://www.usatoday.com/story/news/politics /elections/2018/11/07/2018-midterms-gop-candidates-racist-rhetoric-campaign-ads /1919980002/. For an empirical examination of how racial resentment bolsters GOP policies, see Jonathan M. Metzl, *Dying of Whiteness: How the Politics of Racial Resentment Is Killing America's Heartland* (New York: Hachette, 2019).

51. Jardina, *White Identity Politics*; Sides, Tesler, and Vavreck, *Identity Crisis*.

52. For several notable exceptions, see Marisa Abrajano and Zoltan L. Hajnal, *White Backlash: Immigration, Race, and American Politics* (Princeton, NJ: Princeton University Press, 2017); Gest, *The New Minority*; Hochschild, *Strangers in Their Own Land*; Jardina, *White Identity Politics*; Metzl, *Dying of Whiteness*; Sides, Tesler, and Vavreck, *Identity Crisis*.

53. Feagin, *The White Racial Frame*.

54. Feagin, *White Party, White Government*; Haney López, *Dog Whistle Politics*.

55. For several notable exceptions, see Paul R. Croll, "Modeling Determinants of White Racial Identity: Results from a New National Survey," *Social Forces* 86, no. 2 (2007): 613–642; Hartmann, Gerteis, and Croll, "An Empirical Assessment of Whiteness Theory"; and McDermott and Samson, "White Racial and Ethnic Identity."

56. For several notable exceptions, see chapter 2.

57. Alice McIntyre, *Participatory Action Research* (Thousand Oaks, CA: Sage, 2007).

58. Case and Deaton, *Deaths of Despair*; Gest, *The New Minority*.

APPENDIX

Epigraphs: Marjorie DeVault, *Liberating Method: Feminism and Social Research* (Philadelphia: Temple University Press, 1999), 84; Bruce L. Berg, *Qualitative Research Methods for the Social Sciences*, 6th ed. (London: Pearson, 2007), 3; Robert S. Weiss, *Learning from Strangers: The Art and Method of Qualitative Interview Studies* (New York: Free Press, 1994), 1.

1. John W. Creswell, *Qualitative Inquiry and Research Design: Choosing among Five Approaches* (Thousand Oaks, CA: Sage, 2013), 42.

2. Berg, *Qualitative Research Methods for the Social Sciences*; Robert K. Yin, *Qualitative Research from Start to Finish* (New York: Guilford, 2015).

3. Berg, *Qualitative Research Methods for the Social Sciences*; Creswell, *Qualitative Inquiry*; Yin, *Qualitative Research from Start to Finish*.

4. Creswell, *Qualitative Inquiry*; Norman K. Denzin and Yvonna S. Lincoln, *The Landscape of Qualitative Research* (New York: Sage, 2008); Yin, *Qualitative Research from Start to Finish*.

5. Kathy Charmaz, *Constructing Grounded Theory* (Thousand Oaks, CA: Sage, 2014); Creswell, *Qualitative Inquiry*.

6. Berg, *Qualitative Research Methods for the Social Sciences*; Creswell, *Qualitative Inquiry*; Denzin and Lincoln, *The Landscape of Qualitative Research*; Weiss, *Learning from Strangers*.

7. Irving Seidman, *Interviewing as Qualitative Research: A Guide for Researchers in Education and the Social Sciences*, 4th ed. (New York: Teachers College Press, 2013); Weiss, *Learning from Strangers*.

8. Herbert J. Rubin and Irene S. Rubin, *Qualitative Interviewing: The Art of Hearing Data* (Thousand Oaks, CA: Sage, 2011).

9. Michael Crotty, *The Foundations of Social Research: Meaning and Perspective in the Research Process* (Thousand Oaks, CA: Sage, 1998); Denzin and Lincoln, *The Landscape of Qualitative Research*; Rubin and Rubin, *Qualitative Interviewing*.

10. Rubin and Rubin, *Qualitative Interviewing*.

11. Rubin and Rubin, *Qualitative Interviewing*, 7.

12. Charmaz, *Constructing Grounded Theory*; Juliet M. Corbin and Anselm Strauss, "Grounded Theory Research: Procedures, Canons, and Evaluative Criteria," *Qualitative Sociology* 13, no. 1 (1990): 3–21; Barney G. Glaser and Anselm L. Strauss, *The Discovery of Grounded Theory: Strategies for Qualitative Research* (Chicago: Aldire, 1967); Rubin and Rubin, *Qualitative Interviewing*.

13. Glaser and Strauss, *The Discovery of Grounded Theory*.

14. Charmaz, *Constructing Grounded Theory*; Corbin and Strauss, "Grounded Theory Research"; Glaser and Strauss, *The Discovery of Grounded Theory*.

15. Rubin and Rubin, *Qualitative Interviewing*.

16. Imelda T. Coyne, "Sampling in Qualitative Research: Purposeful and Theoretical Sampling; Merging or Clear Boundaries?," *Journal of Advanced Nursing* 26, no. 3 (1997): 623–630.

17. Rubin and Rubin, *Qualitative Interviewing*.

18. Berg, *Qualitative Research Methods for the Social Sciences*; Patrick Biernacki and Dan Waldorf, "Snowball Sampling: Problems and Techniques of Chain Referral Sampling," *Sociological Methods and Research* 10, no. 2 (1981): 141–163.

19. Berg, *Qualitative Research Methods for the Social Sciences*, 43–44.

20. Mark S. Handcock and Krista J. Gile, "Comment: On the Concept of Snowball Sampling," *Sociological Methodology* 41, no. 1 (2011): 367–371.

21. I actually recruited over fifty teachers. However, due to data saturation, I settled on thirty-two interviews.

22. A brief, nonexhaustive list includes Terry Arendell, "Reflections on the Researcher-Researched Relationship: A Woman Interviewing Men," *Qualitative Sociology* 20, no. 3 (1997): 341–368; Amy L. Best, "Doing Race in the Context of Feminist Interviewing: Constructing Whiteness through Talk," *Qualitative Inquiry* 9, no. 6 (2003): 895–914; DeVault, *Liberating Method*; Marc L. Hill, "Representin(g): Negotiating Mul-

tiple Roles and Identities in the Field and behind the Desk," *Qualitative Inquiry* 12, no. 5 (2006): 926–949; Reuben A. B. May, "When the Methodological Shoe Is on the Other Foot: African American Interviewer and White Interviewees," *Qualitative Sociology* 37, no. 1 (2014): 117–136; Robert K. Merton, "Insiders and Outsiders: A Chapter in the Sociology of Knowledge," *American Journal of Sociology* 78, no. 1 (1972): 9–47; Nancy A. Naples, "A Feminist Revisiting of the Insider/Outsider Debate: The 'Outsider Phenomenon' in Rural Iowa," *Qualitative Sociology* 19, no. 1 (1996): 83–106; France W. Twine and Jonathan W. Warren, eds., *Racing Research, Researching Race: Methodological Dilemmas in Critical Race Studies* (New York: NYU Press, 2000); Christine L. Williams and E. Joel Heikes, "The Importance of Researcher's Gender in the In-Depth Interview: Evidence from Two Case Studies of Male Nurses," *Gender and Society* 7, no. 2 (1993): 280–291; Maxine B. Zinn, "Field Research in Minority Communities: Ethical, Methodological and Political Observations by an Insider," *Social Problems* 27, no. 2 (1979): 209–219; Zuberi and Bonilla-Silva, *White Logic, White Methods*.

23. Merton, "Insiders and Outsiders"; Williams and Heikes, "The Importance of Researcher's Gender."

24. Bonilla-Silva, *Racism without Racists*; DiAngelo and Sensoy, "Getting Slammed"; McKinney, *Being White*.

25. The first instance was a younger teacher who had been out of college for only two years. She openly admitted that she was interested in attending graduate school, and that whiteness in education was something that she wanted to study in greater detail. The second instance was Mr. Marsh, who flatly stated that he would not sit down for an interview until he had better familiarized himself with the concept of whiteness. I provided them both with a comprehensive list of readings that included literature on whiteness in education, whiteness and the law, white racial identity, white racial discourse, the history of whiteness, and white antiracism.

26. Rubin and Rubin, *Qualitative Interviewing*, 192.

27. Rubin and Rubin, *Qualitative Interviewing*, 190.

28. Rubin and Rubin, *Qualitative Interviewing*, 194–195.

29. Glenn A. Bowen, "Naturalistic Inquiry and the Saturation Concept: A Research Note," *Qualitative Research* 8, no. 1 (2008): 140.

30. Charmaz, *Constructing Grounded Theory*; Corbin and Strauss, "Grounded Theory Research"; Glaser and Strauss, *The Discovery of Grounded Theory*; Rubin and Rubin, *Qualitative Interviewing*.

31. Rubin and Rubin, *Qualitative Interviewing*.

32. DeVault, *Liberating Method*; Smith, *Decolonizing Methodologies*; Twine and Warren, *Racing Research*; Zuberi and Bonilla-Silva, *White Logic, White Methods*.

33. Howard Winant, "Race and Race Theory," *Annual Review of Sociology* 26, no. 1 (2000): 169–185.

34. Martin Bulmer and John Solomos, eds., *Researching Race and Racism* (New York: Routledge, 2004).

35. Bulmer and Solomos, *Researching Race and Racism*; DeVault, *Liberating Method*; Smith, *Decolonizing Methodologies*; Twine and Warren, *Racing Research*; Zuberi and Bonilla-Silva, *White Logic, White Methods*.

36. Best, "Doing Race in the Context of Feminist Interviewing."

37. Marjorie L. DeVault, "Ethnicity and Expertise: Racial-Ethnic Knowledge in Sociological Research," *Gender and Society* 9, no. 5 (1995): 612–631.

38. Collins, *Black Feminist Thought*; DeVault, *Liberating Method*.

39. To be clear, not every teacher engaged in this behavior. During my fieldwork, only a small minority of teachers displayed outright racism. The much more common occurrence was repeating racial stereotypes. Still, even here, they were rarely repeated in a hateful or malicious manner. In fact, there were multiple occasions where it appeared as though interviewees did not fully realize the implications of what they were saying. When I followed up, just for clarification purposes, they often appeared embarrassed by, and ashamed about, their own words.

BIBLIOGRAPHY

Abrajano, Marisa, and Zoltan L. Hajnal. *White Backlash: Immigration, Race, and American Politics*. Princeton, NJ: Princeton University Press, 2017.

Adams, David W. *Education for Extinction: American Indians and the Boarding School Experience, 1875–1928*. Lawrence: University Press of Kansas, 1995.

Ahmed, Sara. "A Phenomenology of Whiteness." *Feminist Theory* 8, no. 2 (2007): 149–168.

Alba, Richard D. *Ethnic Identity: The Transformation of White America*. New Haven, CT: Yale University Press, 1990.

Alcoff, Linda Martin. "Epistemologies of Ignorance: Three Types." In *Race and Epistemologies of Ignorance*, edited by Shannon Sullivan and Nancy Tuana. Albany: SUNY Press, 2007.

Alcoff, Linda Martin. *The Future of Whiteness*. Cambridge, MA: Polity, 2015.

Aldridge, Delores P. *Imagine a World: Pioneering Black Women Sociologists*. Lanham, MD: University Press of America, 2008.

Almaguer, Tomas. *Racial Fault Lines: The Historical Origins of White Supremacy in California*. Berkeley: University of California Press, 2008.

Amico, Robert P. *Exploring White Privilege*. New York: Routledge, 2017.

Anderson, Carol. *White Rage: The Unspoken Truth of Our Racial Divide*. New York: Bloomsbury, 2016.

Anderson, Elijah. *Code of the Street: Decency, Violence, and the Moral Life of the Inner City*. New York: Norton, 2000.

Anderson, Elijah. "The Iconic Ghetto." *Annals of the American Academy of Political and Social Science* 642, no. 1 (2012): 8–24.

Anderson, Elijah. "The White Space." *Sociology of Race and Ethnicity* 1, no. 1 (2015): 10–21.

Anderson, James D. *The Education of Blacks in the South, 1860–1935*. Chapel Hill: University of North Carolina Press, 1988.

Anderson, Karen. *Little Rock: Race and Resistance at Central High School*. Princeton, NJ: Princeton University Press, 2013.

Apel, Dora. *Imagery of Lynching: Black Men, White Women, and the Mob*. New Brunswick, NJ: Rutgers University Press, 2004.

Arendell, Terry. "Reflections on the Researcher-Researched Relationship: A Woman Interviewing Men." *Qualitative Sociology* 20, no. 3 (1997): 341–368.

Arnesen, Eric. "Whiteness and the Historians' Imagination." *International Labor and Working-Class History* 60, no. 3 (2001): 3–32.

Bailey, Alison. "Strategic Ignorance." In *Race and Epistemologies of Ignorance*, edited by Shannon Sullivan and Nancy Tuana, 77–94. Albany: SUNY Press, 2007.

Baugh, Joyce A. *The Detroit School Busing Case*: Milliken v. Bradley *and the Controversy over Desegregation*. Lawrence: University Press of Kansas, 2011.

Berg, Bruce L. *Qualitative Research Methods for the Social Sciences*. 6th ed. London: Pearson, 2007.

Berlak, Ann, and Sekani Moyenda. *Taking It Personally: Racism in the Classroom from Kindergarten to College*. Philadelphia: Temple University Press, 2001.

Best, Amy L. "Doing Race in the Context of Feminist Interviewing: Constructing Whiteness through Talk." *Qualitative Inquiry* 9, no. 6 (2003): 895–914.

Best, Amy L. *Representing Youth: Methodological Issues in Critical Youth Studies*. New York: NYU Press, 2007.

Biernacki, Patrick, and Dan Waldorf. "Snowball Sampling: Problems and Techniques of Chain Referral Sampling." *Sociological Methods and Research* 10, no. 2 (1981): 141–163.

Blee, Kathleen M. "White on White: Interviewing Women in US White Supremacist Groups." In *Racing Research, Researching Race: Methodological Dilemmas in Critical Race Studies*, edited by France W. Twine and Jonathan W. Warren, 93–109. New York: NYU Press, 2000.

Blumer, Herbert. *Symbolic Interactionism: Perspective and Method*. Berkeley: University of California Press, 1986.

Bobo, Lawrence. "Whites' Opposition to Busing: Symbolic Racism or Realistic Group Conflict?" *Journal of Personality and Social Psychology* 45, no. 6 (1983): 1196–1210.

Bobo, Lawrence D. "Somewhere between Jim Crow and Post-racialism: Reflections on the Racial Divide in America Today." *Daedalus* 140, no. 2 (2011): 11–36.

Bobo, Lawrence D., and Camille Z. Charles. "Race in the American Mind: From the Moynihan Report to the Obama Candidacy." *Annals of the American Academy of Political and Social Science* 621, no. 1 (2009): 243–259.

Bobo, Lawrence D., Camille Z. Charles, Maria Krysan, and Alicia D. Simmons. "The Real Record on Racial Attitudes." In *Social Trends in American Life: Findings from the General Social Survey since 1972*, edited by Peter V. Marsden, 38–83. Princeton, NJ: Princeton University Press, 2012.

Bobo, Lawrence, and James R. Kluegel. "Opposition to Race-Targeting: Self-Interest,

Stratification Ideology, or Racial Attitudes?" *American Sociological Review* 58 (1993): 443–464.

Bobo, Lawrence, James R. Kluegel, and Ryan A. Smith. "Laissez-Faire Racism: The Crystallization of a Kinder, Gentler, Antiblack Ideology." In *Racial Attitudes in the 1990s: Continuity and Change*, edited by Steven A. Tuch and Jack K. Martin, 15–44. Westport, CT: Praeger, 1997.

Bonilla-Silva, Eduardo. "The Linguistics of Color Blind Racism: How to Talk Nasty about Blacks without Sounding 'Racist.'" *Critical Sociology* 28, nos. 1–2 (2002): 41–64.

Bonilla-Silva, Eduardo. *Racism without Racists: Color-Blind Racism and the Persistence of Racial Inequality in the United States*. Lanham, MD: Rowman and Littlefield, 2006.

Bonilla-Silva, Eduardo. "Rethinking Racism: Toward a Structural Interpretation." *American Sociological Review* 62, no. 3 (1997): 465–480.

Bonilla-Silva, Eduardo, and David Dietrich. "The Sweet Enchantment of Color-Blind Racism in Obamerica." *Annals of the American Academy of Political and Social Science* 634, no. 1 (2011): 190–206.

Bonilla-Silva, Eduardo, and Tyrone A. Forman. "'I Am Not a Racist But . . .': Mapping White College Students' Racial Ideology in the USA." *Discourse and Society* 11, no. 1 (2000): 50–85.

Bonilla-Silva, Eduardo, Tyrone A. Forman, Amanda E. Lewis, and David G. Embrick. "'It Wasn't Me!': How Will Race and Racism Work in 21st Century America." *Research in Political Sociology* 12, no. 1 (2003): 111–134.

Bonilla-Silva, Eduardo, Carla Goar, and David G. Embrick. "When Whites Flock Together: The Social Psychology of White Habitus." *Critical Sociology* 32, nos. 2–3 (2006): 229–253.

Bonilla-Silva, Eduardo, Amanda Lewis, and David G. Embrick. "'I Did Not Get That Job Because of a Black Man . . .': The Story Lines and Testimonies of Color-Blind Racism." *Sociological Forum* 19, no. 4 (2004): 555–581.

Bourdieu, Pierre, and Loïc Wacquant. *An Invitation to Reflexive Sociology*. Chicago: University of Chicago Press, 1992.

Bowen, Glenn A. "Naturalistic Inquiry and the Saturation Concept: A Research Note." *Qualitative Research* 8, no. 1 (2008): 137–152.

Brewer, Rose M. "Theorizing Race, Class and Gender: The New Scholarship of Black Feminist Intellectuals and Black Women's Labor." In *Theorizing Black Feminisms: The Visionary Pragmatism of Black Women*, edited by Stanlie M. James and Abena P. A. Busia, 13–30. New York: Routledge, 1993.

Bridges, Tristan, and Cheri J. Pascoe. "Hybrid Masculinities: New Directions in the Sociology of Men and Masculinities." *Sociology Compass* 8, no. 3 (2014): 246–258.

Brodkin, Karen. *How Jews Became White Folks and What That Says about Race in America*. New Brunswick, NJ: Rutgers University Press, 1998.

Browne-Marshall, Gloria J. *Race, Law, and American Society: 1607–Present*. 2nd ed. New York: Routledge, 2013.

Brown Givens, Sonja M., and Jennifer L. Monahan. "Priming Mammies, Jezebels, and

Other Controlling Images: An Examination of the Influence of Mediated Stereo-types on Perceptions of an African American Woman." *Media Psychology* 7, no. 1 (2005): 87–106.

Brown Henderson, Cheryl, and Steven M. Brown. "*Brown versus Board* at 62: March-ing Back into the Future." *Education, Citizenship and Social Justice* 12, no. 3 (2017): 244–251.

Bucholtz, Mary. "The Whiteness of Nerds: Superstandard English and Racial Marked-ness." *Journal of Linguistic Anthropology* 11, no. 1 (2001): 84–100.

Bulmer, Martin, and John Solomos, eds. *Researching Race and Racism*. New York: Routledge, 2004.

Burke, Meghan. *Colorblind Racism*. Cambridge: Polity, 2018.

Burke, Meghan A. "Colorblind Racism: Identities, Ideologies, and Shifting Subjectivi-ties." *Sociological Perspectives* 60, no. 5 (2017): 857–865.

Calhoun, Craig, ed. *Sociology in America: A History*. Chicago: University of Chicago Press, 2007.

Camp, Jordan T. *Incarcerating the Crisis: Freedom Struggles and the Rise of the Neolib-eral State*. Berkeley: University of California Press, 2016.

Carr, Leslie G. *"Color-Blind" Racism*. Thousand Oaks, CA: Sage, 1997.

Carter, Dan T. *The Politics of Rage: George Wallace, the Origins of the New Conserva-tism, and the Transformation of American Politics*. Baton Rouge: LSU Press, 2000.

Case, Anne, and Angus Deaton. *Deaths of Despair and the Future of Capitalism*. Princeton, NJ: Princeton University Press, 2020.

Case, Kim A., and Annette Hemmings. "Distancing Strategies: White Women Pre-service Teachers and Antiracist Curriculum." *Urban Education* 40, no. 6 (2005): 606–626.

Charles, Camille Z. "The Dynamics of Racial Residential Segregation." *Annual Review of Sociology* 29, no. 1 (2003): 167–207.

Charmaz, Kathy. *Constructing Grounded Theory*. Thousand Oaks, CA: Sage, 2014.

Charmaz, Kathy, Scott R. Harris, and Leslie Irvine. *The Social Self and Everyday Life: Understanding the World through Symbolic Interactionism*. Hoboken, NJ: Wiley-Blackwell, 2019.

Charon, Joel M. *Symbolic Interactionism: An Introduction, an Interpretation, an Integra-tion*. London: Pearson, 2010.

Chemerinsky, Erwin. "The Segregation and Resegregation of American Public Educa-tion: The Court's Role." *NCL Review* 81 (2002): 1597–1622.

Choo, Hae Yeon, and Myra Marx Ferree. "Practicing Intersectionality in Sociologi-cal Research: A Critical Analysis of Inclusions, Interactions, and Institutions in the Study of Inequalities." *Sociological Theory* 28, no. 2 (2010): 129–149.

Clotfelter, Charles T. *After* Brown: *The Rise and Retreat of School Desegregation*. Princ-eton, NJ: Princeton University Press, 2011.

Clotfelter, Charles T. "School Desegregation, 'Tipping,' and Private School Enrollment." *Journal of Human Resources* 11, no. 1 (1976): 28–50.

Cobb, Jessica S. "Inequality Frames: How Teachers Inhabit Color-Blind Ideology." *So-ciology of Education* 90, no. 4 (2017): 315–332.

Collins, Patricia H. *Black Feminist Thought: Knowledge, Consciousness, and the Politics of Empowerment.* New York: Routledge, 2002.

Condron, Dennis J., and Vincent J. Roscigno. "Disparities Within: Unequal Spending and Achievement in an Urban School District." *Sociology of Education* 76, no. 1 (2003): 18–36.

Cooley, Charles H. *Human Nature and the Social Order.* New York: Charles Scribner's Sons, 1902.

Corbin, Juliet M., and Anselm Strauss. "Grounded Theory Research: Procedures, Canons, and Evaluative Criteria." *Qualitative Sociology* 13, no. 1 (1990): 3–21.

Corsaro, William A. *The Sociology of Childhood.* Los Angeles: Sage, 2017.

Cox, Daniel, Rachel Lienesch, and Robert P. Jones. "Beyond Economics: Fears of Cultural Displacement Pushed the White Working Class to Trump." PRRI/*Atlantic*, May 9, 2017. https://www.prri.org/research/white-working-class-attitudes-economy-trade-immigration-election-donald-trump/.

Coyne, Imelda T. "Sampling in Qualitative Research: Purposeful and Theoretical Sampling; Merging or Clear Boundaries?" *Journal of Advanced Nursing* 26, no. 3 (1997): 623–630.

Craig, Maureen A., and Jennifer A. Richeson. "More Diverse Yet Less Tolerant? How the Increasingly Diverse Racial Landscape Affects White Americans' Racial Attitudes." *Personality and Social Psychology Bulletin* 40, no. 6 (2014): 750–761.

Craig, Maureen A., and Jennifer A. Richeson. "On the Precipice of a 'Majority-Minority' America: Perceived Status Threat from the Racial Demographic Shift Affects White Americans' Political Ideology." *Psychological Science* 25, no. 6 (2014): 1189–1197.

Crenshaw, Kimberlé. "Mapping the Margins: Intersectionality, Identity Politics, and Violence against Women of Color." *Stanford Law Review* 43 (1991): 1241–1299.

Crespino, Joseph. *In Search of Another Country: Mississippi and the Conservative Counterrevolution.* Princeton, NJ: Princeton University Press, 2009.

Creswell, John W. *Qualitative Inquiry and Research Design: Choosing among Five Approaches.* Thousand Oaks, CA: Sage, 2013.

Crichlow, Warren. *Race, Identity, and Representation in Education.* New York: Routledge, 2013.

Croll, Paul R. "Modeling Determinants of White Racial Identity: Results from a New National Survey." *Social Forces* 86, no. 2 (2007): 613–642.

Crotty, Michael. *The Foundations of Social Research: Meaning and Perspective in the Research Process.* Thousand Oaks, CA: Sage, 1998.

Dalton, Harlon. "Failing to See." In *White Privilege: Essential Readings on the Other Side of Racism*, 5th ed., edited by Paula S. Rothenberg, 15–18. New York: Worth, 2016.

Danbold, Felix, and Yuen J. Huo. "No Longer 'All-American'? Whites' Defensive Reactions to Their Numerical Decline." *Social Psychological and Personality Science* 6, no. 2 (2015): 210–218.

Delgado, Richard, and Jean Stefancic, eds. *Critical White Studies: Looking behind the Mirror.* Philadelphia: Temple University Press, 1997.

Delmont, Matthew F. *Why Busing Failed: Race, Media, and the National Resistance to School Desegregation.* Berkeley: University of California Press, 2016.

Delpit, Lisa. *Other People's Children: Cultural Conflict in the Classroom.* New York: New Press, 2006.

Denton, Nancy A. "The Persistence of Segregation: Links between Residential Segregation and School Segregation." *Minnesota Law Review* 80 (1995): 795–824.

Denzin, Norman K. *Symbolic Interactionism and Cultural Studies: The Politics of Interpretation.* Cambridge, MA: Blackwell, 1992.

Denzin, Norman K., and Yvonna S. Lincoln. *The Landscape of Qualitative Research.* Thousand Oaks, CA: Sage, 2008.

Desmond, Matthew. *Evicted: Poverty and Profit in the American City.* New York: Broadway Books, 2016.

Desmond, Matthew, and Mustafa Emirbayer. *Racial Domination, Racial Progress: The Sociology of Race in America.* New York: McGraw-Hill, 2010.

Desmond, Matthew, and Mustafa Emirbayer. "What Is Racial Domination?" *Du Bois Review* 6, no. 2 (2009): 335–355.

DeVault, Marjorie L. "Ethnicity and Expertise: Racial-Ethnic Knowledge in Sociological Research." *Gender and Society* 9, no. 5 (1995): 612–631.

DeVault, Marjorie L. *Liberating Method: Feminism and Social Research.* Philadelphia: Temple University Press, 1999.

DeVault, Marjorie L. "Talking and Listening from Women's Standpoint: Feminist Strategies for Interviewing and Analysis." *Social Problems* 37, no. 1 (1990): 96–116.

Dewey, John. "The Reflex Arc Concept in Psychology." *Psychological Review* 3, no. 4 (1896): 357–370.

DiAngelo, Robin J. *What Does It Mean to Be White? Developing White Racial Literacy.* New York: Peter Lang, 2016.

DiAngelo, Robin J. "White Fragility." *International Journal of Critical Pedagogy* 3, no. 3 (2011): 54–70.

DiAngelo, Robin J. *White Fragility: Why It's So Hard for White People to Talk about Racism.* Boston: Beacon, 2018.

DiAngelo, Robin J. "'Why Can't We All Just Be Individuals?': Countering the Discourse of Individualism in Anti-racist Education." *InterActions: UCLA Journal of Education and Information Studies* 6, no. 1 (2010). https://escholarship.org/uc/item/5fm4h8wm.

DiAngelo, Robin J., and David Allen. 2006. "'My Feelings Are Not about You': Personal Experience as a Move of Whiteness." *InterActions: UCLA Journal of Education and Information Studies* 2, no. 2 (2006). https://escholarship.org/uc/item/6dk67960.

DiAngelo, Robin, and Özlem Sensoy. "Getting Slammed: White Depictions of Race Discussions as Arenas of Violence." *Race, Ethnicity and Education* 17, no. 1 (2014): 103–128.

Doane, Ashley W., and Eduardo Bonilla-Silva, eds. *White Out: The Continuing Significance of Racism.* New York: Routledge, 2003.

Doane, Woody. "Rethinking Whiteness Studies." In *White Out: The Continuing Signif-*

icance of Racism, edited by Ashley W. Doane and Eduardo Bonilla-Silva, 3–18. New York: Routledge, 2003.

Downey, Douglas B. "Black/White Differences in School Performance: The Oppositional Culture Explanation." *Annual Review of Sociology* 34 (2008): 107–126.

Downey, Douglas B., and James W. Ainsworth-Darnell. "The Search for Oppositional Culture among Black Students." *American Sociological Review* 67, no. 1 (2002): 156–164.

Dray, Philip. *At the Hands of Persons Unknown: The Lynching of Black America*. New York: Random House, 2003.

Du Bois, W. E. B. *Darkwater: Voices from within the Veil*. Mineola, NY: Dover, 1999.

Du Bois, W. E. B. *The Souls of Black Folk*. New York: Barnes and Noble Classics, 2003.

Durkheim, Émile. *The Rules of Sociological Method*. New York: Free Press, 1938.

Dyer, Richard. "The Matter of Whiteness." In *White Privilege: Essential Readings on the Other Side of Racism*, 5th ed., edited by Paula Rothenberg, 9–14. New York: Worth, 2016.

Elder, Larry. *Stupid Black Men: How to Play the Race Card—and Lose*. New York: Macmillan, 2008.

Elliott, Delbert S., William J. Wilson, David Huizinga, Robert J. Sampson, Amanda Elliott, and Bruce Rankin. "The Effects of Neighborhood Disadvantage on Adolescent Development." *Journal of Research in Crime and Delinquency* 33, no. 4 (1996): 389–426.

Erickson, Ansley T. *Making the Unequal Metropolis: School Desegregation and Its Limits*. Chicago: University of Chicago Press, 2016.

Evans, Gary W. "The Environment of Childhood Poverty." *American Psychologist* 59, no. 2 (2004): 77–92.

Fabricant, Michael, and Michelle Fine. *Charter Schools and the Corporate Makeover of Public Education: What's at Stake?* New York: Teachers College Press, 2015.

Fairlie, Robert W., and Alexandra M. Resch. "Is There 'White Flight' into Private Schools? Evidence from the National Educational Longitudinal Survey." *Review of Economics and Statistics* 84, no. 1 (2002): 21–33.

Farley, Reynolds, Howard Schuman, Suzanne Bianchi, Diane Colasanto, and Shirley Hatchett. "'Chocolate City, Vanilla Suburbs': Will the Trend toward Racially Separate Communities Continue?" *Social Science Research* 7, no. 4 (1978): 319–344.

Farley, Reynolds, Charlotte Steeh, Tara Jackson, Maria Krysan, and Keith Reeves. "Continued Racial Residential Segregation in Detroit: 'Chocolate City, Vanilla Suburbs' Revisited." *Journal of Housing Research* 4, no. 1 (1993): 1–38.

Feagin, Joe R. *Systemic Racism: A Theory of Oppression*. New York: Routledge, 2013.

Feagin, Joe R. *White Party, White Government: Race, Class, and US Politics*. New York: Routledge, 2012.

Feagin, Joe R. *The White Racial Frame: Centuries of Racial Framing and Counterframing*. New York: Routledge, 2010.

Feagin, Joe R., and Vera Hernan. *White Racism: The Basics*. New York: Routledge, 2000.

Feagin, Joe R., and Eileen O'Brien. *White Men on Race: Power, Privilege, and the Shaping of Cultural Consciousness*. Boston: Beacon, 2003.

Feagin, Joe R., and Melvin P. Sikes. *Living with Racism: The Black Middle-Class Experience*. Boston: Beacon, 1994.

Feagin, Joe R., and Debra Van Ausdale. *The First R: How Children Learn Race and Racism*. Lanham, MD: Rowman and Littlefield, 2001.

Ferguson, Ann A. *Bad Boys: Public Schools in the Making of Black Masculinity*. Ann Arbor: University of Michigan Press, 2000.

Fine, Michelle, Lois Weis, Judi Addelston, and Julia Marusza. "Secure Times: Constructing White Working-Class Masculinities in the Late 20th Century." *Gender and Society* 11, no. 1 (1997): 52–68.

Firebaugh, Glenn, and Kenneth E. Davis. "Trends in Antiblack Prejudice, 1972–1984: Region and Cohort Effects." *American Journal of Sociology* 94, no. 2 (1988): 251–272.

Fischbach, Jonathan, Will Rhee, and Robert Cacace. "Race at the Pivot Point: The Future of Race-Based Policies to Remedy De Jure Segregation after Parents Involved in Community Schools." *Harvard Review* 43 (2008): 491–538.

Ford, Richard T. *The Race Card: How Bluffing about Bias Makes Race Relations Worse*. New York: Macmillan, 2008.

Fordham, Signithia, and John U. Ogbu. "Black Students' School Success: Coping with the 'Burden of "Acting White."'" *Urban Review* 18, no. 3 (1986): 176–206.

Forman, Tyrone A., and Amanda E. Lewis. "Racial Apathy and Hurricane Katrina: The Social Anatomy of Prejudice in the Post–Civil Rights Era." *Du Bois Review* 3, no. 1 (2006): 175–202.

Frankenberg, Erica, and Gary Orfield. *The Resegregation of Suburban Schools: A Hidden Crisis in American Education*. Cambridge, MA: Harvard Education Press, 2012.

Frankenberg, Ruth. *White Women, Race Matters: The Social Construction of Whiteness*. Minneapolis: University of Minnesota Press, 1993.

Freund, David M. *Colored Property: State Policy and White Racial Politics in Suburban America*. Chicago: University of Chicago Press, 2010.

Fryer, Roland G. "'Acting White': The Social Price Paid by the Best and Brightest Minority Students." *Education Next* 6, no. 1 (2006): 52–60.

Gadsden, Vivian L., and Ezekiel J. Dixon-Roman. "'Urban' Schooling and 'Urban' Families: The Role of Context and Place." *Urban Education* 52, no. 4 (2017): 431–459.

Gallagher, Charles A. "Color-Blind Privilege: The Social and Political Functions of Erasing the Color Line in Post-race America." *Race, Gender and Class* 10, no. 4 (2003): 22–37.

Gallagher, Charles A. "Playing the White Ethnic Card: Using Ethnic Identity to Deny Contemporary Racism." In *White Out: The Continuing Significance of Racism*, edited by Ashley W. Doane and Eduardo Bonilla-Silva, 145–158. New York: Routledge, 2003.

Gallagher, Charles A. "White Racial Formation: Into the Twenty-First Century." In *Critical White Studies: Looking behind the Mirror*, edited by Richard Delgado and Jean Stefancic, 6–11. Philadelphia: Temple University Press, 1997.

Gest, Justin. *The New Minority: White Working Class Politics in an Age of Immigration and Inequality*. New York: Oxford University Press, 2016.

Gilens, Martin. *Why Americans Hate Welfare: Race, Media, and the Politics of Antipoverty Policy.* Chicago: University of Chicago Press, 2009.

Glaser, Barney G., and Anselm L. Strauss. *The Discovery of Grounded Theory: Strategies for Qualitative Research.* Chicago: Aldine, 1967.

Glenn, Evelyn N. "Yearning for Lightness: Transnational Circuits in the Marketing and Consumption of Skin Lighteners." *Gender and Society* 22, no. 3 (2008): 281–302.

Goffman, Erving. *The Presentation of Self in Everyday Life.* 1956. Repr., New York: Random House, 2008.

Goldstein, Dana. *The Teacher Wars: A History of America's Most Embattled Profession.* New York: Anchor Books, 2015.

Goldstone, Lawrence. *Inherently Unequal: The Betrayal of Equal Rights by the Supreme Court, 1865–1903.* New York: Walker, 2011.

Gordon, Linda. *Pitied but Not Entitled: Single Mothers and the History of Welfare.* Cambridge, MA: Harvard University Press, 1994.

Gotanda, Neil. "A Critique of 'Our Constitution Is Color-Blind.'" *Stanford Law Review* 44, no. 1 (1991): 1–68.

Gregory, Anne, and Pharmicia M. Mosely. "The Discipline Gap: Teachers' Views on the Over-representation of African American Students in the Discipline System." *Equity and Excellence in Education* 37, no. 1 (2004): 18–30.

Gregory, Anne, Russell J. Skiba, and Pedro A. Noguera. "The Achievement Gap and the Discipline Gap: Two Sides of the Same Coin?" *Educational Researcher* 39, no. 1 (2010): 59–68.

Guglielmo, Thomas A. *White on Arrival: Italians, Race, Color, and Power in Chicago, 1890–1945.* New York: Oxford University Press, 2003.

Hagerman, Margaret A. *White Kids: Growing Up with Privilege in a Racially Divided America.* New York: NYU Press, 2018.

Hale, Grace Elizabeth. *Making Whiteness: The Culture of Segregation in the South, 1890–1940.* New York: Vintage Books, 2010.

Hall, Stuart, and Paul du Gay, eds. *Questions of Cultural Identity.* London: Sage, 1996.

Halley, Jean, Amy Eshleman, and Ramya M. Vijaya. *Seeing White: An Introduction to White Privilege and Race.* Lanham, MD: Rowman and Littlefield, 2011.

Handcock, Mark S., and Krista J. Gile. "Comment: On the Concept of Snowball Sampling." *Sociological Methodology* 41, no. 1 (2011): 367–371.

Haney López, Ian. *Dog Whistle Politics: How Coded Racial Appeals Have Reinvented Racism and Wrecked the Middle Class.* New York: Oxford University Press, 2015.

Haney López, Ian. "'A Nation of Minorities': Race, Ethnicity, and Reactionary Colorblindness." *Stanford Law Review* 59 (2007): 985–1064.

Haney López, Ian. *White by Law: The Legal Construction of Race.* New York: NYU Press, 1997.

Harding, Sandra G. *The Feminist Standpoint Theory Reader: Intellectual and Political Controversies.* New York: Routledge, 2004.

Harris, Angel L. "I (Don't) Hate School: Revisiting Oppositional Culture Theory of Blacks' Resistance to Schooling." *Social Forces* 85, no. 2 (2006): 797–834.

Harris, Cheryl I. "Whiteness as Property." *Harvard Law Review* 106, no. 8 (1993): 1707–1791.

Hartigan, John. *Racial Situations: Class Predicaments of Whiteness in Detroit.* Princeton, NJ: Princeton University Press, 1999.

Hartmann, Douglas, Paul R. Croll, Ryan Larson, Joseph Gerteis, and Alex Manning. "Colorblindness as Identity: Key Determinants, Relations to Ideology, and Implications for Attitudes about Race and Policy." *Sociological Perspectives* 60, no. 5 (2017): 866–888.

Hartmann, Douglas, Joseph Gerteis, and Paul R. Croll. "An Empirical Assessment of Whiteness Theory: Hidden from How Many?" *Social Problems* 56, no. 3 (2009): 403–424.

Harvey, David. *A Brief History of Neoliberalism.* New York: Oxford University Press, 2007.

Helms, Janet E. *Black and White Racial Identity: Theory, Research, and Practice.* Westport, CT: Greenwood, 1990.

Henricks, Kasey. "When Questions Do Not Yield Answers: Foreclosures of Racial Knowledge Production." *Sociology Compass* 10, no. 11 (2016): 1028–1037.

Herrnstein, Richard J., and Charles Murray. *The Bell Curve: Intelligence and Class Structure in American Life.* New York: Simon and Schuster, 1994.

Hewitt, John P. *Self and Society: A Symbolic Interactionist Social Psychology.* London: Pearson, 1976.

Higham, John. *Strangers in the Land: Patterns of American Nativism, 1860–1925.* New Brunswick, NJ: Rutgers University Press, 2002.

Hill, Jane H. *The Everyday Language of White Racism.* Hoboken: John Wiley and Sons, 2009.

Hill, Marc L. "Representin(g): Negotiating Multiple Roles and Identities in the Field and behind the Desk." *Qualitative Inquiry* 12, no. 5 (2006): 926–949.

Hill, Mike. *Whiteness: A Critical Reader.* New York: NYU Press, 1997.

Hochschild, Arlie R. *Strangers in Their Own Land: Anger and Mourning on the American Right.* New York: New Press, 2018.

Hochschild, Jennifer L., and Nathan Scovronick. *The American Dream and the Public Schools.* New York: Oxford University Press, 2003.

Hodes, Martha. "The Sexualization of Reconstruction Politics: White Women and Black Men in the South after the Civil War." *Journal of the History of Sexuality* 3, no. 3 (1993): 402–417.

Hodes, Martha. *White Women, Black Men: Illicit Sex in the Nineteenth-Century South.* New Haven, CT: Yale University Press, 2014.

Hofstader, Ralph. *Great Issues in American History.* New York: Vintage, 1982.

hooks, bell. *Ain't I a Woman: Black Women and Feminism.* Boston: South End, 1981.

hooks, bell. *Representing Whiteness in the Black Imagination.* New York: Routledge, 1992.

Hughey, Matthew W. "The (Dis)Similarities of White Racial Identities: The Conceptual Framework of 'Hegemonic Whiteness.'" *Ethnic and Racial Studies* 33, no. 8 (2010): 1289–1309.

Hughey, Matthew W. *White Bound: Nationalists, Antiracists, and the Shared Meanings of Race*. Palo Alto, CA: Stanford University Press, 2012.

Hunter, Margaret L. "Buying Racial Capital: Skin-Bleaching and Cosmetic Surgery in a Globalized World." *Journal of Pan African Studies* 4, no. 4 (2011): 142–164.

Hursh, David. "Assessing No Child Left Behind and the Rise of Neoliberal Education Policies." *American Educational Research Journal* 44, no. 3 (2007): 493–518.

Hursh, David. "The Growth of High-Stakes Testing in the USA: Accountability, Markets and the Decline in Educational Equality." *British Educational Research Journal* 31, no. 5 (2005): 605–622.

Hurwitz, Jon, and Mark Peffley. "Playing the Race Card in the Post–Willie Horton Era: The Impact of Racialized Code Words on Support for Punitive Crime Policy." *Public Opinion Quarterly* 69, no. 1 (2005): 99–112.

Hyde, Cheryl. "The Meanings of Whiteness." *Qualitative Sociology* 18, no. 1 (1995): 87–95.

Hytten, Kathy, and John Warren. "Engaging Whiteness: How Racial Power Gets Reified in Education." *International Journal of Qualitative Studies in Education* 16, no. 1 (2003): 65–89.

Ignatiev, Noel. *How the Irish Became White*. New ed. New York: Routledge, 2009.

Irving, Debby. *Waking Up White and Finding Myself in the Story of Race*. Cambridge, MA: Elephant Room, 2016.

Isenberg, Nancy. *White Trash: The 400-Year Untold History of Class in America*. New York: Penguin, 2017.

Ispa-Landa, Simone, and Jordan Conwell. "'Once You Go to a White School, You Kind of Adapt': Black Adolescents and the Racial Classification of Schools." *Sociology of Education* 88, no. 1 (2015): 1–19.

Iyer, Aarti, Colin Wayne Leach, and Faye J. Crosby. "White Guilt and Racial Compensation: The Benefits and Limits of Self-Focus." *Personality and Social Psychology Bulletin* 29, no. 1 (2003): 117–129.

Jacobson, Matthew F. *Whiteness of a Different Color: European Immigrants and the Alchemy of Race*. Cambridge, MA: Harvard University Press, 1999.

James, William. *The Principles of Psychology*. 1890. Repr., New York: Cosimo Classics, 2007.

Jardina, Ashley. *White Identity Politics*. Cambridge: Cambridge University Press, 2019.

Jargowsky, Paul A. *Poverty and Place: Ghettos, Barrios, and the American City*. New York: Russell Sage Foundation, 1997.

Jaspin, Elliot. *Buried in the Bitter Waters: The Hidden History of Racial Cleansing in America*. New York: Basic Books, 2008.

Jayakumar, Uma M., and Annie S. Adamian. "The Fifth Frame of Colorblind Ideology: Maintaining the Comforts of Colorblindness in the Context of White Fragility." *Sociological Perspectives* 60, no. 5 (2017): 912–936.

Johnson, Heather B. *The American Dream and the Power of Wealth: Choosing Schools and Inheriting Inequality in the Land of Opportunity*. New York: Routledge, 2014.

Johnson, Heather B., and Thomas M. Shapiro. "Good Neighborhoods, Good Schools: Race and the Good Choices." In *White-Out: The Continuing Significance of Racism*, edited by Ashley W. Doane and Eduardo Bonilla-Silva, 173–187. New York: Routledge, 2003.

Johnson, Lauri. "'My Eyes Have Been Opened': White Teachers and Racial Awareness." *Journal of Teacher Education* 53, no. 2 (2002): 153–167.

Jones, Robert P. *The End of White Christian America*. New York: Simon and Schuster, 2016.

Kaufman, Cynthia. "A User's Guide to White Privilege." *Radical Philosophy Review* 4, nos. 1–2 (2001): 30–38.

Kennedy, Randall. *Nigger: The Strange Career of a Troublesome Word*. New York: Vintage Books, 2008.

Kenny, Lorraine Delia. *Daughters of Suburbia: Growing Up White, Middle Class, and Female*. New Brunswick, NJ: Rutgers University Press, 2000.

Kimmel, Michael. *Angry White Men: American Masculinity at the End of an Era*. Rev. ed. New York: Nation Books, 2017.

Kinder, Donald R., and Lynn M. Sanders. *Divided by Color: Racial Politics and Democratic Ideals*. Chicago: University of Chicago Press, 1996.

Kinder, Donald R., and David O. Sears. "Prejudice and Politics: Symbolic Racism versus Racial Threats to the Good Life." *Journal of Personality and Social Psychology* 40, no. 3 (1981): 414–431.

King, Deborah K. "Multiple Jeopardy, Multiple Consciousness: The Context of a Black Feminist Ideology." *Signs: Journal of Women in Culture and Society* 14, no. 1 (1988): 42–72.

King, Martin L. *Why We Can't Wait*. New York: Penguin, 2000.

Kitwana, Bakari. *Why White Kids Love Hip-Hop: Wankstas, Wiggers, Wannabes, and the New Reality of Race in America*. New York: Civitas Books, 2005.

Klein, Naomi. *The Shock Doctrine: The Rise of Disaster Capitalism*. New York: Picador, 2007.

Kozol, Jonathan. *Savage Inequalities: Children in America's Schools*. 1991. Repr., New York: Broadway Books, 2012.

Kozol, Jonathan. *The Shame of the Nation: The Restoration of Apartheid Schooling in America*. New York: Broadway Books, 2005.

Kruse, Kevin M. *White Flight: Atlanta and the Making of Modern Conservatism*. Princeton, NJ: Princeton University Press, 2013.

Kruse, Kevin M., and Julian E. Zelizer. *Fault Lines: A History of the United States since 1974*. New York: Norton, 2019.

Krysan, Maria. "Prejudice, Politics, and Public Opinion: Understanding the Sources of Racial Policy Attitudes." *Annual Review of Sociology* 26, no. 1 (2000): 135–168.

Krysan, Maria. "Whites Who Say They'd Flee: Who Are They, and Why Would They Leave?" *Demography* 39, no. 4 (2002): 675–696.

Kuhn, Manford H. "Major Trends in Symbolic Interaction Theory in the Past Twenty-Five Years." *Sociological Quarterly* 5, no. 1 (1964): 61–84.

Ladner, Joyce A. *The Death of White Sociology: Essays on Race and Culture*. Baltimore: Black Classic Press, 1998.

Ladner, Joyce A. "Tomorrow's Tomorrow: The Black Woman." In *Imagine a World: Pioneering Black Women Sociologists*, edited by Delores P. Aldridge, 91–101. Lanham, MD: University Press of America, 2009.

Ladson-Billings, Gloria. "It's Not the Culture of Poverty, It's the Poverty of Culture: The Problem with Teacher Education." *Anthropology and Education Quarterly* 37, no. 2 (2006): 104–109.

Landsman, Julie. *A White Teacher Talks about Race*. Lanham, MD: Rowman and Littlefield, 2009.

Lassiter, Matthew D., and Andrew B. Lewis, eds. *The Moderates' Dilemma: Massive Resistance to School Desegregation in Virginia*. Charlottesville: University of Virginia Press, 1998.

Lee, Jaekyung. "Racial and Ethnic Achievement Gap Trends: Reversing the Progress toward Equity?" *Educational Researcher* 31, no. 1 (2002): 3–12.

Leonardo, Zeus. "The Color of Supremacy: Beyond the Discourse of 'White Privilege.'" *Educational Philosophy and Theory* 36, no. 2 (2004): 137–152.

Leonardo, Zeus. *Race, Whiteness, and Education*. New York: Routledge, 2009.

Leonardo, Zeus, and W. Norton Grubb. *Education and Racism: A Primer on Issues and Dilemmas*. New York: Routledge, 2018.

Levine-Rasky, Cynthia. "Framing Whiteness: Working through the Tensions in Introducing Whiteness to Educators." *Race, Ethnicity and Education* 3, no. 3 (2000): 271–292.

Lewis, Amanda E. "Everyday Race-Making: Navigating Racial Boundaries in Schools." *American Behavioral Scientist* 47, no. 3 (2003): 283–305.

Lewis, Amanda E. *Race in the Schoolyard: Negotiating the Color Line in Classrooms and Communities*. New Brunswick, NJ: Rutgers University Press, 2003.

Lewis, Amanda E. "There Is No 'Race' in the Schoolyard: Color-Blind Ideology in an (Almost) All-White School." *American Educational Research Journal* 38, no. 4 (2001): 781–811.

Lewis, Amanda E. "What Group? Studying Whites and Whiteness in the Era of Color-blindness." *Sociological Theory* 22, no. 4 (2004): 623–646.

Lewis, Amanda E. "Whiteness in School: How Race Shapes Black Students' Opportunities." In *Beyond Acting White: Reframing the Debate on Black Student Achievement*, edited by Erin M. Horvat and Carla O'Connor, 176–199. Lanham, MD: Rowman and Littlefield, 2006.

Lewis, Amanda E., and John B. Diamond. *Despite the Best Intentions: How Racial Inequality Thrives in Good Schools*. New York: Oxford University Press, 2015.

Lewis, George. *Massive Resistance: The White Response to the Civil Rights Movement*. London: Hoddor Arnold, 2006.

Lewis, Oscar. 1966. "The Culture of Poverty." *Scientific American* 215, no. 4 (1966): 19–25.

Lipman, Pauline. *The New Political Economy of Urban Education: Neoliberalism, Race, and the Right to the City*. Abingdon, UK: Taylor and Francis, 2013.

Lipsitz, George. *How Racism Takes Place*. Philadelphia: Temple University Press, 2011.

Lipsitz, George. *The Possessive Investment in Whiteness: How White People Profit from Identity Politics*. Philadelphia: Temple University Press, 2006.

Lipsitz, George. "The Racialization of Space and the Spatialization of Race: Theorizing the Hidden Architecture of Landscape." *Landscape Journal* 26, no. 1 (2007): 10–23.

Loewen, James W. *Sundown Towns: A Hidden Dimension of American Racism*. New York: New Press, 2018.

Logan, John R., Elisabeta Minca, and Sinem Adar. "The Geography of Inequality: Why Separate Means Unequal in American Public Schools." *Sociology of Education* 85, no. 3 (2012): 287–301.

Logan, John R., Deirdre Oakley, and Jacob Stowell. "School Segregation in Metropolitan Regions, 1970–2000: The Impacts of Policy Choices on Public Education." *American Journal of Sociology* 113, no. 6 (2008): 1611–1644.

Lord, J. Dennis. "School Busing and White Abandonment of Public Schools." *Southeastern Geographer* 15, no. 2 (1975): 81–92.

Love, Bettina L., and Brandelyn Tosolt. "Reality or Rhetoric? Barack Obama and Post-racial America." *Race, Gender and Class* 17, nos. 3–4 (2010): 19–37.

Lubienski, Christopher. "Innovation in Education Markets: Theory and Evidence on the Impact of Competition and Choice in Charter Schools." *American Educational Research Journal* 40, no. 2 (2003): 395–443.

Lum, Lydia. "The Obama Era: A Post-racial Society?" *Diverse: Issues in Higher Education* 25, no. 26 (2009): 14–16.

Mahadeo, Rahsaan. "Why Is the Time Always Right for White and Wrong for Us? How Racialized Youth Make Sense of Whiteness and Temporal Inequality." *Sociology of Race and Ethnicity* 5, no. 2 (2019): 186–199.

Major, Brenda, Alison Blodorn, and Gregory Major Blascovich. "The Threat of Increasing Diversity: Why Many White Americans Support Trump in the 2016 Presidential Election." *Group Processes and Intergroup Relations* 21, no. 6 (2016): 931–940.

Majors, Richard, and Janet M. Billson. *Cool Pose: The Dilemma of Black Manhood in America*. New York: Simon and Schuster, 1993.

Massey, Douglas S., and Nancy A. Denton. *American Apartheid: Segregation and the Making of the Underclass*. Cambridge, MA: Harvard University Press, 1993.

May, Reuben A. B. "When the Methodological Shoe Is on the Other Foot: African American Interviewer and White Interviewees." *Qualitative Sociology* 37, no. 1 (2014): 117–136.

McCall, Leslie. "The Complexity of Intersectionality." *Signs: Journal of Women in Culture and Society* 30, no. 3 (2005): 1771–1800.

McCarthy, Cameron, Warren Crichlow, Greg Dimitriadis, and Nadine Dolby. *Race, Identity, and Representation in Education*. New York: Routledge, 2013.

McDermott, Monica. "Color-Blind and Color-Visible Identity among American Whites." *American Behavioral Scientist* 59, no. 11 (2015): 1452–1473.

McDermott, Monica. *Working-Class White: The Making and Unmaking of Race Relations*. Berkeley: University of California Press, 2006.

McDermott, Monica, and Frank L. Samson. "White Racial and Ethnic Identity in the United States." *Annual Review of Sociology* 31 (2005): 245–261.

McGirr, Lisa. *Suburban Warriors: The Origins of the New American Right*. Princeton, NJ: Princeton University Press, 2015.

McIntosh, Peggy. "White Privilege: Unpacking the Invisible Knapsack." *Peace and Freedom Magazine*, July/August 1989, 10–12.

McIntyre, Alice. *Making Meaning of Whiteness: Exploring Racial Identity with White Teachers*. Albany: SUNY Press, 1997.

McIntyre, Alice. *Participatory Action Research*. Thousand Oaks, CA: Sage, 2007.

McKinney, Karyn D. *Being White: Stories of Race and Racism*. New York: Routledge, 2005.

McWhorter, John H. *Losing the Race: Self-Sabotage in Black America*. New York: Simon and Schuster, 2000.

Mead, George H. *Mind, Self, and Society: From the Standpoint of a Social Behaviorist*. Edited by Charles W. Morris. Chicago: University of Chicago Press, 1934.

Mead, George H. "Social Consciousness and the Consciousness of Meaning." *Psychological Bulletin* 7, no. 12 (1910): 397.

Mendelberg, Tali. *The Race Card: Campaign Strategy, Implicit Messages, and the Norm of Equality*. Princeton, NJ: Princeton University Press, 2017.

Merton, Robert K. "Insiders and Outsiders: A Chapter in the Sociology of Knowledge." *American Journal of Sociology* 78, no. 1 (1972): 9–47.

Metzl, Jonathan M. *Dying of Whiteness: How the Politics of Racial Resentment Is Killing America's Heartland*. New York: Hachette, 2019.

Meyer, Stephen G. *As Long as They Don't Move Next Door: Segregation and Racial Conflict in American Neighborhoods*. Lanham, MD: Rowman and Littlefield, 2000.

Mills, Charles W. *The Racial Contract*. Ithaca, NY: Cornell University Press, 1997.

Mills, Charles W. *The Sociological Imagination*. New York: Oxford University Press, 2000

Mills, Charles W. "White Ignorance." In *Race and Epistemologies of Ignorance*, edited by Shannon Sullivan and Nancy Tuana, 26–31. Albany: SUNY Press, 2007.

Modica, Marianne. "Unpacking the 'Colorblind Approach': Accusations of Racism at a Friendly, Mixed-Race School." *Race, Ethnicity and Education* 18, no. 3 (2015): 396–418.

Morris, Aldon D. "Sociology of Race and W. E. B. DuBois: The Path Not Taken." In *Sociology in America: A History*, edited by Craig Calhoun, 503–534. Chicago: University of Chicago Press, 2007.

Morris, Edward W. *An Unexpected Minority: White Kids in an Urban School*. New Brunswick, NJ: Rutgers University Press, 2006.

Morris, Monique. *Pushout: The Criminalization of Black Girls in Schools*. New York: New Press, 2016.

Morrison, Toni. *Playing in the Dark: Whiteness and the Literary Imagination*. New York: Vintage Books, 1993.

Mueller, Jennifer C. "Producing Colorblindness: Everyday Mechanisms of White Ignorance." *Social Problems* 64, no. 2 (2017): 219–238.

Naples, Nancy A. "A Feminist Revisiting of the Insider/Outsider Debate: The 'Outsider Phenomenon' in Rural Iowa." *Qualitative Sociology* 19, no. 1 (1996): 83–106.

Neubeck, Kenneth J., and Noel A. Cazenave. *Welfare Racism: Playing the Race Card against America's Poor*. New York: Routledge, 2002.

Noguera, Pedro A. "The Trouble with Black Boys: The Role and Influence of Environmental and Cultural Factors on the Academic Performance of African American Males." *Urban Education* 38, no. 4 (2003): 431–459.

Norton, Michael I., and Samuel R. Sommers. "Whites See Racism as a Zero-Sum Game That They Are Now Losing." *Perspectives on Psychological Science* 6, no. 3 (2011): 215–218.

Oakes, Jeannie. *Keeping Track: How Schools Structure Inequality*. New Haven, CT: Yale University Press, 2005.

Oeur, Freeden Blume. *Black Boys Apart: Racial Uplift and Respectability in All-Male Public Schools*. Minneapolis: University of Minnesota Press, 2018.

Ogbu, John U., ed. *Minority Status, Oppositional Culture, and Schooling*. New York: Routledge, 2008.

Ogletree, Charles J. *All Deliberate Speed: Reflections on the First Half Century of* Brown v. Board of Education. New York: Norton, 2004.

Omi, Michael, and Howard Winant. *Racial Formation in the United States: From the 1960s to the 1990s*. New York: Routledge, 1994.

Orfield, Gary, and Susan E. Eaton. *Dismantling Desegregation: The Quiet Reversal of* Brown v. Board of Education. New York: New Press, 1996.

Orfield, Gary, Erica D. Frankenberg, and Chungmei Lee. "The Resurgence of School Segregation." *Educational Leadership* 60, no. 4 (2003): 16–20.

Orfield, Gary, and Chungmei Lee. "Why Segregation Matters: Poverty and Educational Inequality." Civil Rights Project at Harvard University, January 2005. https://eric.ed .gov/?q=Why+Segregation+Matters%3a+Poverty+and+Educational+Inequality &id=ED489186.

Outten, H. R., Michael T. Schmitt, Daniel A. Miller, and Amber L. Garcia. "Feeling Threatened about the Future: Whites' Emotional Reactions to Anticipated Ethnic Demographic Changes." *Personality and Social Psychology Bulletin* 38, no. 1 (2012): 14–25.

Painter, Nell I. *The History of White People*. New York: Norton, 2010.

Park, Robert E. "Reflections on Communication and Culture." *American Journal of Sociology* 44, no. 2 (1938): 187–205.

Parks, Gregory S., and Matthew W. Hughey, eds. *The Obamas and a (Post) Racial America?* New York: Oxford University Press, 2011.

Peffley, Mark, Jon Hurwitz, and Paul M. Sniderman. "Racial Stereotypes and Whites' Political Views of Blacks in the Context of Welfare and Crime." *American Journal of Political Science* 41, no. 1 (1997): 30–60.

Perry, Pamela. *Shades of White: White Kids and Racial Identities in High School*. Durham, NC: Duke University Press, 2002.

Perry, Pamela. "White Means Never Having to Say You're Ethnic: White Youth and the Construction of 'Cultureless' Identities." *Journal of Contemporary Ethnography* 30, no. 1 (2001): 56–91.

Pettigrew, Thomas F. "Justice Deferred a Half Century after *Brown v. Board of Education*." *American Psychologist* 59, no. 6 (2004): 521–529.

Phillips, Steve. *Brown Is the New White: How the Demographic Revolution Has Created a New American Majority*. New York: New Press, 2018.

Picower, Bree. "The Unexamined Whiteness of Teaching: How White Teachers Maintain and Enact Dominant Racial Ideologies." *Race, Ethnicity and Education* 12, no. 2 (2009): 197–215.

Plaut, Victoria C., Flannery G. Garnett, Laura E. Buffardi, and Jeffrey Sanchez-Burks. "'What about Me?': Perceptions of Exclusion and Whites' Reactions to Multiculturalism." *Journal of Personality and Social Psychology* 101, no. 2 (2011): 337–353.

Posey-Maddox, Linn. *When Middle-Class Parents Choose Urban Schools: Class, Race, and the Challenge of Equity in Public Education*. Chicago: University of Chicago Press, 2014.

Pratto, Felicia, Jim Sidanius, Lisa M. Stallworth, and Bertram F. Malle. "Social Dominance Orientation: A Personality Variable Predicting Social and Political Attitudes." *Journal of Personality and Social Psychology* 67, no. 4 (1994): 741–763.

Quadagno, Jill S. *The Color of Welfare: How Racism Undermined the War on Poverty*. New York: Oxford University Press, 1994.

Rasmussen, Birgit B., Eric Klinenberg, Irene J. Nexica, and Matt Wray. *The Making and Unmaking of Whiteness*. Durham, NC: Duke University Press, 2001.

Ravitch, Diane. *Reign of Error: The Hoax of the Privatization Movement and the Danger to America's Public Schools*. New York: Vintage Books, 2013.

Reardon, Sean F. "The Widening Academic Achievement Gap between the Rich and the Poor: New Evidence and Possible Explanations." *Whither Opportunity* 1, no. 1 (2011): 91–116.

Reardon, Sean F., and Ann Owens. "60 Years after *Brown*: Trends and Consequences of School Segregation." *Annual Review of Sociology* 40 (2014): 199–218.

Reardon, Sean F., and John T. Yun. "Private School Racial Enrollments and Segregation." Civil Rights Project at Harvard University, June 26, 2002. https://eric.ed.gov /?q=Private+School+Racial+Enrollments+and+Segregation&id=ED467108.

Reny, Tyler T., Loren Collingwood, and Ali A. Valenzuela. "Vote Switching in the 2016 Election: How Racial and Immigration Attitudes, Not Economics, Explain Shifts in White Voting." *Public Opinion Quarterly* 83, no. 1 (2019): 91–113.

Rios, Victor M. *Punished: Policing the Lives of Black and Latino Boys*. New York: NYU Press, 2011.

Roda, Allison, and Amy Stuart Wells. "School Choice Policies and Racial Segregation: Where White Parents' Good Intentions, Anxiety, and Privilege Collide." *American Journal of Education* 119, no. 2 (2013): 261–293.

Roediger, David R. *Black on White: Black Writers on What It Means to Be White*. New York: Random House, 2010.

Roediger, David R. *The Wages of Whiteness: Race and the Making of the American Working Class*. New York: Verso, 1992.

Roediger, David R. *Working toward Whiteness: How America's Immigrants Became White; The Strange Journey from Ellis Island to the Suburbs*. New York: Basic Books, 2006.

Rossell, Christine H. "School Desegregation and White Flight." *Political Science Quarterly* 90, no. 4 (1975): 675–695.

Roth, Benita. *Separate Roads to Feminism: Black, Chicana, and White Feminist Movements in America's Second Wave*. Cambridge: Cambridge University Press, 2004.

Rothenberg, Paula S., ed. *White Privilege: Essential Readings on the Other Side of Racism*. 5th ed. New York: Worth, 2016.

Rothstein, Richard. *The Color of Law: A Forgotten History of How Our Government Segregated America*. New York: Norton, 2017.

Rubin, Herbert J., and Irene S. Rubin. *Qualitative Interviewing: The Art of Hearing Data*. Thousand Oaks, CA: Sage, 2011.

Saini, Angela. *Superior: The Return of Race Science*. Boston: Beacon, 2019.

Sampson, Robert J. *Great American City: Chicago and the Enduring Neighborhood Effect*. Chicago: University of Chicago Press, 2012.

Sampson, Robert J., Jeffrey D. Morenoff, and Thomas Gannon-Rowley. "Assessing 'Neighborhood Effects': Social Processes and New Directions in Research." *Annual Review of Sociology* 28, no. 1 (2002): 443–478.

Satter, Beryl. *Family Properties: Race, Real Estate, and the Exploitation of Black Urban America*. New York: Macmillan, 2009.

Schaffner, Brian F., Matthew MacWilliams, and Tatishe Nteta. "Understanding White Polarization in the 2016 Vote for President: The Sobering Role of Racism and Sexism." *Political Science Quarterly* 133, no. 1 (2018): 9–34.

Schuman, Howard, Charlotte Steeh, Lawrence Bobo, and Maria Krysan. *Racial Attitudes in America: Trends and Interpretations*. Cambridge, MA: Harvard University Press, 1997.

Seamster, Louise, and Victor Ray. "Against Teleology in the Study of Race: Toward the Abolition of the Progress Paradigm." *Sociological Theory* 36, no. 4 (2018): 315–342.

Sears, David O., Carl P. Hensler, and Leslie K. Speer. "Whites' Opposition to 'Busing': Self-Interest or Symbolic Politics?" *American Political Science Review* 73, no. 2 (1979): 369–384.

Sears, David O., and Donald R. Kinder. "Whites' Opposition to Busing: On Conceptualizing and Operationalizing Group Conflict." *Journal of Personality and Social Psychology* 48, no. 5 (1985): 1141–1147.

Sears, David O., Colette Van Laar, Mary Carrillo, and Rick Kosterman. "Is It Really Racism? The Origins of White Americans' Opposition to Race-Targeted Policies." *Public Opinion Quarterly* 61, no. 1 (1997): 16–53.

Seidman, Irving. *Interviewing as Qualitative Research: A Guide for Researchers in Education and the Social Sciences*. 4th ed. New York: Teachers College Press, 2013.

Shapiro, Thomas M., and Heather B. Johnson. "Good Neighborhoods, Good Schools: Race and the Good Choices of White Families." In *White Out: The Continuing Significance of Racism*, edited by Ashley W. Doane and Eduardo Bonilla-Silva, 173–187. New York: Routledge, 2003.

Sharkey, Patrick. *Stuck in Place: Urban Neighborhoods and the End of Progress toward Racial Equality*. Chicago: University of Chicago Press, 2013.

Shedd, Carla. *Unequal City: Race, Schools, and Perceptions of Injustice*. New York: Russell Sage, 2015.

Sides, John, Michael Tesler, and Lynn Vavreck. *Identity Crisis: The 2016 Presidential*

Campaign and the Battle for the Meaning of America. Princeton, NJ: Princeton University Press, 2018.

Sleeter, Christine E. "How White Teachers Construct Race." In *Race, Identity, and Representation in Education,* edited by Cameron McCarthy, Warren Crichlow, Greg Dimitriadis, and Nadine Dolby, 157–171. New York: Routledge, 1993.

Small, Mario L., David J. Harding, and Michèle Lamont. Introduction to "Reconsidering Culture and Poverty," special issue, *Annals of the American Academy of Political and Social Science* 629, no. 1 (2010): 6–27.

Small, Mario L., and Katherine Newman. "Urban Poverty after the Truly Disadvantaged: The Rediscovery of the Family, the Neighborhood, and Culture." *Annual Review of Sociology* 27, no. 1 (2001): 23–45.

Smedley, Audrey, and Brian D. Smedley. "Race as Biology Is Fiction, Racism as a Social Problem Is Real: Anthropological and Historical Perspectives on the Social Construction of Race." *American Psychologist* 60, no. 1 (2005): 16–26.

Smith, Linda T. *Decolonizing Methodologies: Research and Indigenous Peoples.* 2nd ed. London: Zed Books, 2013.

Sniderman, Paul M., and Thomas L. Piazza. *The Scar of Race.* Cambridge, MA: Harvard University Press, 1993.

Snow, David A. "Extending and Broadening Blumer's Conceptualization of Symbolic Interactionism." *Symbolic Interaction* 24, no. 3 (2001): 367–377.

Solomona, R. Patrick, John P. Portelli, Beverly J. Daniel, and Arlene Campbell. "The Discourse of Denial: How White Teacher Candidates Construct Race, Racism and 'White Privilege.'" *Race, Ethnicity and Education* 8, no. 2 (2005): 147–169.

Steele, Shelby. *The Content of Our Character: A New Vision of Race in America.* New York: St. Martin's, 1990.

Steele, Shelby. *White Guilt: How Blacks and Whites Together Destroyed the Promise of the Civil Rights Era.* New York: HarperCollins, 2009.

Steinberg, Stephen. *Turning Back: The Retreat from Racial Justice in American Thought and Policy.* Boston: Beacon, 1995.

Stoll, Laurie C. "Constructing the Color-Blind Classroom: Teachers' Perspectives on Race and Schooling." *Race, Ethnicity and Education* 17, no. 5 (2014): 688–705.

Stoll, Laurie C. *Should Schools Be Colorblind?* Cambridge: Polity, 2019.

Stryker, Sheldon. *Symbolic Interactionism: A Social Structural Version.* San Francisco: Benjamin-Cummings, 1980.

Sugrue, Thomas J. *The Origins of the Urban Crisis: Race and Inequality in Postwar Detroit.* Princeton, NJ: Princeton University Press, 2014.

Sullivan, Shannon, and Nancy Tuana, eds. *Race and Epistemologies of Ignorance.* Albany: SUNY Press, 2007.

Taeuber, Karl E., and David R. James. "Racial Segregation among Public and Private Schools." *Sociology of Education* 55, no. 2 (1982): 133–143.

Tatum, Beverly D. *Can We Talk about Race? And Other Conversations in an Era of School Resegregation.* Boston: Beacon, 2007.

Tatum, Beverly D. *Why Are All the Black Kids Sitting Together in the Cafeteria? And Other Conversations about Race.* 20th anniv. ed. New York: Basic Books, 2017.

Tesler, Michael. *Post-Racial or Most-Racial? Race and Politics in the Obama Era*. Chicago: University of Chicago Press, 2016.

Tesler, Michael, and David O. Sears. *Obama's Race: The 2008 Election and the Dream of a Post-racial America*. Chicago: University of Chicago Press, 2010.

Theoharis, Jeanne, Gaston Alonso, Noel S. Anderson, and Celina Su. *Our Schools Suck: Students Talk Back to a Segregated Nation on the Failures of Urban Education*. New York: NYU Press, 2009.

Thernstrom, Stephan, and Abigail Thernstrom. *America in Black and White: One Nation, Indivisible*. New York: Simon and Schuster, 1999.

Trepagnier, Barbara. *Silent Racism: How Well-Meaning White People Perpetuate the Racial Divide*. 2nd ed. London: Routledge, 2017.

Trounstine, Jessica. *Segregation by Design: Local Politics and Inequality in American Cities*. Cambridge: Cambridge University Press, 2018.

Twine, France W., and Jonathan W. Warren. *Racing Research, Researching Race: Methodological Dilemmas in Critical Race Studies*. New York: NYU Press, 2000.

US National Commission on Excellence in Education. *A Nation at Risk: The Imperative for Education Reform*. Washington, DC: National Commission on Excellence and Education, 1983.

Vaught, Sabina E., and Angelina E. Castagno. "'I Don't Think I'm a Racist': Critical Race Theory, Teacher Attitudes, and Structural Racism." *Race, Ethnicity and Education* 11, no. 2 (2008): 95–113.

Wacquant, Loïc. *Punishing the Poor: The Neoliberal Government of Social Insecurity*. Durham, NC: Duke University Press, 2009.

Warren, John T. "Doing Whiteness: On the Performative Dimensions of Race in the Classroom." *Communication Education* 50, no. 2 (2001): 91–108.

Warren, John T. *Performing Purity: Whiteness, Pedagogy, and the Reconstitution of Power*. New York: Peter Lang, 2003.

Waters, Mary C. *Ethnic Options: Choosing Identities in America*. Berkeley: University of California Press, 1990.

Watkins, William H. *The White Architects of Black Education: Ideology and Power in America, 1865–1954*. New York: Teachers College Press, 2001.

Watson, Dyan. "Norming Suburban: How Teachers Talk about Race without Using Race Words." *Urban Education* 47, no. 5 (2012): 983–1004.

Watson, Dyan. "'Urban, but Not Too Urban': Unpacking Teachers' Desires to Teach Urban Students." *Journal of Teacher Education* 62, no. 1 (2011): 23–34.

Watson, Dyan. "What Do You Mean When You Say 'Urban'? Speaking Honestly about Race and Students." *Rethinking Schools* 26, no. 1 (2011): 48–50.

Webb, Clive, ed. *Massive Resistance: Southern Opposition to the Second Reconstruction*. New York: Oxford University Press, 2005.

Weber, Lynn. "A Conceptual Framework for Understanding Race, Class, Gender, and Sexuality." *Psychology of Women Quarterly* 22, no. 1 (1998): 13–32.

Weiss, Robert S. *Learning from Strangers: The Art and Method of Qualitative Interview Studies*. New York: Free Press, 1994.

Wellman, David T. *Portraits of White Racism.* Cambridge: Cambridge University Press, 1993.

Wells, Ida B. *Southern Horrors: Lynch Law in All Its Phases.* 1892. Repr., Auckland: Floating Press, 2014.

Wildman, Stephanie M., and Adrienne D. Davis. "Making Systems of Privilege Visible." In *Critical White Studies: Looking behind the Mirror,* edited by Richard Delgado and Jean Stefancic, 314–319. Philadelphia: Temple University Press, 1997.

Wilkerson, Isabel. *The Warmth of Other Suns: The Epic Story of America's Great Migration.* New York: Vintage Books, 2011.

Williams, Christine L., and E. Joel Heikes. "The Importance of Researcher's Gender in the In-Depth Interview: Evidence from Two Case Studies of Male Nurses." *Gender and Society* 7, no. 2 (1993): 280–291.

Williams, Linda. *Playing the Race Card: Melodramas of Black and White from Uncle Tom to O. J. Simpson.* Princeton, NJ: Princeton University Press, 2002.

Wilson, William J. *The Declining Significance of Race: Blacks and Changing American Institutions.* Chicago: University of Chicago Press, 1978.

Wilson, William J. *The Truly Disadvantaged: The Inner City, the Underclass, and Public Policy.* Chicago: University of Chicago Press, 2012.

Wilson, William J. *When Work Disappears: The World of the New Urban Poor.* New York: Vintage Books, 2011.

Wimmer, Andreas. "Race-Centrism: A Critique and a Research Agenda." *Ethnic and Racial Studies* 38, no. 13 (2015): 2186–2205.

Winant, Howard. "The Dark Side of the Force: One Hundred Years of the Sociology of Race." In *Sociology in America: A History,* edited by Craig Calhoun, 535–571. Chicago: University of Chicago Press, 2007.

Winant, Howard. "Race and Race Theory." *Annual Review of Sociology* 26, no. 1 (2000): 169–185.

Wing, Jean Yonemura. "Beyond Black and White: The Model Minority Myth and the Invisibility of Asian American Students." *Urban Review* 39, no. 4 (2007): 455–487.

Winkler, Erin N. *Learning Race, Learning Place: Shaping Racial Identities and Ideas in African American Childhoods.* New Brunswick, NJ: Rutgers University Press, 2012.

Wise, Tim. *Colorblind: The Rise of Post-racial Politics and the Retreat from Racial Equity.* San Francisco: City Lights Books, 2010.

Wise, Tim. *White like Me: Reflections on Race from a Privileged Son.* New York: Soft Skull, 2011.

Wray, Matt. *Not Quite White: White Trash and the Boundaries of Whiteness.* Durham, NC: Duke University Press, 2006.

Yancy, George. *Backlash: What Happens When We Talk Honestly about Racism in America.* Lanham, MD: Rowman and Littlefield, 2018.

Yancy, George. *Black Bodies, White Gazes: The Continuing Significance of Race in America.* 2nd ed. Lanham, MD: Rowman and Littlefield, 2016.

Yancy, George. *Look, a White! Philosophical Essays on Whiteness.* Philadelphia: Temple University Press, 2012.

Yin, Robert K. *Qualitative Research from Start to Finish*. New York: Guilford, 2015.

Yinger, John. *Closed Doors, Opportunities Lost: The Continuing Costs of Housing Discrimination*. New York: Russell Sage Foundation, 1995.

Yu, Tianlong. "Challenging the Politics of the 'Model Minority' Stereotype: A Case for Educational Equality." *Equity and Excellence in Education* 39, no. 4 (2006): 325–333.

Zhang, Qin. "Asian Americans beyond the Model Minority Stereotype: The Nerdy and the Left Out." *Journal of International and Intercultural Communication* 3, no. 1 (2010): 20–37.

Zinn, Maxine B. "Field Research in Minority Communities: Ethical, Methodological and Political Observations by an Insider." *Social Problems* 27, no. 2 (1979): 209–219.

Zuberi, Tukufu, and Eduardo Bonilla-Silva. *White Logic, White Methods: Racism and Methodology*. Lanham, MD: Rowman and Littlefield, 2008.

INDEX

abstract liberalism, 120, 123

affirmative action, 10, 90, 120, 122, 145

African American history, ix, 39, 53

African Americans, 18, 90, 134, 140; affluence, 45; criminal justice system and, viii, 179n2; dehumanization of, 36; as demographic, 6; hostility toward, 15; postracialism and, 128; racial discrimination and, 58, 93–95, 115, 126, 142, 144; stereotypes and, 81, 108, 145, 176

alt-right, 160, 211n31

American Sociological Society (American Sociological Association), 19

antiracism, ix, 123–124, 126, 151, 216n25

antiracist activism, 124, 126. *See also* social justice warriors

antiwhiteness, 75, 90, 110, 112–113, 126; as bias, 67; and discrimination, 3, 137, 142, 152; as prejudice, 13; as racism, 98, 114, 136; as ubiquitous in black schools, 96, 146. *See also* black privilege

Asian Americans, 127, 129–130, 163

Atlantic, 86

authentic grievance, 131, 140–141, 143–147, 149, 152

backlash, viii, 14, 43, 61, 81, 157

Baldwin High School, 74

Baltimore, Maryland, viii

Ben and Jerry's, ix

Beyoncé, 129

black bodies, 52, 57, 96, 104, 204n34

black culture, 12, 57, 75, 79, 204n33; hostility toward, 15; perception of, 39, 50–52; as white performative act, 111–112, 204n35

blackface, 38

Black History Month, 52, 74

Black Lives Matter, viii, x, 80, 156, 201n41

blackness, ix, 10, 40, 52, 61, 72, 97, 110, 198n76

black privilege, 13, 97, 109–110, 115–116; as advantage with black students, 114; antiwhiteness and, 112–113; as pedagogical tool, 111. *See also* antiwhiteness; collective whiteness; reverse discrimination

black racism, 144

black schools, 37, 53, 76, 110, 167, 172, 201n35; racialization of urban schools as, 11, 39–40, 48–50; white disadvantage in, 114, 133; white identity in, 69, 71–73, 78, 84, 154, 170–171; white ideology and, 118, 136; white race card and, 87, 97

black spaces, 41, 50. *See also* white spaces

Boyd, Alexa (Mrs.), 53, 93

Bradley, Denise (Mrs.), 88–89, 109, 148–150

Brown, Mike, viii, 207n34

Brown v. Board of Education (1954), 40, 42, 48, 195n48

Bush, George W., 46, 196n61

capitalism, 47, 197n65

Castile, Philando, viii

charter schools. *See* neoliberalism: and education policy

Chasing Higher Education program (Brick City School District), 48

Chauvin, Derek, viii

Chinese exclusion, 130, 208n42

civil rights, 38–39, 43, 160

civil rights movement, 27–28, 43, 92, 118, 120, 133, 151, 197n67

Civil War (US), 118

Clark, Chelsea (Mrs.), 112–113, 132, 149–150

Clark, Stephon, viii

class, 4, 14, 24–25, 66, 68, 210n20

Clinton, Hillary, 160, 212n32, 213n46

collective whiteness, 97, 104–106, 108–109, 115–116. *See also* black privilege; reverse discrimination

color-consciousness, 13, 119, 121–126, 131, 134–136, 138–140, 150–152. *See also* race-consciousness

compulsory busing, 43–44

Costa, Amanda (Mrs.), 59–61, 69, 117

Coulter, Ann, 158

Crawford, John, viii

crime, x, 45, 93, 156, 207n34, 210n13

critical whiteness studies, 5, 20, 183n11

cultural shift, 156, 157

Daily Caller, 86

Darling, Rebecca (Mrs.), 63, 141–142

data analysis, 172–174

Davidson, Clay (Mr.), 73, 79, 171

de facto segregation. *See* segregation

de jure segregation. *See* Jim Crow

Democratic National Convention, 160

Democratic Party, 43, 157–160, 211n24, 212n32

demographic classification of white, 4, 18, 21

demographic gap, 6, 8, 113, 170, 209n3

desegregation, 43–44, 195n48. *See also* segregation

DeYoung, Mrs., 105–106

Douglass, Frederick, 52

Doyle, Mrs., 55–56

Du Bois, W. E. B., 19

East Genesee Middle School, 117

Edwards, Tiffany (Mrs.), 50–51, 102–103, 113–114, 127–128, 204n36, 208n40

egalitarianism, x, 118–119, 122, 127, 154, 162

Electoral College, 151, 158, 211n24

Emerson Middle School, 113

environment, 84, 115, 169; inequitable, 45; local, xi, 3, 12; neighborhood, 52; people as products of, 65–66; racialized, 4, 7, 39, 57–58, 61, 64, 67–69, 164, 184n21; residential, 163; social, 10, 65; toxins, 47; workplace, 136, 144, 171

ethnicity, 19, 21, 29, 33, 35–36, 208n44. *See also* white deflection

Federalist, 86

Ferguson, Missouri, viii, 123

fieldwork, 171–172

Floyd, George Perry, Jr., viii–x, 179n1, 179n3

Fox News, 152, 157–158

Gardener Middle School, 49–50, 57

Garner, Eric, viii, x, 179n1

gender, 19, 29, 66, 68, 72, 103; as distancing strategy, 32, 36–37; methodology and, 173, 175–176, 177; as recognized identity, 21, 28–31, 33

gentrification, 46, 197n65

geography, 24, 46, 50, 61

ghetto, 39, 41

Gray, Freddy, viii

Gray, Mrs., 74–75, 90

Great Recession, 46, 197n65, 197n69

Great Society, 46

Hall, Allison (Ms.), 22–23, 88, 129–130, 189n21

Harlan, John Marshall, 117, 205n2

hate crimes, x

Hayes, Stephen (Mr.), 92

hegemonic whiteness, 156

heterogeneity, 5, 42

Holder, Eric, 124

Hurricane Katrina, 46, 197n65

identity construction, 5, 67–68; compensatory, 79–80, 83; protectionary, 79–81, 83

immigrants/immigration, 34–36, 50, 130, 159–160, 163
in-group solidarity, 159–160
Innovation Area Schools (Brick City School District), 48
interactional practice, 10, 32, 39, 61, 64–65, 67, 111, 161
intersectionality, 24, 32–33, 162
invisibility of whiteness, 18, 21–22, 26–27, 37; as the norm, 12, 28, 154; as privileged identity, 3; to racial other, 19, 68–69, 72–73, 78. *See also* white normativity
Irish identity, 33–34, 35. *See also* ethnicity; white deflection
Italian identity, 34–35. *See also* ethnicity; white deflection

Jackson, Jesse, 124
Jackson Middle School, 58
James, LeBron, 129
Japanese American internment, 122, 129–130, 208n42
Jarvis, Cynthia (Ms.), 25–26, 49–50, 57, 142–144
Jay Z, 129
Jean, Botham, viii
Jim Crow, 43–44, 89, 116, 117, 120, 195n48. *See also* segregation

King, Martin Luther, Jr., viii, 52, 151

Ladner, Joyce, 19
Latino Americans, 163
Limbaugh, Rush, 158
Livingston, Ms., 71–72, 73, 122–123, 138–140

Malcolm X, 38–39, 52–53
Marsh, Richard (Mr.), 27–28, 140, 216n25
Marshall, Thurgood, 52
Martin, Erica (Mrs.), 22, 38–39, 52–53, 58–59, 110–111, 125–126
Martin, Trayvon, 55–56, 58, 178n2, 198n80
McCormick, Jessi (Mrs.), 70–71, 73, 121
McDonald, LaQuan, viii
Meredith, Kate (Mrs.), 33–35, 52, 76–77, 98–100, 134–135

meritocracy, 10, 46, 89, 93, 114, 197n67, 204n36
Microsoft, ix
Miller, Dennis, 158
Milliken v. Bradley (1974), 44
misogyny, 29, 36
model minority myth, 127, 129. *See also* Asian Americans
modes of dress, 4, 12, 39, 50–52, 78–79
momentary minority status, 5, 66–68
Mothers of the Movement, 160

NASCAR, ix
National Review, 86
Nation at Risk (1983), 45
Native Americans, 122, 163
NBA, ix
Nelson, Mrs., 90–91, 123
neoliberalism, 10, 40, 46–48, 197nn67–68; colorblindness and, 205n2; and education policy, 11, 45–46, 48, 185n36; rugged individualism and, 35
New Republic, 86
New Yorker, 86
NFL, ix
nonwhite racialized spaces, 5–6, 9–10, 72, 87, 97, 152, 164

Obama, Barack, 118, 124, 127–129, 151, 157, 159–160, 208n40
O'Reilly, Bill, 152, 157–158

Palmer, Bryan (Mr.), 104, 108–109, 133–135
Parents Involved in Community Schools v. Seattle School District No. 1 (2007), 44
Parks, Rosa, 52
pathological discourse, 12, 92, 120, 156, 213n39
patriarchy, 21, 29, 31–32, 36
Pattengill Middle School, 108, 133
pedagogy, 2, 46, 79, 81, 106, 111, 114, 138
Plessy v. Ferguson (1896), 117
police brutality, ix–x
political correctness, 91–92, 95, 202n45; as perceived problem, 87–88, 156; to police white behavior, 89–90; politics and, 160

postracialism, 11–13, 116, 118, 141; antiwhite racism and, 131–132, 136; black celebrity and, 126–128; colorblindness and, 144, 146, 148, 151; as universal good, 130. *See also* race-consciousness

poverty, 45, 58, 93, 128, 207n36; federal line, 47, 197n69; fighting, 148; methodology and, 198n76; racialized, 41, 68; student, 48, 125, 198n75

private property, 4, 10

privatization, 46, 185n36. *See also* neoliberalism

psychic freedom, 104–105, 109

public schools, 13, 195n48, 197n65, 209n3; desegregation in, 43; disinvestment in, 11; inner-city, xi, 5, 45, 93, 170; as majority-minority institutions, 155; as racialized spaces, 42; resegregation in, 6, 44, 164

purposeful sampling, 5, 169

qualitative methods, 166–167

race-consciousness, 118, 120–121, 125. *See also* color-consciousness

racial autonomy, 7, 67

racial classification, 3, 9–10, 41, 44, 64, 118, 121, 141, 195n48

racial discrimination, 3, 13, 35, 120–122, 131–133; color-consciousness and, 123, 126, 131; dismissal of, 118; postracialism and, 127–129; the race card and, 86–87; racial recognition as, 58, 61, 95, 97; skepticism of, 141–142; victim mentality and, 92–93, 115; white race card and, 96, 144, 146

racial disparity, xi, 6, 92, 120

racial experience, 36, 74, 96, 131–132, 140, 148, 151; methodology, 4, 14, 163–164

racial inequality, ix, xii, 10, 93–94, 115, 176, 213n39; colorblindness and, 120–124; justification of, 118–119; political correctness and, 91–92; significance of, 13; student discourse on, 39, 55–56; study of, 19–20

racialization, 11–12, 32–33, 39–42; and United States, 161–163; urban schools and, 48, 52–53, 57, 62, 72; white, 5, 14, 64, 162, 164, 170

racialized discourse, 12, 53–55, 56–58, 91

racialized experience, 4, 86, 96, 98, 131, 171–172; in black schools, 136, 142, 144, 146–147; colorblindness and, 148–150; white ideology and, 118–119

racialized social system, 9, 58

racialized stress, 16, 81, 152

racial minority, 3, 99, 132, 142, 147, 149–151, 171; as demographic, 155–156, 205n38; ethnicity and, 35–36; identity and, 115; as lived experience, 140; occupational status as, 7; political efficacy and, 158, 161–162

racial mistrust, 71, 108–109

racial oppression, 73, 119, 122

racial other, 3, 12–13, 72, 75, 79, 97

racial politics, 44, 102–103, 159–160

racial prejudice, 2, 121

racial progress, x, 61, 121, 130

racial rationalization, 131, 136, 138–140, 146–147, 152

racial recognition, 58–59, 61, 78, 151

racial socialization, 2, 7, 25, 28, 35, 37, 64, 84, 202n46

racial status, 57, 74, 132, 147, 149, 151

racial stereotypes, 15–16, 51, 82–83, 144–146, 176, 217n39

racial stratification system, 4, 67, 121, 124

racial victimization, 13, 86–87, 89, 92–94, 115–116, 152; authenticity of, 119–120, 131, 133, 140–146, 149; claims of, 95–96, 118, 137–138; methodology of, 161, 164, 175, 208n50; as social construction, 116; and spatial construction of, 97–98; white versus nonwhite, 109. *See also* white racial victimization

racism: antiblack, ix, 36, 127; antiwhite, and postracialism, 131–132, 136; antiwhiteness as, 98, 114, 136; black, 144; institutional, viii, 9, 85–86, 142–143, 145, 160, 205n37; minimization of, 120, 123; white, 72, 93–96, 102, 108–109, 112, 209n10. *See also* antiracism

Radke, Dan (Mr.), 84, 88, 125–126, 137–138, 140

Reagan, Ronald, 45, 158

reflexivity, 175–177

reluctant recognition, 131–132, 147, 149–152

Republican Party, 43, 157, 196n61, 211n24, 212n32

resegregation, 6, 43–44, 164

responsive interview model, 167–169, 175–177

resocialization, 11
reverse discrimination, 10, 13, 109, 115–116, 140, 197n68; as barrier to career advancement, 102–104; as form of antiwhite hostility, 98–100; loss of power and, 67; whiteness as badge of inferiority and, 97
rhetorical incoherence, 24, 84, 152, 154; color-blindness and, 132, 134–135, 139; white race-lessness and, 21, 25, 28, 37; spatial negotiation and, 131; subject of whiteness and, 18–19; as thematic concept, 12
Rhodes, James (Mr.), 49, 128
Rice, Susan, 124
Rice, Tamir, viii
riots, 123, 124, 133, 156, 179n3
Romney, Mitt, 157–158, 211n24

Satter, Candice, 54, 98
school uniforms, 52. See also modes of dress
Scott, Melanie (Mrs.), 29, 30–32, 36, 80
Scott, Walter, viii
segregation: economic, 46–47; housing, 6; Jim Crow, 116–117; racial, 42, 61, 121; school, 40, 43–44, 195n48. See also Jim Crow; resegregation
sexism, 29, 36
Sexton High School, 85, 88, 137
Sharpton, Al, 124
situated racial identity, 3, 13. See also black privilege; reverse discrimination
slavery, chattel, x, 116, 118, 120, 122, 129, 145
slurs, 54, 56, 59, 102
Smith, Will, 129
snowball sampling, 5, 170–171
social justice warriors, 124, 144–145. See also antiracist activism
spatial victimization, 96–97, 103, 105, 109, 111, 115
special negotiation, 119, 131
speech patterns, 39, 50, 79, 80
Stacey, Ms., 72–73, 107–108
standardized tests. See neoliberalism: and education policy
stigmatism, 2, 3, 75–76, 78, 97, 104, 164
suburbs, viii, 43, 45–46, 47, 61
surveillance, 46–47
symbolic interactionism, 65–66

Taft Middle School, 148
Taylor, Breonna, viii
Taylor, Sophia (Mrs.), 24–25, 147
theoretical sampling, 169
theoretical saturation, 174–175
Thompson, Leah (Mrs.), 8, 63–64, 78, 99–100
Thornhill, Isaac (Mr.), 144–146
Trump, Donald, 14, 158–161, 165, 210n20, 211n31, 212n32
Tubman, Harriet, 52, 156

unconscious bias, 160
United States Supreme Court, 44, 116

victim mentality, 92–93, 95–96, 109, 115
Vincent, Paige (Mrs.), 17–18, 34–35, 94, 127
violence, x, 1, 32, 40, 41, 156, 160, 210n13

Walker, Hanna (Mrs.), 23–24, 153–154
Walnut Middle School, 63–64
Washington, Booker T., 52
Weaver, Carrie (Mrs.), 29–30, 81–83
Wells, Ida B., 19
Western, Jennifer (Ms.), 100–101, 124
white allies, 86, 91, 205n37
white deflection, 12, 19, 21, 28–29, 35–37, 84. See also ethnicity
white ethnic card, 35. See also racial socialization
white habitus, 146, 152, 162
white identity construction, 5, 64, 66–68
white nationalism, x, 14, 158, 160, 165, 212n32
white normativity, 10–11, 14, 67, 116–118, 123, 138–139, 151, 197n67
white privilege, ix, 24–25, 67–68, 72, 142, 160, 209n10
white racial awareness, 7, 10, 62, 67, 160, 174
white racial domination, 9, 123
white racial frame, 118–119, 130, 161
white racial invisibility. See invisibility of whiteness
white racial victimization, 13, 87, 103–104, 112, 115, 118–120, 152, 161, 164, 205n37; authentic grievance and, 131, 133, 140–143; black privilege and, 112; colorblindness and, 135, 137, 175; as experiential reality, 136, 138;

white racial victimization (*continued*)
    political correctness and, 89, 92; race card
    and, 86–87, 95; and rejection of nonwhite
    racial victimization, 93–94, 144–146; re-
    luctant recognition and, 149; reverse dis-
    crimination and, 103–104; white race card
    and, 96
white spaces, 7, 13–14, 26, 37, 41, 42, 53, 184n21.
    See also black spaces

white supremacy, ix–x, 119, 120
Wilkes, Mrs., 1–3, 7, 16, 170
Winfrey, Oprah, 129
womanhood, 32, 36

xenophobia, 160, 212n32

Zimmerman, George, 55–56

www.ingramcontent.com/pod-product-compliance
Lightning Source LLC
Chambersburg PA
CBHW071736270326
41928CB00013B/2702